Praise for *Wise Effort*

"*Wise Effort* is a transformative guide to living with heart and integrity. Diana Hill invites us to turn inward—with curiosity, compassion, and courage—and align our lives with what truly matters. Drawing from both contemplative practice and psychological insight, this book offers a pathway home to presence, purpose, and the quiet joy of living true to our hearts."

Tara Brach
author of *Radical Acceptance* and *Radical Compassion*

"*Wise Effort* helps you use your energy more intentionally. This approach encourages us to do what matters without burning out. Blending insights from Buddhism, psychology, and neuroscience, psychologist Diana Hill offers a practical, compassionate guide for high achievers ready to work smarter, not harder."

Nedra Glover Tawwab, LCSW
LCSW, *New York Times* bestselling author
of *Set Boundaries, Find Peace*

"When we learn how our brains work, we open ourselves up to so many possibilities for changing habits, channeling our energy where it matters most, and living fulfilling and impactful lives. Diana Hill's book is the perfect blend of neuroscience and daily practices that will help you leverage your strengths and set you on a path toward wise effort."

Judson Brewer, MD, PhD
New York Times bestselling author of *Unwinding Anxiety*

"Diana Hill shows how you can connect your body, heart, and mind into a wise, caring, effective rhythm of life."

Jack Kornfield
author of *A Path with Heart*

"Diana Hill offers down-to-earth wisdom and a wonderful tool kit for anyone searching for the path you were meant to be on. Whether you're feeling stuck in a particular area of your life or looking to bring fresh awareness and energy to the life you're already living, you'll find rich, actionable insights in these pages."

Robert J. Waldinger, MD
director of the Harvard Study of Adult Development, *New York Times* bestselling coauthor of *The Good Life*

"*Wise Effort* is a beautifully crafted guide to channeling human energy in ways that align with the neurobiological foundations of connection, safety, and resilience. Personally, I found her approach deeply resonant. Diana invites readers to listen to their bodies, focus their energy with intention, and cultivate a life anchored in meaning and vitality. *Wise Effort* is a compassionate and practical resource for anyone seeking to live with greater coherence, curiosity, and courage."

Stephen W. Porges, PhD
cofounder of the Polyvagal Institute, author of *The Polyvagal Theory*

"This book is a practical guide for living with more clarity, alignment, and vitality. It reminds us that energy—not time—is our most meaningful resource. With her *Wise Effort* method, Diana offers a powerful path to help you reclaim your focus and aliveness and direct it toward what really matters. The reflection prompts are thoughtful and honest—and they'll nudge you to listen to your own wisdom more deeply."

Sonya Looney, MS, MAPP
world champion mountain miker and mental performance coach

"Diana Hill's energy and her ability to communicate how best to employ daily practices that lift our spirits, guide us to do good work, and be good people are vital right now!"

Allison Aubrey
NPR correspondent

"This is not just a book—it's a map for living with purpose without burning out. *Wise Effort* is the rare book that blends deep psychological insight with practical, grounded wisdom. Diana Hill offers a compassionate, clear-eyed path for high achievers and sensitive souls alike, those who care deeply, strive earnestly, and still find themselves stuck. With powerful metaphors, actionable tools, and profound heart, Diana helps readers transform their unique energy into a force for clarity, connection, and real change."

Marcela Matos, PhD
clinical psychologist and auxiliary researcher at the Center for Research in Neuropsychology and Cognitive and Behavioral Intervention, University of Coimbra, Portugal

"A gentle guide to living with purpose, presence, and inner freedom."

Christiana Figueres
coauthor of *The Future We Choose*

wise effort

wise effort

How to Focus Your Genius Energy on What Matters Most

Diana Hill, PhD

sounds true
BOULDER, COLORADO

Sounds True
Boulder, CO

© 2025 Diana Hill

Foreword © 2026 Rick Hanson

Sounds True is a trademark of Sounds True Inc.

All rights reserved. No part of this book may be used or reproduced in any manner without written permission from the author(s) and publisher.

No AI Training: Without in any way limiting the author's and publisher's exclusive rights under copyright, any use of this publication to "train" generative artificial intelligence (AI) technologies to generate text is expressly prohibited. The author reserves all rights to license uses of this work for generative AI training and development of machine learning language models.

This book is not intended as a substitute for the medical recommendations of physicians, mental health professionals, or other health-care providers. Rather, it is intended to offer information to help the reader cooperate with physicians, mental health professionals, and health-care providers in a mutual quest for optimal well-being. We advise readers to carefully review and understand the ideas presented and to seek the advice of a qualified professional before attempting to use them.

Published 2025

Cover, jacket, and book design by Charli Barnes

Printed in the United States of America

BK07098

Cataloging-in-Publication data for this book is available from the
    Library of Congress.
ISBN: 9781649633361
eBook ISBN: 9781649633378

This book is for my clients. Some appear in stories; others are between the lines. You show me the way of wise effort.

To straighten the crooked, you must first do a harder thing—straighten yourself.

—The Dhammapada

contents

Foreword xi

Introduction: What Is Wise Effort? 1

Wise Effort Task #1: Get Curious

1. What Is Your Genius? 11
2. What Is Your Struggle? 27
3. How Is Your Genius Also Your Problem? 43
4. How Does Your Environment Impact Your Genius? 59
5. What Are Your Values? 79

Wise Effort Task #2: Open Up

6. Open Up Your Mind 99
7. Open Up Your Feelings 115
8. Open Up Your Wise Self 135
9. Open Up to Change 151

Wise Effort Task #3: Focus Your Energy

10. Wise Effort in Relationships 171
11. Wise Effort with Your Body 187

12   Wise Effort at Work   203

13   Wise Effort in Creativity   217

14   Wise Effort in Community   227

Conclusion: Wise Effort Is Now   245

Acknowledgments   246

Additional Resources   249

Notes   250

About the Author   269

foreword

I nearly drowned one day when I was sixteen. I'd been skin diving in the Pacific Ocean, off the coast of Los Angeles, and became trapped in a forest of kelp. Running out of air, I thrashed and thrashed, tightening the leathery seaweed around me. I was strong and determined, a nerdy shy kid who'd fight back if he had to, but all that was only making things worse. I lost a fin and my mask slid down my neck. I was going to die.

Then from somewhere—I know not where—a clear voice spoke: "Cool it." Calm replacing panic, slowly pulling the binding strands apart, gently rising through beautiful orange-brown leaves, rising and rising toward a silvery surface lit by sun. And that first breath of air.

I can't explain the "why" of that day. But the "what" of it is clear. I was surely getting an A for effort! But a whole bunch of strengths that served me well in other settings were now about to kill me. Through grace or mystery or the deep unconscious, my efforts became adapted to the situation, now more skillful, sustained, effective . . . in a word, wise.

Throughout history, there have been many different descriptions of "wise effort." While playing poker, we need to know "when to hold 'em, and when to fold 'em." In the Serenity Prayer, we ask for the courage to change the things we can, the serenity to accept the things we cannot change, and the wisdom to know the difference. Born with HIV/AIDS and before dying at twelve, Nkosi Johnson invited us to "Do all you can with all you have in the time you have in the place you are." In his poem Ash Wednesday, T.S. Eliot writes:

> Teach us to care and not to care
> Teach us to sit still.

In the Buddhist tradition, wise effort is part of the eightfold path. Applied to thoughts, words, and deeds . . . it consists of beginning, sustaining, and increasing what is beneficial to others and oneself . . . as well as preventing, decreasing, and ending what is harmful to others and oneself. The ancient texts describe this as a path "of the noble ones." This is an inner nobility of character that has nothing to do with caste or class. What is already noble within you is drawn to wise effort, and further ennobled by it.

Efforts that are wise usually involve intersections of two or more qualities. A Zen meditator can be "soft in the front, firm in the back." Psychologist Daniel Ellenberg writes of strength with heart. Think globally while acting locally. Have fierce compassion. Use mind/body medicine. Stay in the present while taking the long view. Trust but verify. The starship Enterprise needs both Mr. Spock and Dr. McCoy.

Good advice, and coming from many times and places.

But easier said than done.

So *how* do we do it, how do we find that sweet spot of intersection, how do we slip into that flow of effortless effort in which the dancer becomes the dance? What are the efforts we need to make—skillfully, effectively, wisely—to actually engage in wise effort?

Diana Hill's genius has been to look freshly and deeply into this fundamental question. I've known her for years, and she embodies multiple intersections herself. As you'll see in these pages, she integrates scientific knowledge, clinical skills, heartfelt compassion, and childlike wonder. She is hyper-logical and intuitive, tender and tough, practical and playful. It is rare to find a book that is so good at combining breadth and depth, rigor and accessibility, the academic and the personal, soaring ideas and down-to-earth helpfulness. Her writing is conversational, inviting, encouraging, deeply insightful, and always clear.

Her personal journey of unwise effort provides a narrative backbone, and grounds this book in the seriousness of its subject. As she will tell you, in her youth she was an elite athlete with outstanding grades, good friends, and loving parents—and an eating disorder that put her in the hospital. Diana and I share a haunting bond with many others: our unwise efforts nearly killed us.

If we race about in our modern, busy, often fragmented lives—chasing gold rings and stressing along the way, pushing others and being pushed by them, pressing ourselves with self-criticism and relentless demands—we are definitely making efforts. But at what cost? Anxieties and resentments grow, and a gradual numbing, a quiet despair at the never-ending hamster wheel, and a wondering "Is this it? Is this what I'm chasing? Do I really care?" What is the collateral damage of those kinds of efforts in your body? Your well-being? Your relationships? Allostatic load accumulates, the gradual wear and tear of chronic stress. Thousands of studies have shown the costs to health, happiness, families and friendships, and lovers and mates of the unwise efforts many of us make each day.

People may say, "OK, but I need to stay hungry. I need to push hard or I'll fall behind. I can't let anyone down. I have to keep driving and then one day I'll be able to take it easier."

One of the great merits of this book is how Dr. Hill addresses this understandable concern. Brilliantly, she exposes the ways in which our efforts become unwise when we misuse our *genius*: our particular talents, virtues, and other strengths. We give our weaknesses some distance and scrutiny, but we identify with our strengths and don't realize we've become seduced by them. The world rewards this and calls for more, more. They become a familiar go-to, especially when under pressure. With repetition, they crowd out other things inside that would be good to develop—like how, for me, intellect crowded out heart for many years.

Dr. Hill brings her own genius to the joys and sorrows of genius itself. In great useful detail, she explains how to apply three key qualities of truly wise effort—curiosity, openness, and focus—to specific areas of one's life, including relationships, the body, work, creativity, and community. She draws on her mastery of ACT—Acceptance and Commitment Therapy (or Training), developed by Dr. Steven Hayes—as well as her deep roots in mindfulness and compassion training, to help readers identify their own "genius profile" and how it has been affected by both their childhood and their current environment and relationships. With the tools and support she offers, you can accept yourself more fully, soften inside, come home to the best within yourself, and continue to dream big dreams and pursue them with gusto and grace in your own best ways—without paying the price of unwise efforts.

The heart of all this is choice. Choosing to use your genius rather than being used by it. Clarifying your values and selecting your highest priorities to guide the wisest expressions of your genius. Getting on your own side, focusing on what is truly in your best interests, and leaning toward a greater happiness over a lesser one.

Choice is a sacred power, even if sometimes it can only be applied to the inner world when the outer one has no options. No one can stop you from using that sacred power, from how you learn and heal and grow in the pages ahead to how you channel and empower your different kinds of genius in the efforts you make wisely in the days and years to come. And throughout, you have with you a trustworthy guide, a genuinely kind and caring person who has been down this path herself, sharing her own mistakes and lessons, and wishing you the very best along your way.

Rick Hanson, PhD
San Rafael, California

introduction

what is wise effort?

My family lives in the foothills of coastal California, where we often leave our kitchen door open to welcome the breeze. Every so often, we get unexpected visitors—hummingbirds, blue jays, chickadees, and even a few blue-bellied lizards make their way in. The moment a bird flies in, their instinct guides them straight for the large kitchen window, mistaking it for the way out. And then, bam! They collide with the glass and tumble to the floor.

What happens next feels almost painfully human. Dazed but determined, they gather themselves and try again, this time with more force, more urgency. Bam! Again, they crash. It's a heartbreaking cycle—a mix of determination and misdirection, effort without clarity.

It's so relatable, isn't it? We are going about our lives, doing our thing, and then find ourselves stuck—maybe in a relationship, an unhealthy habit, a work problem, or our creative pursuits. And we do the exact same thing those birds do. We think if we just fly harder, go faster, or push ourselves more, we will get out. We put our immense energy into overdrive, persisting even if it hurts us. Or we freeze, paralyzed by the fear of failing or getting hurt again. Dazed and confused, we hesitate, overthink it, doubt ourselves, hide, hold back, and eventually we stop flying altogether. We find ourselves sitting on the kitchen floor of our life, feeling trapped, defeated, and exhausted, wondering, *How did I get here? And how do I get free?*

This book is about just that—how the way you use your energy shapes your life. When your energy is overused, underused, or directed toward the wrong things, it keeps you stuck, burns you out, and leaves you spinning your wheels. But when your energy is channeled with wisdom, it can take you to extraordinary places. How you spend your energy is everything. It fuels your ability to get things done, brings vitality and vibrancy to your life, and draws others toward you. Yet it's also the force that, if unmanaged, can leave you overwhelmed, depleted, and going nowhere.

If you picked up this book, you probably yearn to turn your energy around. You're likely tired of overextending yourself beyond what is sustainable, or you may feel an urgency to make a shift in your career, relationships, leadership roles, or physical pursuits. You are a striver—a flyer—you care a lot and have big goals, but sometimes you struggle to get started or keep your momentum going, and at other times you find yourself working relentlessly at things even if it means neglecting your health, loved ones, and personal needs and values. You might feel discouraged or baffled by the fact that you keep ending up at square one no matter how hard you try. No matter how good your life looks on the outside, you don't feel quite satisfied. Perhaps you can relate to one of my clients who said, "I have a constant feeling of not doing enough and doing too much at the same time. I am simultaneously overcommitted and underinvolved."

Wise effort is the answer to this dilemma. It's how you can find the open door that is waiting for you and fly toward the open sky of your life.

Using Your Energy Wisely

I first encountered the concept of wise effort over twenty years ago while studying with Zen master Thich Nhat Hanh. During a retreat at his monastery in Plum Village, France, a soldier stood up and asked whether he should leave his job. After learning about the peaceful practices of mindfulness and compassion, this man was questioning his vocation. To paraphrase Thich Nhat Hanh's response, "It is people like you we need behind the gun." His words conveyed a powerful truth: wise effort isn't about avoiding difficulty; it's about bringing your genius energy to bear in ways that are aligned with your values, no matter the circumstance.

Decades after hearing Thich Nhat Hanh's lesson for the soldier, I was on a retreat with meditation teacher Jack Kornfield. I asked for his counsel on the framework for this book.

"What is your intention?" he asked.

"I want to help people live their fullest expression without losing themselves," I replied.

With a smile, he said, "That sounds like wise effort."

Wise effort is a concept described in the Buddhist Eightfold Path. In the traditional teaching, wise effort is preventing and letting go of harmful ways of being while cultivating and maintaining wholesome ways of being.[1] In this book, we'll take a consilient approach, integrating insights from many fields of study, including contemplative practice, modern psychology, neuroscience, ancestral wisdom, and your personal embodied experience.[2] The goal is to discover what wise effort looks like uniquely for you so that you can apply it to your daily life.

In my career as a psychologist, I have focused on working with high achievers and strivers who feel stagnant or as if they're spiraling in the wrong direction. These are creative entrepreneurs, parents, executives, health-care workers, thought leaders, young professionals, and good-hearted people who are going about their efforts in ways that are depleting them and causing them to wonder if it's all worth it. Sometimes they are putting big energy into what they value, but it is burning them out because they are not being wise about it. Other times they are playing small, holding back, and not doing the thing that they really want to do. In my search to help these clients and myself, I became curious about how modern psychological approaches like Acceptance and Commitment Therapy (ACT, pronounced as one word) intersect with ancient teachings on wise use of energy.

To understand how our striving gets us stuck, I have interviewed hundreds of thought leaders, spiritual teachers, and researchers on the topic of wise effort. What can psychological science tell us about why humans repeat behaviors that clearly don't work for them? How can contemplative practice guide us toward something more effective? I have also worked closely with the developers of ACT and trained thousands of mental health professionals in the processes that underlie this method. Psychological flexibility is central to wise energy use. We all fall into unwise effort from time to time, as you will hear in this book. As I often tell my clients, our mess is our message.

As such, the Wise Effort model is woven from psychological science; contemplative teachings; my personal embodied practice; and fifteen years of applying the Wise Effort method in my clinical work as a therapist, trainer, and executive consultant.

Here's what I know: wise effort is about feeling alive; being engaged; asking bigger questions; and making decisions from your body, head, *and* heart. It's about getting to know who you are and contributing what you have to offer the world with passion and generosity. And it will change your life.

Wise effort offers a way for you to use your energy more effectively. It's renewable energy, meaning you get as much out as you put in. It isn't always about slowing down; sometimes it's spreading your wings and going full force at something that's right for you.

Wise Effort Is How You Fly

In every person I work with, I see an inner fortitude and powerful energy that, when directed with wisdom, can carry you through the winds of life and lead you to do great things. It is important to get to know this energy—what I call your genius energy. It's the force behind your strengths, talents, interests, and superpowers. Everyone has their own one-of-a-kind combination of genius energy. It's vast, timeless, and—dare I say it as an evidence-based psychologist—magical.

The word *genius* is not meant to be used to put yourself above others. You aren't "special" or better than others because of it. Rather, it honors your personal spark; indescribable essence; or intangible, fascinating qualities that make you *you*. If the word *genius* is not a fit for you, you may substitute words like *gift*, *personal strengths*, *life force*, or *je ne sais quoi*. The goal here is to democratize the word *genius* as our unique and true nature—we all have it. And you are going to spend some time figuring yours out.

You will also learn that your genius energy is both a gift and a challenge. Sometimes your genius energy isn't easy to manage and can be co-opted by unwise effort. You might have felt this when you overused your talents to try to prove yourself or ran away from your feelings by staying busy. When it gets off track, your genius can become your problem. In the pages ahead, you will learn to recognize when your energy is out of balance and skillfully redirect it with wise effort. This skill of turning your energy around can become your most powerful resource. Note that we will not tone *down* our genius energy. You might have heard people say things like "Don't be so loud, such a striver, such a perfectionist, such a dreamer." "You are too much of this or that." "Stop being so [enter your genius here]." Has anyone ever told you that? It can be frustrating and disheartening to be told to suppress your life force. You won't hear that here.

That's because being asked to tone it down is actually an attack on your genius energy. Those very quirks, traits, and characteristics have helped you survive life up to this point, whether you've experienced a less-than-stellar childhood, awkward tween years, a heavy breakup, or the trials of building families and businesses. My genius energy of persistence and emotional sensitivity are what got me through a nasty eating disorder to a PhD and a place where I could write this book for you. I wouldn't want to give up those qualities. And I bet you don't want to give up yours, either.

Don't stop being who you are. There's nothing wrong with you or your sensitivities, strengths, and differences. You don't have to dampen your light or pretend to care less than you do. Please don't stop flying. The world needs your genius.

Instead, you will learn how to apply wise effort so you can use your genius energy skillfully in any corner of your life, whether you are dealing with a work environment that's crushing your soul, facing a health crisis, deciding how to prioritize competing creative opportunities, having another fight with your partner/mother-in-law/teenager/sister/neighbor, or doing something as small as debating whether to turn off Netflix and go to sleep.

I've seen firsthand how the Wise Effort method works. Clients reclaim their energy, find their direction, and move more freely, even in the midst of difficult life circumstances. When you put wise effort into practice, you bring into being the person you want to be. It's a remarkable thing to experience.

To be clear, wise effort won't get rid of your problems. That's not the point. The issues you may be having in life often aren't the problem; it's how you relate to them that matters most.

With this book, you'll learn to engage with your energy *wisely* so it works for you—not against you or others. You'll be able to lean on what's already inside you and act on what's truest to live a more fulfilled, connected, and vibrant life.

Wise effort is contagious. Like the clients and thought leaders who eagerly agreed to let me share parts of their stories in these pages (some with identifying elements changed), once you experience it, you'll find yourself wanting to spread it, too.

The Three Wise Effort Tasks

Throughout the book, you will practice three Wise Effort tasks—Get Curious, Open Up, and Focus Your Energy—to ensure that wise effort guides your genius energy. I call them tasks because it takes *work* to be skillful with your energy use. But unlike all the other tasks piling up on your to-do list, these will free you up!

To support this work, I recommend that you get a new, unlined journal for writing and drawing assignments. Your personal Wise Effort Journal. Don't just skim the exercises in this book—if you want to reclaim and direct your energy in a meaningful way, you need to actually put some effort into this. Do the work. Answer the questions. Practice the experiential exercises. Draw the drawings. Put pen to paper. Research has suggested that writing things by hand can help you process and remember information more effectively. By engaging in the Wise Effort method, you'll develop the skills to choose moments of aliveness—to make decisions that restore and replenish your energy.

Personally, I choose wise effort, even on my busiest days, when I take my ten-minute break between clients to step outside. Instead of pushing myself to catch up on emails or going to the cupboard for a quick hit of sugar, I put down my laptop, walk down the gravel path, and exhale. I release the energy I'm holding from the client I just saw. I return to my breath, remembering my values of presence and care. I make space to welcome what (and who) comes next. My genius energy flows best when I am clear, steady, and here. Wise effort connects me to something bigger than the million never-ending to-dos that always seem to demand my attention. It's a small, personal example, but choosing wise effort has consequences that ripple throughout my life. That walk outside is a practice for how I want to walk into an important podcast interview. And *that* is a practice for how I want to show up with my kids, friends, family, clients, and community: curious, open, and wise.

It always comes back to these three simple actions: Get Curious, Open Up, and Focus Your Energy. When you combine these three Wise Effort tasks into an ongoing practice, you become the person you want to be. You learn to trust yourself more so you can make wiser decisions, big and small. With wise effort, you will utilize your genius energy in the right amount, at the right time, and in the right place. You will create a life you love and contribute to a world we all want to live in.

Let's begin.

wise effort task #1

get curious

Have patience with everything unresolved in your heart and try to love the questions themselves.

—Rainer Maria Rilke, *Letters to a Young Poet*

1
what is your genius?

One of the gifts of being a therapist is that, for the most part, people don't put themselves together to come see you. They want to see you the most when things are falling apart. Sometimes clients start crying before they put their keys on the table or before their video feed pops up on my computer screen. They are escaping their hectic lives to figure things out and arrive just as they are.

No matter how someone shows up, I see a genius energy within every person I meet—an array of strengths, talents, and interests that have served them well in life. It might be hidden, misdirected, or used in ways that are unhelpful (more on that later), but it's in there. And so is yours. Your genius energy is not a comparison between you and someone. It's about you and the qualities that make you tick. You have multiple geniuses that make up your genius energy. When channeled with wisdom, this genius energy will help you fly out of whatever kitchen you find yourself stuck in. This is the essence of wise effort—harnessing your genius energy wisely. It's expansive, it's open, and it looks and feels very different from the tangle of your struggle. Picture something like this:

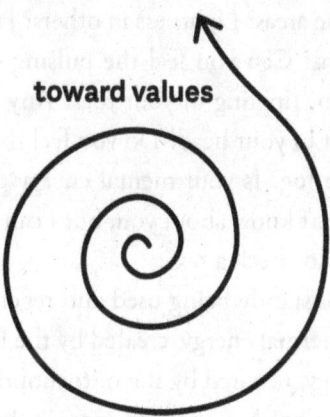

The open, expansive energy of your genius moving toward your values.

Your energy is everything—the basis of all life, including yours. In this chapter, you will get curious about the nature of energy itself. You'll explore what genius energy means to you and how you express its five aspects. Then you will observe genius energy in others and in nature. By the end of this chapter, you will have a clear definition of your unique genius energy and be ready to uncover how you can use it more wisely.

What Is Energy Really?

I've always been sensitive to the energy in a room. As soon as a client sits down, I can feel their nervous energy as they bounce their knees, the dull, sinking energy of depression as they slump into the couch, but also the wave of vitality when they talk about what they love. Then there's that energetic pull to fill an uncomfortable silence or an energetic push to problem-solve. Have you felt that before? Your energy or someone else's?

To make energy more tangible, try or imagine quickly rubbing your hands together and then holding them a few inches in front of your face. Do you feel their heat? Now rub them together again and put them one inch apart, slowly moving them back and forth. Can you feel the electrical charge?

What about the energy in your body? What do you notice? Do you feel heaviness in some areas? Lightness in others? How about the energy of physical sensations? Can you feel the pulsing of blood in your fingers? The sensation of tingling in your toes? Any energy in your chest or belly? What about in your head? Do you feel the buzz of thinking or the dullness of brain fog? Is your mental energy pulled in many directions right now? I don't know about you, but I can feel my energy being pulled to my phone to check a text.

Your energy is constantly being used and regenerated in a dynamic cycle. Whether it's thermal energy, created by the friction between your hands; physical energy, restored by the mitochondria within your cells; emotional energy, replenished through meaningful social connections;

or mental energy, renewed while you sleep, your vitality is always in motion. Every action you take, from movement to rest, from focus to relaxation, is made up of energy.

Through this lens, you may notice that nearly every field of study revolves around the concept of energy. Physicists define energy as the capacity to do work or cause change. Kinetic energy moves things, potential energy is stored up for later use, and heat energy warms us up. In essence, energy allows things to happen or move and can be converted from one form to another.

Neuroscientists talk about energy driving the connections between our neurons: what fires together wires together. Biologists describe how plants convert the sun's energy into sugar through photosynthesis. Energy also flows between us. Musicians describe the energy they draw from audience engagement as "electric," and athletes can transform the energy of a cheering crowd into a home-team advantage.

Have you ever felt a jolt of sexual energy across a room? That's the flow of energy. Our nervous systems communicate with each other before we are even conscious of it. When you catch the smiling eyes of a person at a coffee shop, your body's nervous system picks up the energy of someone else's emotional state.[1] Even something as small as a contraction of the orbicularis oculi muscles around other people's eyes gives us the message that it's safe to connect.[2]

To take this concept a bit further, consider the idea of "life force energy." In yoga, it's called our *prana*; in Egypt, they call it *sekhen*; in traditional Chinese medicine, it's your *qi*; in Finland, it's your *sisu*; and in France, it's your *élan vital*. In the understanding of many of the Indigenous peoples of the Americas, spirit energy is the life force that flows through all living things—humans, animals, plants, and the Earth itself. Numerous rituals, such as sweat lodges in the Chumash tradition and totem poles among the Haida, Tlingit, and Kwakwaka'wakw tribes of the Pacific Northwest, are performed to purify and honor this sacred energy.[3]

Even as a child, you might have felt this kind of life force energy expand when creating art or running on the sports field and multiply when playing with your best friend. You could feel it contract when you sensed a caregiver's anxiety or feel it drain when you overperformed to persuade others to like you. As I've come to learn more about life force energy through yoga, meditation, and psychological science, I've noticed that a particular form of it comes alive when we are engaging our talents and strengths. This is what I call your genius energy.

The Five Aspects of Genius Energy

Maybe you are thinking that "genius" is overstating things a bit. You know you have gifts, but does that make you a genius? Again, when I say genius, I'm not talking about your score on the Stanford-Binet Intelligence Scale. This is not your IQ. We often think about genius in relation to intellectual capabilities, but the word *genius* has its roots in an ancient Roman religion in which the genius was a guardian spirit believed to watch over a family or community.[4] Over time, the word came to mean a character of your spirit whose role was to protect moral character. If we keep closer to the roots of the word, we can think about your genius as a unique energy that you can use to protect yourself and offer outward. When I say "genius," I'm talking about a well of energy that you can tap into—specific characteristics, personality pattern, talents, habits of mind, or strengths that you have always been able to depend on.

Your genius lies in the abilities that come easily to you but may be hard for others. It's your artistic, practical, spatial, or emotional intelligence that you can use to do good in the world. It's your capacity for compassion, perseverance, innovative thinking, insightfulness, or self-discipline. It's your ability to solve complex problems or produce groundbreaking work but also your skill at making people feel welcome in your home.

In the book *Your Hidden Genius*, Betsy Wills and Alex Ellison use science-backed methods to uncover three components of your hidden genius: personality pattern, aptitude, and interests.[5] I've added two constructs from clinical and positive psychology—character strengths and emotional intelligence—to highlight your social and emotional geniuses as well. These five aspects form a spiral of your unique genius energy. You can think of these qualities as what lights you up.

1. Personality

Your personality shapes the expression of your genius—for example, extroversion and charm can amplify your leadership and networking skills, while high openness fuels your creativity and innovation. Your personality pattern is how you approach the world and develops from your temperament, early attachment, and life experiences. No one is extroverted all the time or always open to new experiences, but you may naturally lean in certain directions. For example, you might be the one who can brighten up a boring work meeting with humor or the reliable friend who always follows through or the one people call when they want to go on an adventure. Perhaps you're the glue that brings people together or the one who stays vigilant and prepared for potential crises. Your personality pattern helps you approach life's challenges in a way that is unique to you.[6] To explore how your personality shapes your genius, title a page in your Wise Effort Journal "My Genius Energy—Personality" and answer these questions:

- What characteristics of my personality (e.g., conscientiousness, introversion, agreeableness) elevate my work, relationships, or creativity?

- Do I thrive in social settings, or do I recharge best in solitude?

- How do I typically approach new experiences?

- How do I best respond to setbacks?

- What places and people are the best match for my temperament?

2. Talents

The second aspect of your genius energy is your talents in problem-solving, reasoning, physical pursuits, and creativity. Talents include things like

- Spatial visualization skills: Are you great at arranging a room, staging it so everything flows? Or assembling IKEA furniture without breaking a sweat?

- Idea generation: Do you thrive on brainstorming at a whiteboard, or is your genius in focusing others' ideas and turning them into bullet points?

- Problem-solving skills: Can you quickly diagnose problems, even when there are gaps in information? Or maybe you prefer to fact-check everything—it takes you weeks to pick out a mattress, but you get the best one!

- Information organization: Can you turn chaos into logical order? Or perhaps you excel at following a system someone else has set up?

- Physical talents: What are your physical skills? Do you have great endurance? Are you quick on your feet, great at balancing, or a natural at sports that require hand-eye coordination?

- Creative talents: What are your musical, artistic, design, or creative writing skills?

Cognitive aptitudes are best assessed through psychometric tools such as numerical, verbal, and logical reasoning tests. Remember that test where you had to imagine folding a paper, then punch holes in it and unfold it in your mind? That was a psychometric test of your visuospatial tools. If you want a low-cost test of your cognitive talents,

I recommend the one at youscience.com.[7] But you can also explore your aptitudes and talents by titling a page "Genius Energy—Talents" and answering these questions:

- How do I best solve problems?

- What do people say I am a whiz at?

- How do I best organize information?

- What physical activities come easily to me?

- What are my creative and artistic talents?

3. Interests

The third aspect of your genius energy is what intrigues you and draws you in. Interests are like emotional fuel—when you engage in them, you might experience what psychologist Mihaly Csikszentmihalyi called "flow," an immersive focus and complete absorption in what you are doing.[8]

Science shows that interests are highly susceptible to change—they evolve over time and are influenced by whom you sat next to last night at dinner, what's trending on social media, and your past experiences. For example, you may have interests like reading historical novels, latte art, fostering cats, or politics. To get to know this form of genius energy, you need to sample widely across different areas or maybe resurrect some interests you have let fall by the wayside. Follow even small sparks of curiosity to see what they might grow into. An interest in digital design, mountain biking, drone videography, crochet, or martial arts could blossom into a major part of your life. Answer these questions in your Wise Effort Journal under the title "Genius Energy—Interests":

- What are activities that make me feel energized, excited, or "in the zone"?

- What interested me most as a child? What did I intrinsically want to learn more about or do with my free time?

- What interests have I let drift that I want to bring back?

- What are some new interests that I haven't tried that I want to explore?

4. Character Strengths

The fourth aspect of genius energy is positive character strengths and virtues. Martin Seligman, considered the father of positive psychology, researched prosocial traits across cultures, religions, and philosophies and boiled them down to twenty-four character strengths that contribute to personal well-being but also our greater community.[9] They include a wide range of human virtues, such as creativity, zest, honesty, bravery, fairness, leadership, gratitude, and hope. For example, maybe you can't tolerate lying, you are always on time, and you are good at doing hard things when you know they are the right thing to do. VIAcharacter.org offers a scientifically valid measure of character strengths.[10] You can also do a little self-exploration through journaling. Answer these questions in your Wise Effort Journal under the title "Genius Energy—Character Strengths":

- When faced with challenges, what character strengths and virtues (e.g., gratitude, love of learning, bravery, teamwork) do I rely on most?

- What do people often thank me for?

- How do I inspire and support others around me?

- What makes me a good person?

5. Emotional Intelligence

The final aspect of genius energy is your emotional intelligence. This is your ability to recognize, understand, and manage your emotions while also being attuned to the emotions of others. Are you a genius at reading the room? Maybe you know how to say no gracefully, when to keep your mouth shut, where you can best help, or how to sit with someone who is grieving. These skills play an important role in personal and professional success, often rivaling traditional measures of intelligence. They allow you to regulate your emotions, connect with others deeply, build trust, and maintain meaningful relationships. Answer these questions in your Wise Effort Journal under the title "Genius Energy—Emotional Intelligence":

- What helps me stay attuned to my inner world?
- What skills do I lean on when my emotions are strong?
- How do I best show up for others who are struggling?
- When I am at my best, how do I respond to conflict?
- What are my best qualities when it comes to meeting new people?

Each of the five aspects of genius energy—personality, talents, interests, character strengths, and emotional intelligence—is expressed in your genius energy. Together they create a vibrant spiral of your greatest strengths. Can you see how unique and powerful your genius energy is? It infuses every domain of your life, and when you learn to channel it with wise effort, it can be your secret weapon in achieving a successful and fulfilling life. It's likely you have seen this kind of phenomenal genius energy in others as well.

Spotting Other People's Genius

My husband, a teacher for over twenty-five years, has a genius for patience. He can sit for hours with a student struggling with a math problem without getting frustrated. In fact, he finds it interesting. He's in flow when a fifteen-year-old can't determine how to solve an equation, knowing what to ask to unlock the mystery. Another example is my good friend Sonya Looney, world champion in twenty-four-hour women's mountain biking. She has a genius for stamina and determination that allows her to pick up her bike and cross a river in the middle of the night, raise two small children, and return to school to get her degree in positive psychology. She likes to call it her "chip on her shoulder"; if someone tells her she can't do something, she will. But I see it as her genius.

Think about your three closest friends. Can you identify their geniuses? I bet you can. Now, how about your family members or coworkers? When you start to look for it, you'll begin to see the genius in everyone. You'll recognize the genius energy in your financial analyst, who makes you feel inspired to create and stick to a budget; in your grocery clerk, who knows how to find a common humanity with you in two minutes flat while simultaneously ringing up your food and making sure your coupons go through; and in a family member who has a knack for keeping family traditions going. There's genius all around us.

Just the other day, I assigned a client to look for other people's genius, and he returned and said, "Did you ever watch Blondie live in concert in the '70s? Debbie Harry's a nuclear bomb. She's raw and punk and hot as a blowtorch. I couldn't stop watching the show. There's someone who's stepped into their genius energy." You may not be world-class like Debbie Harry, but when you sing your song, make your moves, and do what you love, you rock it like no one else because you are offering your innate gifts.

Learning from Nature's Genius

Everyone and everything has genius energy. From where I sit in my office, for example, there's a view of an oak forest. I've always been sensitive to plants, and when I feel stuck with a client, I like to look out at the thick, craggy gray branches and borrow a bit of the trees' energy.

In *The Hidden Life of Trees*, Peter Wohlleben writes about oaks' stabilizing force, "There is a scientific observation to this: The blood pressure of forest visitors . . . calms down and falls in stands of oaks."[11] The stability of the oaks surrounding my office is an unspoken reassurance to me and, I imagine, to my clients. The oaks outside my office have overheard hundreds of hours of therapy but also were here well before the Spanish colonized this Chumash land. The small surface area of their leaves allows them to preserve water during years of drought, and many of them have burn scars from past wildfires. Most importantly, an oak tree does not try to be a pine or palm tree; it has its own way of being, just like you.

Nature's genius energy is easy to spot. I encourage you to get curious and look for the life force energy in the nature that surrounds you. It might be as big as the pull of the moon or as tiny as a stream of ants working together to find their way. Nature can teach us a lot about trust, communication, and regenerative ways of living.[12]

Often, but not always, our genius is developed and strengthened out of the hardship, challenges, and changes we face in life. We evolved these qualities to survive. Just as the firefly evolved its bioluminescence as a defense mechanism against predators, you may have developed your bright, cheery spirit to get through your parents' divorce. And like a succulent that developed its thick leaves to conserve water, you might have developed your ability to remain calm and self-sufficient because very few people have been around to help you out in life. Hardship often creates the most beautiful genius energy.

Can you think of a life challenge that may have contributed to your genius energies? Were certain characteristics or temperaments favored in your household? What significant life events or transitions have contributed to the development of your strengths? How has your genius served you in getting through hard times?

The Many Forms of Genius Energy

Now that you've practiced spotting genius energy in other people and in nature, let's refine the way you describe your own unique genius energies. What would you call your genius energy if you could give it a name? Or perhaps you have many names and many different kinds of genius energy that show up in different contexts. Remember that you're not putting yourself in a rigid box; rather, you are describing sources of energy that come naturally to you, bring you vitality, and, when used well, create a positive impact.

Here are a few ideas to get you started:

Idea Generator

You are full of ideas and energize others with your wealth of new projects and initiatives. You generate energy in others with your enthusiasm. This genius can become your problem when you struggle to finish what you start or spin so many plates that you can't spin any of them very well. When overused, your generative force may dilute your ability to focus on what matters most. When it is underused, you are left with great ideas that never come to fruition.

Calming Force

You are the grounding force that people look to when things become chaotic. You can stay calm under pressure, soothe others, and have a measured response when others are losing their cool. However, this genius becomes your problem when people interpret your coolness as apathy or when it prevents you from taking action. When it is overused, you spend a lot of energy cutting yourself off from your emotions or trying to keep others calm. When it is underused, you may not be able to offer yourself the calming force you need.

Emotional Sensor

You have an incredible ability to pick up on the energy in a room. You can read others' emotions before they say a word. You are tuned in to people's facial expressions, tone of voice, and gestures in ways that others aren't.

This genius becomes your problem when you can't regulate your own emotions because you are caught up in everyone else's and when you constantly adjust your own behaviors to meet others' emotional needs. When it is overused, you are a roller coaster of others' emotions, and when it is underused, you fail to check in with your own.

Helping Hero

People call on you to help and know you will show up when they need it. You are the person who will pitch in when no one else does, and it feels great to be of service. However, this genius energy becomes your problem when you help others at the expense of your own well-being or when you become resentful that you have to do it all without much appreciation. When it is overused, you become a martyr. When it is underused, you don't help yourself or you fail to offer help when you know it's needed.

Organizer

You are skilled at seeing structure and turning chaos into order. Whether it's organizing a spreadsheet, someone's desk, or a creative idea, you are great at setting up systems. This genius becomes your problem when you get lost in the details, when you spend so much time organizing things that you don't see the big picture, or when you work to the point of no longer enjoying the process. When it is overused, you can become rigid in your thinking and lack creativity. When it is underused, you don't allow yourself to offer order where it is needed most.

Determined Stamina

When others give up, you keep going. You can persevere through physical, emotional, or mental challenges that set you apart. This genius becomes your problem when you are so focused on finishing that you don't take time to reset, reflect, or rest. You lose track of the why behind your effort. When it is overused, you become narrowly focused and don't know when to stop. When it is underused, you don't even get started because you are afraid of failing or embracing your power.

Articulator
You write and speak clearly, concisely, and persuasively. You can convey complex ideas in a way that others can understand without losing nuance. This genius becomes your problem when you overthink what you are going to say and lose spontaneity in your speech or writing. When it is overused, you hyperfocus on the details of your communication. When it is underused, you second-guess yourself and don't say anything at all.

Justice Defender
You know what is right and wrong, and you want to defend people or animals who are being treated unfairly. You sense injustice when others walk right past it, and you stand up for what you believe is right. This genius becomes your problem when your drive for justice puts you or others in dangerous positions or leads you to dismiss other perspectives. When it is overused, you can be one-sided. When it is underused, you don't share this gift of fairness with yourself.

Social Glue
You bring people together effortlessly, whether you're networking, connecting friends, matchmaking, or building teams. This genius can become your problem when you lack boundaries and prioritize everyone's connections over your own. When it is overused, you spread yourself too thin to maintain your relationships or get overinvolved in others' lives. When it is underused, you don't connect with yourself and your needs.

Planner
You are a genius at strategizing and creating a step-by-step plan. You reach your long-term goals—whether they are vacations, work goals, or your next social event—because you think ahead. This genius

can become your problem when you miss out on the here and now because you are always planning or when you become rigid in your planning and lose out on play and spontaneity. When it is overused, you are always looking ahead, hyperfocused on perfecting your plans, and miss out on your life right now. When it is underused, you leave things to chance out of fear of commitment.

Do you resonate with any of these expressions of genius? What would you add? How would you describe your genius in a way that fits you? Maybe you relate to a combination of these or something else entirely. It's important to note that your genius is not a static trait or state, and there is not just one kind. It's a form of energy, so you likely have a wide variety of geniuses that you use in different places and different ways. Take a stab at it.

Wisdom-Building Questions

Throughout the book, you will be invited to answer Wisdom-Building Questions. Please note that these questions aren't here for you to just glance over; they are central to our Wise Effort tasks. This is your work. So get out your Wise Effort Journal, title this section "My Genius Energy," and work through these prompts. The goal is to write a concise definition of your genius energy.

- Name a time in your life when you were under pressure or stress and rose to the occasion. What strengths did you rely on to help you do that?

- Go through the five aspects of genius energy and see if you can list some of your strengths—personality, interests, aptitudes, emotional intelligence, and character strengths.

- What geniuses do you see in others? What about in nature? What do these observations say about the genius in you?

- How have your early-childhood experiences or challenging life events helped shape your genius?

- Based on these answers, can you boil your genius(es) into a few sentences? Can you give it (them) a name?

Everyone has their own genius, and I want you to celebrate yours. For example, your calming force may be just what is needed when your spouse is looking for a new job or your kid is freaking out about college. And your ability to generate ideas will serve you well at your next team meeting. The only thing is, sometimes we are so tangled up in our problems that we can't see that we have a genius, or its energy gets misdirected and co-opted in unwise ways. Let's look at a struggle you are having and start to untangle it a bit to see how your genius might help or hinder the situation.

2
what is your struggle?

It's 2 a.m., and you're wide awake. You lie in bed for about twenty minutes, tossing and turning, until you grab for your phone. Breaking all the sleep advice you've gotten, you check your news app. It's not good. Your finger automatically cruises over to email, the unread messages you've been avoiding, then over to your Instagram account. Wired but tired, you head to the kitchen to get a glass of water. Out of habit, you open the fridge. You eye the wine, think about ice cream. But nothing sounds right. What is really happening here? You're struggling, but with what exactly? Lack of sleep is not the real issue; it's a symptom of something else.

Every week I get emails from potential clients sharing the struggles they want to work on in therapy:

- *I'm anxious about work.*

- *My mother is driving me up the wall.*

- *I want to be a more confident leader.*

- *I'm chasing the wrong kind of relationship.*

- *I don't know what to do next with my life.*

Likely from as far back as we can remember, we've had problems—ones that we can't seem to fix or that morph into new problems. I'll schedule a client who says their mother is driving them up the wall. However, by the time they arrive at my office, it's not their mother anymore; it's their sister. In one session, a client shares that they're anxious about work, and the next week, it's their vacation. A client who comes in to figure out their career gets cancer. A client who comes in to work on their body image loses their dad. It seems like no matter what we do, problems keep finding us. I've come to understand that it's not the problems themselves that are the issue. Problems will keep rolling in; it's what's happening inside us when they show up that we need to be most curious about.

In our sessions, I invite clients to talk about their experiences, and I've found that they often follow similar themes: "I thought it would be this way, but it turned out like that." "I keep doing more, but it's never enough." "I am getting through my day, but I am not really present in my day." When you are caught in unwise effort, you are inflexible in your thinking, avoiding your emotions, and not acting from your heart. In these instances, your genius energy has gotten off track and you've lost touch with your Wise Self. Unwise effort might look and feel like the following:

- Your attention is scattered or overfocused on unhelpful things.

- You're running from your feelings.

- You're stuck in a story about yourself.

- You're avoiding doing that thing you know you need to do.

- You feel like it's up to you alone to figure everything out.

When we are in this space of unwise effort, we are trapped in fixed views of who we are and who we are not. We may be working hard, but we're going nowhere and are often headed toward unhelpful escape routes. How did we get here? Is there a wiser way to relate to and engage with the problems that show up? Yes, there is! That is exactly what this book is about.

Think of your current struggle like the top of a Rubik's Cube—it's the most obvious pain point right now. But it isn't your only struggle, and it can change from day to day or even hour to hour. By using the Wise Effort method, you'll uncover the deeper patterns that run through many of your problems. It's less about which side of the cube you're trying to solve and more about how you approach it. When new challenges arise—at work, with family, or concerning your health—you can focus on whichever issue is most pressing. Ultimately, it's the skills you're developing that matter most because you can apply them to any problem, anytime.

So to start, let's get curious! What struggle is at the top of your Rubik's Cube right now?

Interest Curiosity

Sometimes it doesn't feel good to look at our struggles. Maybe you feel embarrassed that you are stuck again or dread looking too closely at your problem because you'll have to deal with whatever you find. That's why we are leaning into curiosity, which is about discovery, exploration, and asking questions, not just seeking answers. This creates an opening for wisdom to seep in. Dr. Judson Brewer, a neuroscientist at Brown University and author of *The Craving Mind*, says that curiosity is like ice cream; it comes in different flavors. There's Deprivation Curiosity, which motivates us to seek answers but also ends when we find them, and Interest Curiosity, which is more about discovery.[1] Research has suggested that this type of curiosity can turn social anxiety into an exhilarating conversation and small talk at a mundane dinner party into intimate connection. Curiosity can even make you more innovative and motivated at work.[2]

Curiosity can make anything magnetic because it activates the brain's reward centers—releasing dopamine and energizing areas linked to pleasure and motivation.[3] Whether you're feeling trapped in a rut of addiction, have lost the spark in your long-term relationship, or are bored during your commute, curiosity is how you begin to breathe some life back in.

When approaching your struggle, it's helpful to set judgment aside and look at it with a beginner's mind. You've probably rehashed a million possible solutions, and I want you to look at your problem in a different way. Zen koans are a great way to do this. They are clever riddles that open your mind to a new way of seeing things, and the best ones leave you questioning yourself a bit. You'll hear a few of my favorite koans throughout this book, but this first one is the most important to keep in mind. It's about staying curious. As I retell it, consider the places where your energy feels off track and which cups fit for you.

> A student went to visit a famous Zen master. The student was eager to learn and thought he already knew a great deal about Zen. The Zen master poured the tea until it reached the top of the cup, then kept on pouring as it spilled out. The student was confused. Upon reflection with the teacher, the student realized there are five types of cups:
>
> - **The Full Cup:** You are so full of other people's ideas, self-help strategies, rules, and shoulds that you can't let your innate wisdom in.
>
> - **The Upside-Down Cup:** You are shutting out new ideas because you are afraid to open up and try something different.
>
> - **The Dirty Cup:** You have a layer of unhelpful stories about yourself and others that make it hard to see clearly.
>
> - **The Cup with a Hole:** You are distracted and not present, and you can't hold on to anything that works.
>
> - **The Empty Cup:** You are open, right side up, clean, and ready to receive.

When we feel stuck in a problem—trying the same thing and getting the same result—we need to check our cup. Is it upside down? Too full? Full of holes? Dirty? If so, no biggie; turn it over, empty it, and wipe it clean. This gives you the best chance to relate to your struggle in a new way.

Draw Your Struggle

Let's explore your struggle with an empty cup in the way I do with clients and podcast guests. For example, in one particularly meaningful episode of the *Wise Effort* show, I asked the confidence coach Michael the same question I want you to ask yourself now: What do you want to work on? What is your impossible puzzle? What decision are you struggling with? What old pattern are you having trouble finding your way out of?

Here is what Michael said:[4]

> I've built a beautiful life here in Vienna over the past ten years. And I'm also at a place where I can make my business take off with a hard and dedicated push. However, with my neuromuscular condition steadily progressing, I am on the verge of losing my independence in the not-too-distant future (end of year?). That means that I have to move back to Germany to get the support I will need. I struggle with deciding how to spend the remainder of my time here to make it meaningful. Spending half the day taking care of my health and the other half working on my business may hardly be the best use of my time. Going into leisure mode and burning through my savings might lack the purpose that I need. And doing a tiny bit of each (health, work, leisure) would probably mean I'm half-assing all of it.

Michael, currently using an electric wheelchair, lives independently, but his condition is likely to progress to where he'll need help getting out of bed, holding a cup of coffee, or using the bathroom. At the same time, he's a high-achieving podcaster, coach, and influential speaker. His genius energy shines at work and in his social life. He's captivating, funny, relatable, and a natural motivator with a career that's taking off. Michael loves life in Vienna, where he feels energized sitting in the sun with friends, sharing a beer, and soaking in the good life. Yet with his declining health, time-intensive care needs, and a long, dark winter ahead, Michael was befuddled by the mystery of how to balance it all—health, career, and leisure. How to use his limited time and energy felt like a puzzle that was impossible to solve.

Take a moment to think about how you would describe where and how you're stuck. Visualize what this feels like inside. Where is your energy going when you are caught in this struggle? What does it feel like in your mind and body? What shape, design, or texture does it have? Now get out your Wise Effort Journal, label the top of the page "My Struggle," and draw it. It doesn't have to be perfect; just capture the emotional texture of being stuck. Perhaps it's a messy, tangled knot; a chaotic flight path; or something else. Here's one I drew recently. No skill required.

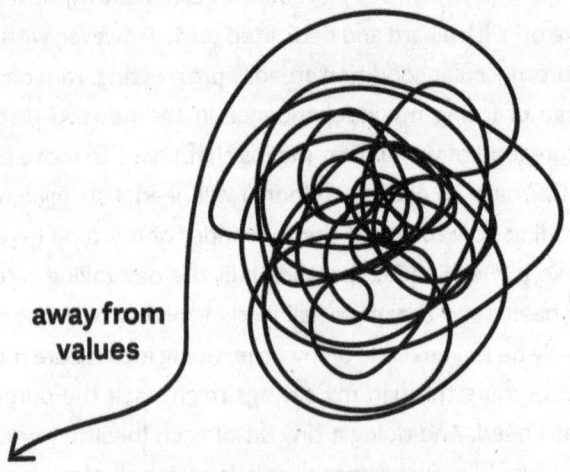

The tangled energy of your struggle.

Explore Your Inner World

Now let's get curious about what's going on inside that tangle of energy. When you are caught up in your thoughts, entangled in your emotions, and turning away from your values, you are what ACT calls psychologically inflexible. Your genius energy gets lost and misdirected in battling your problems.

But when you are psychologically flexible, your energy can flow. You are present. You have the capacity to be with difficult thoughts and feelings. You don't get caught up in a story but rather feel connected to a larger Wise Self. You know what matters to you. And you take action from that place of care. Like a river flowing freely, you are unobstructed and directed toward something bigger.

It turns out that being psychologically flexible just may be the best predictor of your well-being, over and above the problem itself.[5] A meta-analysis of over fifty thousand studies, one of the largest of its kind ever conducted, showed that it's psychological flexibility, along with mindfulness, that is responsible for change in therapy.[6] It's not just the problem that we are interested in here but also how you are using your energy in the midst of it.

Let's take a personalized look at how you relate to your struggle by looking at six dimensions of your psychology.[7] Are you flexible or rigid in how you relate to your thoughts, emotions, attention, sense of self, motivation, and behavior? As you'll see in later chapters, wise effort isn't about eliminating difficulty. You can experience discomfort while still moving forward by getting curious, opening up, and focusing your energy where it matters most.

The first step is becoming a wise observer of how you respond inside to what's happening on the outside. Think of it like lifting the hood of a car to understand how your engine runs. Few people take the time to do this, but when you do, you uncover the deeper patterns that keep you stuck. Take a moment to reflect on the following questions about your current struggle in your Wise Effort Journal on a page titled "My Inner World":

Your thoughts: Think about something that is bothering you. What thoughts run through your mind about it? Which thoughts are loudest? Do you feel trapped in your thinking, or can you be flexible with your thoughts?

Your attention: When you are caught up in the struggle, where is your attention focused? Are you worrying about the future? Stuck in the past? Scattered or overly focused? Are you able to bring your attention back to the present?

Your feelings: What are you feeling? Are you overwhelmed by your feelings? Are you avoiding them? Do you even know what you feel? Can you allow your feelings to move through you without running from them?

Your sense of self: How do you see yourself in this struggle? Do you blame yourself or feel alone in it all? Can you connect with a Wise Self, even with this problem present?

Your motivation: Do you know what your values are in this struggle? Are you chasing things that don't bring fulfillment? Motivated by external rewards? Or can you find a sense of bigger purpose and meaning in this problem?

Your behavior: How are you acting? Are you acting in ways that don't line up with the type of person you want to be? What are you doing that's effective? What's not effective?

As you can see, your inner psychology impacts how you feel in your struggle. If we respond with openness and curiosity, we can handle even the most difficult situations much better. But when we are inflexible in our inner world, we can turn even the smallest problem into a nightmare. Which brings us to the next question: If you don't turn your energy around, where might you end up that you don't want to go?

Your Nightmare Review

The next question I asked Michael during the podcast was the same question that book coach Jennie Nash asked me when I started writing this book: "What's your Nightmare Book Review?" But here, instead of a nightmare book review, we're talking about something even bigger: What is the Nightmare Review of your life?

Imagine yourself a year from now, reading a review of how you used your energy unwisely. What would it say? How do you not want it to go? If you were to use your energy ineffectively, what might happen? Keep in mind that I'm talking about things that are within your control—how you are responding to your circumstances, not the circumstances themselves. You may not have chosen to have a health condition, go through a divorce, or be depressed, but what about those things do you have control over? Can you identify any parts where you can use your energy differently? What would your Nightmare Review look like?

Here is what Michael said in his Nightmare Review:

> **Two Stars: Olympic-Level Procrastinator Misses Out on It All**
> Michael spent his time working on projects he didn't like and that didn't pay off. He spent too much time procrastinating on what needed to be done instead of getting through tasks as quickly as possible and then enjoying the rest of his time. In the last months, Michael wasn't proactive enough in facilitating time to spend with friends.

It can be difficult to write out the negative outcomes we fear, but remember, this book is about energy use. No matter what your external circumstances are, you always have a choice in where you put your energy. This Nightmare Review could be the catalyst that inspires you to make changes.

Take a moment now to write your Nightmare Review. Picture yourself a year from now, reading a review of your life where you didn't use your energy the way you intended. What would it say? To help you get started, here are a couple more examples.

> **Two Stars: She Played It Safe**
> She stayed in her uninspiring job, where she's undervalued, underpaid, and unmotivated. Despite having all the skills to start her own practice, she didn't trust herself enough to take the leap. Instead, she played it safe, staying stuck and stagnant. A year later, she hasn't moved forward—except to sink deeper into self-doubt and regret.
>
> **Three Stars: The Year of Pushing Too Hard**
> They spent the year trying to get their loved one to change—dropping hints, offering advice, and escalating to arguments when nothing worked. They poured their energy into fixing behaviors that weren't theirs to fix, convinced it was the only way to help. But instead of bringing them closer, it created distance. Their loved one grew defensive and pulled away, and the effort only left them feeling frustrated, unheard, and stuck in the same dynamic. A year later, nothing has changed except the added strain on their relationship.

These Nightmare Reviews clearly reveal how disappointing and frustrating it can be when our energy gets off track. Reflecting on your worst-case scenario like this might even provoke anxiety, but doesn't your mind do that to you all the time anyway? The difference here is that you're pausing with intention and getting curious about where you don't want to go so you can start choosing a different way. Your Nightmare Review can reveal exactly where and how to shift your energy toward something better—something that, deep inside, you really yearn for.

Human Yearnings

We humans yearn to have meaningful, rich, and connected lives. We long to grow, get better at things, have an impact on others, and experience the full range of what it means to be human. These yearnings aren't random; they are foundational to a fulfilling life. And they are a sign not of something wrong but of something profoundly right: they guide us toward what matters most.

In his book *A Liberated Mind*, Steven Hayes, the founder of ACT, writes that our core yearnings are not just desires but essential needs deeply rooted in human nature.[8] They orient us, helping us align our actions with our values and choose a life that feels truly worthwhile. These universal yearnings can be distilled into six key areas. Generally, all humans yearn to

1. **Connect with others:** We yearn for belonging and understanding; for meaningful relationships, intimacy, and inclusion; and to be part of the group.

2. **Make sense of things:** We yearn to understand ourselves and our context, for our thoughts to align with our experience.

3. **Feel deeply:** We yearn for emotional depth and the freedom to express the full range of human emotions.

4. **Be oriented:** We yearn to ground ourselves in the here and now, to be present in our lives.

5. **Have purpose:** We yearn to feel like our life matters and has a sense of chosen purpose and values.

6. **Develop competence:** We yearn for growth, to learn new skills, achieve goals, and build mastery.

Engaging in wise effort can help you fulfill these yearnings in authentic and healthier ways. Instead of chasing things that aren't satisfying and lead you to your Nightmare Review, you commit to creating a Five-Star Genius Life. But to do that, you need to get a clear sense of the genius strengths that we explored in the last chapter. Let's go there next.

Wisdom-Building Questions

Take a moment to reflect on what came up for you while reading this chapter and answer the questions below in your Wise Effort Journal on a page titled "My Struggle":

- Write a brief paragraph about your current struggle. Where are you stuck? How long have you had this problem? How does it impact your life?

- Reflect on the questions about how your struggle impacts your thoughts, attention, feelings, sense of self, motivation, and behavior.

- Next, write your Nightmare Review. Give it a title. What will your life be like a year from now if it is exactly how you hope it *doesn't* turn out?

- What does your Nightmare Review say about what you long for and how you might want to use your genius energy differently going forward?

- Which core yearnings in your life are the most unmet right now? Why?

Before we move further into the Wise Effort method, let's take a mini-assessment of where you are right now in five main areas—each of which you will be diving more deeply into in the chapters ahead. This is not a scientifically validated measure but more of a self-check. Mark the boxes that reflect where you are right now, and record in your Wise Effort Journal your sum score in each category. In the upcoming chapters, you will actively engage in practices across these areas to cultivate and deepen your experience of wise effort. At the end of the book, you'll get another chance to assess yourself to see what has shifted.

Wise Effort Self-Assessment

Values

UNWISE EFFORT	WISE EFFORT
☐ I am chasing external rewards like money, other people's approval, or status.	☐ I am motivated from the inside.
☐ I don't have a sense of purpose.	☐ I know what matters to me and what I want out of life.
☐ Life is lackluster. It feels like something is missing.	☐ I feel a sense of aliveness and vitality.
☐ I am stuck in regrets.	☐ I use my regrets to motivate change.
Sum of boxes checked:	Sum of boxes checked:

Feelings

UNWISE EFFORT	WISE EFFORT
☐ I am overwhelmed by my emotions.	☐ I can center myself.
☐ I have a hard time recognizing my emotions.	☐ I can identify and name my feelings.
☐ I try to suppress or control my emotions.	☐ I can make space for my full range of emotions.
☐ I feel overwhelmed by my feelings.	☐ I know how to take care of my feelings.
Sum of boxes checked:	Sum of boxes checked:

Mind

UNWISE EFFORT	WISE EFFORT
☐ I get entangled in repetitive thoughts, worries, and ruminations.	☐ I can make space for my thoughts, even the difficult ones.
☐ I believe my thoughts to be true.	☐ I can question my thoughts and act independently from them.
☐ I get caught in either/or thinking.	☐ I can hold two things to be true at once.
☐ I mostly see the negative in things.	☐ I often savor what is good.
Sum of boxes checked:	Sum of boxes checked:

Sense of Self

UNWISE EFFORT	WISE EFFORT
☐ I feel separate, like I don't belong.	☐ I see myself as part of something bigger than just me.
☐ I am held back by self-limiting stories.	☐ I can see beyond the stories my mind creates.
☐ I am self-critical and judgmental of others.	☐ I feel compassion for myself and others.
☐ I don't feel very wise.	☐ I am connected to my Wise Self.
Sum of boxes checked:	Sum of boxes checked:

Behavior

UNWISE EFFORT	WISE EFFORT
☐ I resist discomfort and change.	☐ I can radically accept what is here.
☐ I am stuck in unhealthy habits and routines.	☐ I try new things and can create new habits.
☐ I underuse or overuse my strengths.	☐ I use my talents and strengths wisely.
☐ I act in ways that are out of alignment with who I want to be.	☐ I act in line with my values, even when it's uncomfortable.
Sum of boxes checked:	Sum of boxes checked:

Now that you've taken a look at where you are and have gained clarity regarding where you *don't* want to go, the next step is to get curious about why we engage in unwise effort. What is happening inside us that leads us to act out of alignment with our values, get stuck in our heads, and let our genius get away from us? In the next chapter, we will explore three ways in which your genius becomes your problem.

3

how is your genius also your problem?

In 2021, I experienced my own version of a bird hitting its head against a window. I was cohosting a highly successful podcast with three other psychologists. We had nearly two million downloads and a loyal following and were on the verge of securing sponsorships, which meant we'd finally be paid! On the surface, everything seemed perfect. I was at the top of my game—I could land almost any interview I wanted and regularly spoke with famous psychologists and best-selling authors I used to only read about in books.

Yet secretly, I wanted out.

I had felt for a while that I longed to explore different ideas—ones that skirted the edges of psychology and dabbled in spirituality—but I didn't trust myself to take the leap. I was also feeling an increasingly large gap between my values and the podcast. I needed more room to fly to places beyond the sometimes inflexible space of evidence-based psychology. I was afraid of going it alone and believed my mind's story that I wasn't good enough. The longer I stayed, the more inauthentic I became, and then I started having panic attacks before team meetings. As Bessel van der Kolk says, "The body keeps the score," and mine was screaming for change.[1] I ignored my feelings; didn't trust my intuition; forced myself to stay; and became controlling, competitive, and rigid. Everyone around me could see that I needed to let go, but I held on tightly, persisting on moving deeper into a version of my Nightmare Review.

Not only was my genius energy being misdirected, but it was also becoming my problem. The very genius that had allowed me to be successful in my career—my persistence—was causing me to hold on too long. And I was ignoring my genius for emotional sensitivity when I needed it most.

When directed by wise effort, your genius energy can make extraordinary things happen, like creating a rad podcast with good friends or being a highly responsive and intuitive therapist. But when overused, underused, or misdirected, that same energy can send you in circles, away from what you care about, or even make things worse. This is a golden thread that you will see throughout this book and in your life: **Your genius—that very force that fuels you—becomes your problem if it's used unwisely, but if it's used wisely, it becomes your solution.**

You might already know this. Maybe you've heard that your greatest strength is your greatest weakness, or perhaps you have done some deep Jungian shadow work and unveiled a similar notion. If so, that's great. It will help you here as we uncover how your genius(es) can get tangled up as your problem and how you can redirect this energy for your, and others', benefit. Although we all have an inner genius, that doesn't mean we always apply it in healthy ways. In the chapter ahead, you'll get curious about why your genius gets off track so you can reclaim its power.

It's Hard to Be a Person

In case you're curious, I did eventually leave the podcast. The hardest part? It hurt. Telling my cohosts was painful—I felt like I was giving up. Watching them continue without me was especially hard. I felt deflated, embarrassed, and fearful of what people would think. Plus, I didn't want to let go of the good feeling of having a top-performing show. What if I became irrelevant? My ego took a hit as I started my new podcast from scratch. Although it was far from the hardest thing I've ever done, letting go sucked. At the same time, letting go set me free.

The reality of life is that sometimes it just sucks. It's hard to be a person. This truth is so fundamental that when bad things happen, we often say, "Well, that's life, isn't it?" ACT has a motto: pain and values are two sides of the same coin.[2] It's the things you care about most that are often the most painful to you. What turns pain into suffering is when we divert our energy away from what we value. We suffer when we ignore what we know in our gut is best for us and when we cling too tightly to things we need to let go.

Continuing a podcast that I had lost heart for was uncomfortable. What made it unbearable were the ways I tried to control what was out of my control.

Buddhism teaches a similar lesson. The First Noble Truth is that life includes both pleasant and unpleasant experiences. Although the First Noble Truth is often translated as "Life is suffering," it's more nuanced than that.[3] Not everything in life is 100 percent miserable—there's also joy, serenity, love, and all kinds of good in life. Conditions are always changing, unpredictable, impermanent, and empty until we add to them. What gets us out of joint is when we cling to pleasurable experiences or reject the unwanted ones. The Noble Truths teach us that feeling bad is not a personal failing; it's a universal experience. When we accept that everyone faces challenges, including ourselves, we're more inclined to respond with kindness and compassion.

In English, the word *suffer* comes from the Latin *sufferre*, meaning "to carry."[4] We all have burdens to carry. But what turns life's discomfort into suffering is *how* we carry them. Resisting what is makes life "unsatisfactory," as Vipassana meditation teacher Sylvia Boorstein puts it, like the grade you might have gotten in elementary school.[5] That painful podcast experience showed me that I had some growing up to do, and I will always be grateful to the pain for what it taught me. In the words of neuropsychologist Rick Hanson, let be, let go, and let in.[6]

Your Response Changes Your Experience

When you take a long view of your life, it's clear that you have gains and losses, pleasure and pain, fame and insignificance. What's striking about this perspective is realizing how much your response influences your experience. Sometimes you face hardships and come through more resilient and stronger. Life has a way of surprising us—with moments of serendipity, a sense of awe, and incredible connections that we never could have imagined. You feel like a badass in how you handled your divorce, recognize how your house fire brought your family closer, and are still talking about that time you got stuck in the airport for eight hours with two toddlers and made a game of it. You experience what psychologists call post-traumatic growth: greater meaning, connection, spiritual development, strength, and appreciation for life.[7]

But we (obviously!) don't always handle things well. Sometimes we shut down, turn away, self-sabotage, or behave in ways that don't align with who we want to be. These moments are harder to talk about because they show how we misused, underused, or overused our genius. Your energy got away from you—you either spent it in the wrong places or didn't bring it forth when you needed it most.

Too Little, Too Much, or Misdirected: Genius Frenemies

In positive psychology research, character strengths are seen as dimensional—on a continuum. Overuse occurs when your strength is pushed too far in a given situation, and underuse happens when it's not applied enough. The "optimal strength zone" lies in the middle, representing a balanced expression of that strength (often referred to as the "golden mean").[8] We need the right combination of strengths, to the right degree and in the right situation, to really flourish.[9]

Overusing strengths is as harmful as neglecting them.[10] It's the Goldilocks rule: not too much, not too little, but just the right amount of energy use in the right place. For example, if your genius is the ability to express gratitude even in difficult situations, when it is underused, you are unable to notice the good around you. When it is overused, gratitude could make you feel that you don't deserve more as you self-deprecatingly tell yourself to "just be grateful."

When you know what to look for, you can see this overuse or underuse of genius energy everywhere. It's when your friend, whose genius is humor, uses jokes to avoid uncomfortable feelings or throws themselves under the bus one too many times. Or when your coworker, whose genius is being detail-oriented, packs their reports with so much data that they become confusing.

Related to the underuse and overuse of genius energy is its misuse. Sometimes it's not that we are using our genius too much or too little; it's that it has morphed into another form that isn't our genius at all. In Buddhism, this concept is called "near enemies," or subtle qualities that masquerade as virtues but actually divert us from the wise path.[11] For instance, the near enemy of sympathetic joy (feeling happiness for others) is emotional indulgence. You become clingy and need others to be happy for you to feel happy. I call these near enemies "frenemies." They look a lot like our genius but undermine its power to do good.

Maybe you are great at giving, but this can turn into its frenemy, martyrdom, when you start expecting acknowledgment and praise in return. Or your genius for self-awareness turns into self-absorption: you tell yourself that you're engaging in personal growth, but what you're really doing is bombarding everyone with unsolicited self-help advice and book recommendations. You can see that when your genius becomes your frenemy, it actually becomes your problem.

What are the frenemies of your genius? Does it ever go sideways on you? Take a look at this chart for some examples to get you started.

GENIUS ENERGY	FRENEMY
Generosity	Martyrdom
Leadership	Domination
Humility	Self-deprecation
Appreciating pleasures	Hedonism
Helping others	Pity

GENIUS ENERGY	FRENEMY
Self-awareness	Self-absorption
Persistence	Stubbornness
Loving	Smothering

It's easy to see how overusing, underusing, or misdirecting your genius can lead to problems, but simply knowing this isn't enough to break the cycle. We also need to explore what drives these behaviors. Why do we avoid our genius when it's most needed? Why do we double down when it's clear that our genius is making things worse? And what tangles us up into thinking something is our genius when it's more our frenemy?

Our Genius Power

That example of the podcast wasn't the first time my persistence had gotten away from me. And I imagine that whatever you are struggling with right now isn't the first time you have felt this way, either. The first time I noticed that my genius was my problem was in high school. My genius for emotional sensitivity was in overdrive. I was picking up on everyone's energy, wanted to fit in, and turned to restricting my eating. My genius at persistence made me really good at it. I was running from my feelings—literally—waking up at 4 a.m. to exercise on little to no food.

Some mornings, I'd wake up afraid of myself and my power over what I was doing. Other mornings, I'd wake up proud of myself and my power over what I could do. One morning, I woke up and put my legs over the side of the bed and saw something I hadn't seen before: two long bones like the ones you see at the natural history museum. These bones were my legs. I got up and weighed myself, and I had dropped to seventy-two pounds. The next week, I was on a flight to Florida for inpatient treatment.

It can be a brutal awakening when we find that our genius is our problem. Maybe it's waking up to your affair or hearing yourself yell at your kids or getting caught in your addiction. It's an experience of hovering over yourself and asking, *What the $%!@# is happening here?* Maybe you, too, know what it's like to feel so powerful and so powerless at the same time. Our very genius can kill us . . . or save us.

So why does this happen? What causes our genius energy to go so off track? Let's turn to another koan to open this question.

Tigers Above, Tigers Below

Sometimes when a client is particularly stuck, I pull out my well-worn copy of Pema Chödrön's book *Comfortable with Uncertainty* and read them the Zen koan about a woman running from tigers. I'll paraphrase it:

> A woman is running from tigers. She comes to a cliff and grasps a vine. She starts to lower herself down, only to find tigers below. Then she notices that a mouse is gnawing at the vine. The woman looks around. She sees a patch of strawberries. So she reaches over and eats one. It is the most delicious strawberry she has ever eaten.[12]

Chödrön writes, "Tigers above, tigers below. This is the predicament we are always in."

That's exactly how we feel when caught in unwise efforts. We are running from tigers—except ours aren't real ones with stripes. They are internal: fear, inadequacy, and the stories we invent about what others think of us. Eventually it all unravels because we cling too tightly to control.

But the worst part? We miss out on strawberries—the chance to connect with others who might be feeling the same, the thrill of trying something new, and gratitude for the opportunities right in front of us.

Three Ways Genius Energy Becomes Your Problem

When working with clients who are stuck in a problem, I look less at the problem itself and more at how they are using their energy in it. There are three ways of responding to your struggles that lead to unwise efforts: you are running away from discomfort, you are holding on too tightly, or you are stuck in a story. Let's unpack each of these and how they can throw your genius energy off track.

You Are Running Away

Running from tigers is a good idea if the tigers are real. But in our modern lives, when most of the tigers we face are in our own minds, running from them can make our suffering worse instead of better. Research has shown that this type of experiential avoidance (running from unpleasant thoughts and feelings) is linked to numerous mental health disorders, such as anxiety, substance use disorders, and depression.[13]

It's pretty obvious that if you are feeling terrible and you try to avoid your bad feelings by climbing back into bed, your depression is likely to worsen. And if every time you feel anxious at a social event, you leave early or need to drink to get through it, you're likely to feel more anxious when the next one rolls around. And that project you're procrastinating on only gets more dreadful every day you put it off.

I once had a client who had an email folder called "EMAILS I CAN'T OPEN." These messages made him so anxious that he filed them away so he didn't have to look at them in his inbox. The only problem was that just looking at the folder made him extra-anxious! What's your version of this? What experiences do you run from? How successful have you been at keeping them at bay? And how does your genius play a role?

Then there's the exhausting aftermath of cleaning up the mess when our genius is misdirected. If we don't know how to handle anger, we might lash out at the people we care about most. If we can't sit with the discomfort of disappointing others, we might overcommit or say yes when we shouldn't. All of it piles up, eventually circling back to haunt us. Avoiding our emotions doesn't make them disappear; it decreases our capacity to tolerate them. As Dr. Anna Lembke, author of *Dopamine Nation*, puts it, "We've lost the ability to tolerate even minor forms of discomfort."[14]

How do you run from uncomfortable experiences, and what's the cost? Can you see how avoiding discomfort limits how big you can play with your genius energy? Go down this list and mark which of these experiential avoidance strategies you relate to most.

Common Ways We Run from Discomfort

- **Hiding:** Do you avoid showing your work, speaking up, standing out, or sharing your ideas because you are afraid they will be judged?

- **Overdoing:** Do you stay busy, multitask, overwork, rush through things, or say yes to too many things to avoid your feelings?

- **Bracing with your body:** Do you tense up, clench your jaw, tighten your belly, or hold your breath so you don't have to feel?

- **Numbing out:** Do you use substances, overcaffeinate, overexercise, overeat, or undereat to cover up your feelings?

- **Overthinking:** Do you intellectualize, problem-solve, plan, ruminate, worry, or overanalyze to try to fix your bad feelings?

- **Distracting:** Do you try to think about something else, avoid talking about "it," change the subject, swallow your feelings, or do mental gymnastics to ignore an unwanted experience?

- **Proving your point:** Do you talk over other people's ideas, force others to get on board with your agenda, or listen poorly because it would be uncomfortable to hear what they have to say?

While avoiding pain and discomfort may work in the short term, it drains your energy in the long run. The Wise Effort task here is to get curious when you are struggling and ask, *What am I running from? And how is running away misdirecting my genius?*

You Are Holding on Too Tightly

In the Zen koan, not only was the woman running from tigers, but she was gripping a rope that was unraveling. Holding too tightly to anything makes it hard to respond to life's challenges with flexibility. We grasp at peak experiences, being better than others, staying relevant, or having a life with no problems, and although we may feel a brief sense of power or pride when things go our way, holding on too tightly only leads to disappointment when these things inevitably fade or when they don't give us what we really want.

We often don't actually like the feeling we have while gripping or chasing things. You've probably felt this when receiving praise at work or buying that expensive pair of shoes; you crave these experiences, but once they happen, they're not quite as satisfying as you expected. This makes sense when you consider that brain research has shown that wanting and liking are controlled by two separate neurological systems.[15] While they typically work together (we usually want what we like), over time, these systems can shift. Through a process called "incentive sensitization," repeated exposure makes our wanting system hypersensitive so that we crave more and more, while our liking system builds tolerance, making us enjoy it less.[16] We want that second slice of cake, that third glass of wine, that fourth pair of jeans, but when we get them, we don't really like them as much as we'd hoped. The brain's reward system, driven by dopamine, becomes overactive, making us want more, while the liking system grows more habituated, making us like less.[17] The result? We want a lot but don't like much—and that's no fun!

One thing we tend to hold too tightly is our self-image—especially when it comes to wanting people to like us. We crave those "likes" on our posts and the approval of others. But chasing that kind of validation is exhausting, and it pulls us away from what really matters—like creating meaningful work, loving without conditions, and actually enjoying the journey instead of obsessing over the results.

It's no surprise that research has linked basing your self-worth on external validation to higher levels of stress and unhappiness.[18] When your sense of worth depends on social media likes or hearing a steady stream of "Great job," you're setting yourself up for disappointment. What happens when you get only three likes on your post instead of twelve? Or when you aren't acknowledged for the hard work you put into a project? It's easy to feel deflated or even worthless. And even if the attention keeps coming, it often feels empty. It's not what really fills you up.

On the surface, it may look like we are diligently working toward specific objectives or experiences—work success, lots of followers, a fancy house and car, or a perfect family. But deep down, what we are attached to is how we hope these things will make us *feel*—competent, secure, seen, content, loved. It goes back to those core yearnings we explored in the first chapter. The yearnings make sense, but when you are clinging, you are going about things in an unskillful way.

Take a look at the following list and take note of where and how you may be holding on too tightly. When you hold too tightly, it limits your ability to live out the best expression of your genius energy.

Common Ways We Hold on Too Tightly

- **Controlling:** Do you work hard to control yourself, others, and life in general? Do people tell you that you're rigid or perfectionistic? Do you hold unrealistic expectations for yourself and others?

- **Promoting self-image:** Is it really important to you to *appear* successful in other people's eyes? Do you base your sense of worth on what others have to say about your intelligence, work, performance, appearance, fitness, or finances? Do you spend a lot of time and energy curating and promoting yourself?

- **Pleasing others:** Do you try to please people, ask for reassurance, or seek external validation that you are good enough?

- **Chasing things:** Do you chase more things—a better car, designer clothes, a peak experience, a bigger gig? Are you going for more followers, certifications, degrees, or trophies despite chronic stress and exhaustion?

- **Keeping rigid routines:** Are you attached to a specific routine or habit? Do you work hard to keep things the same, avoid change, or follow a strict schedule? Can you handle it if something goes awry in your routine?

- **Being right:** Are you attached to your beliefs and being right? Do you think other people are wrong or that there's only one solution to problems: yours? Do you think you always have the best answers?

While holding on can seem like the way to secure stability, you end up wanting a lot but not liking much. The Wise Effort task here is to ask yourself when you are struggling, *What am I holding on to here? How is holding too tightly misdirecting my genius?*

You Are Stuck in a Story

The third thing that can trip your genius energy up is believing the stories your mind tells you. Our minds are fantastic storytellers, but not every tale they spin is trustworthy. A lot of these stories are old, outdated, and not even yours to begin with. They come from culture, upbringing, or the collective consciousness, sneaking into your head and shaping how you see yourself and the world.

We tell ourselves things like "There's something wrong with me," "Everyone else has their life together," or "I'm better than them." Sound familiar? We overfill our schedules because we think being busy is just "normal," or we cling to the belief that we have to follow a specific life path to be successful.

And it doesn't stop there. How often do you get stuck in stories about the future—"What if this happens?"—or find yourself replaying the past—"If only I had . . ."? Think about something you did or didn't do ten years ago. Are you still carrying that story? Now consider the stories you're spinning about next week. And don't forget the ones we invent about others: you read a text, fill in a tone that's not there, and assume all sorts of things—"They're ignoring me," "They're upset with me," "They think I'm annoying." The less information we have, the bigger and juicier the story we create. And here's the kicker—we don't even realize we're doing it. As Daniel Kahneman writes, "We can be blind to the obvious, and we are also blind to our blindness."[19]

So here's the big question: what self-stories are you stuck in? And how do these beliefs limit or block your genius energy?

Common Self-Stories

- **Not good enough:** Do you believe you are inadequate or don't measure up? That you must prove your worth and earn love to keep up?

- **I'll be happy when:** Do you believe that your happiness will come sometime in the future? Do you think you will finally be happy when you get through school, get married, get a particular job, make it through a difficult transition, or achieve a certain goal?

- **Don't have enough:** Do you have a scarcity mindset? No matter how much you have, does it never feel like enough? Is it hard to feel satisfied?

- **Better than/worse than:** Do you put yourself above others? Do you think you are more intelligent, influential, or wiser than others? Or perhaps you believe the opposite—that you are inferior, less than, or not as competent as others.

- **It's all up to me:** Do you feel like you are responsible for everything? Do you think that you, as an individual, are in charge of everything that happens in your life? Are you stuck in a story that says there is just one way to do things?

- **They are, they never, they can't:** Do you put other people in boxes? Create stories about what they are capable of or not capable of because of your biases and beliefs?

- **I am, I never, I can't:** Do you box yourself in—believing that you are capable of certain things but not others? Do you stop trying—or never start—because you believe that you will fail?

When do these stories show up for you? How do they block you from living the life you want? When you catch yourself in unwise effort, ask, *What is the story I am believing here, and how is it misdirecting my genius energy?*

Like the woman running from tigers, we all move in and out of unwise efforts. It will get easier to spot over time, but for now, I recommend that when you notice your energy is off track, ask yourself three things:

1. Am I running from discomfort?

2. Am I holding on too tightly?

3. Am I stuck in a story?

Then stop, look around, and eat some strawberries. There is always good to be had in the here and now; don't miss out on it!

Wisdom-Building Questions

Let's look at how your genius can become your problem. Get out your Wise Effort Journal, title a page "My Genius Is Also My Problem," and answer the following questions:

- How are you overusing, underusing, or misusing your genius energy?

- What are your tigers? What thoughts and feelings are you running from?

- How do you run away? What are your avoidance strategies when life gets hard?

- What are you holding on too tightly to? Is it misdirecting your genius? How?

- What are your strawberries? What are you missing out on in your life that you want to pay more attention to?

In this chapter, we discussed how the way in which you respond to your struggles makes a difference in your suffering. But what about context? Your biology, relationships, and environment play big roles in your ability to engage in wise effort, too. After all, we don't live in isolation. To use your genius energy wisely, you need to see the big picture—that's what we will get curious about next.

4

how does your environment impact your genius?

When Tina wakes up, the first things she does are feed her cat, make a pot of coffee, and pull up the shades of her RV—but that's pretty much it for morning routines. She might be looking out the windows at the sun rising over the mountains or perhaps a field of cows; other days, she's looking at her neighbors a few feet away across a parking lot. Tina loves this unpredictable aspect of her life.

Four years ago, Tina was working at a group home for children and adolescents where she was overworked, underpaid, and disenchanted by the politics of her workplace. Sure, it was meaningful work, but her heart and genius were no longer in it. Despite pushback from family and friends who wanted her to use her degree in psychology, she had always dreamed of living on the road. Determined to make it happen, she saved up to buy an RV, started a virtual assistant (VA) business specializing in supporting mental health professionals, and took her work on the road as "The Wandering VA."

This lifestyle is not perfect, but it fits her talents and values. Tina is a genius at planning, mapping out six months of travel as efficiently as she plans her clients' social media strategies. She also has a gift for building quick connections, which she uses to make new friends at RV parks and maintain strong relationships with her clients. Tina says the freedom to work outside, take midday hikes, connect with the RV community, and set up her laptop under her outdoor tent has greatly improved her mental health, creativity, and overall quality of life, and this spills over into supporting her clients. For her, hitting the road was wise effort—directing her genius energy to where it would best thrive.

Maybe, like Tina, you have spaces where you are thriving, and it feels like you've got the wind at your back and your genius energy is flowing right where it needs to go. You also may have other places where it feels exactly the opposite—you are sailing straight into the headwinds of a toxic work environment, an unsupportive spouse, a chronic health condition, or a stressful living situation. You might have nasty coworkers who weigh you down or spend so many hours sitting in front of a screen that your eyes burn at the end of the day. Perhaps there's so much conflict at home that you can't summon the energy to remember that you even have a genius, let alone believe you can use it wisely.

What we often don't look at—or haven't accepted—is how our environment impacts our genius energy. It's not just that you aren't getting enough sleep, aren't exercising enough, or hate your boss; it's that the context of your life—the water you swim in every day—might be hitting you where it hurts most and dampening your unique talents and strengths.

The irony is that when directed with wise effort, your genius energy is the thing that can connect you to healthier spaces. So knowing how context impacts your genius matters—a lot.

With wise effort, you can seek out environments that lift you up, make changes to the environments that deplete you (when possible), and know when to stop exhausting yourself in struggles you simply can't win.

Your Context Matters
Clinical psychology has a long history of ignoring context and societal influences when it comes to mental health and human flourishing. In the traditional medical model of diagnoses, if you were to come into my therapy office complaining of low mood, low energy, feelings of worthlessness, difficulty concentrating, and weight gain, I might diagnose you as having major depressive disorder. Sure, you met the necessary five of the nine symptoms listed in the *Diagnostic and Statistical Manual of*

Mental Disorders (DSM-5) criteria, but what about the other factors that may be contributing to how you feel? Maybe you're exhausted because you've been flying red-eyes for work, or you are devastated because your dog just died, or you can't concentrate because you are trying to figure out how to get your aging dad to admit he can no longer safely drive. Without context, it's hard to know where to intervene.

Another trap that many of us fall into is the fundamental attribution error—we tend to overemphasize dispositional factors and underemphasize situational factors when explaining others' behaviors. This bias is especially present in individualistic cultures, where personal characteristics are often highlighted over contextual influences. For example, in the US, we may call someone lazy or unmotivated for not getting enough exercise and fail to see that they work long hours at a sedentary job, have to commute by car, and have no one to watch their kids after work. It's not laziness; it's context.

Recognizing the broader context that impacts you helps you avoid placing blame on a single cause or falling into the trap of "There's something wrong with me." The environment you inhabit shapes your opportunities, habits, and the way you perceive yourself. For example, the people you engage with may amplify your strengths or make you doubt them. Your physical setting might energize or drain you. Your cultural and societal contexts set expectations that can guide or limit your expression. People often overestimate their ability to overcome environmental toxins. We think we can choose whether something affects us. But if you have been in a bad marriage or workplace for years, no matter how strong your character, you will be changed by it—and probably in ways you don't want to be changed.

This chapter is about identifying how your environmental context—your biology, relationships, workplace, and life circumstances—impact your energy flow. You will get curious about each of these four categories and how they deplete or support your genius. We will not dive right into fixing these, in part because some may not be fixable, but also because I want you to linger in curiosity a little longer. Don't worry; you will get a chance to make tangible changes in the Focus Your Energy section of this book. But before we do that, it's important to slow down, empty your cup, and take a look at how your environment is impacting your energy.

Biological Supporters and Depleters

You've probably read the headlines about how sitting is the new smoking and how we all need to eat more fiber. You likely have a few great health tips in your back pocket, like deep-breathing skills or a seven-minute HIIT workout. But have you taken a close look at how your biology influences your energy? Your biology impacts everything—your outlook, your creativity, your brain fog, your openness to experiences, and yes, your genius energy.

We often ignore our bodies as if they are separate from our minds and mental energy, but they are inherently connected. When you get curious about your biological context, you just might discover how essential your biology is to your energy levels.

For example, I recently had a client who spent weeks procrastinating on starting a newsletter; they finally found the motivation they needed to actually do it after joining an early-morning exercise class. And a friend of mine found that her irritability with her spouse dramatically improved once she and her doctor figured out a good protocol to treat her perimenopause, which was wreaking havoc on her sleep.

That's because the biological basis of energy happens at the cellular level. When we are chronically stressed in an unmanageable way, eat poorly, and don't get deep rest, we speed up the metabolism of our cells (hypermetabolism).[1] Stress ages us faster. When it comes to your energy levels, scientists are particularly interested in your mitochondria. These are like the batteries for your cells, and they need to be regularly recharged. Stress researchers have found that stress, poor nutrition, and lack of sleep age our cells, but deep sleep and exercise are like "mitochondria medicine."[2] If you want your genius energy to thrive, it starts with the body.

Let's take a look at some of the key biological factors that may be impacting your energy at the cellular level. The goal here is to identify aspects of your biological environment that you can address to better support the restoration of your genius energy.

Here's a quick self-assessment to determine whether your genius energy is being depleted or supported by your biological environment. Mark an X along the line that best reflects where you land in each of these areas.

- **Sleep and rest:** How do your sleep and rest impact your energy, focus, and ability to use your talents and gifts? Consider how well rested you feel when you get up in the morning. Do you get enough sleep? What about mini-rests? Do you take breaks throughout your day to recharge your energy levels?

    Depletes Genius Energy   **Supports Genius Energy**

    -5 ——————————— 0 ——————————— +5

- **Movement:** How do your current type and amount of physical activity impact your genius energy? Are you getting the amount, variety, and type of movement you need to feel energized, strong, and physically challenged?

    Depletes Genius Energy   **Supports Genius Energy**

    -5 ——————————— 0 ——————————— +5

- **Eating habits:** How does your eating—both the nutrition you put into your body and the time and space you devote to nourishing yourself—support your energy?

    Depletes Genius Energy   **Supports Genius Energy**

    -5 ——————————— 0 ——————————— +5

- **Health conditions:** How do your health conditions, including pain management, contribute to or detract from your genius energy? Are you getting the support you need?

Depletes Genius Energy   Supports Genius Energy

-5 ———————————— 0 ———————————— +5

- **Substance use:** How does your substance use (perhaps including coffee and alcohol) impact your energy? Do you use substances to boost your energy? Are they working for you long-term?

Depletes Genius Energy   Supports Genius Energy

-5 ———————————— 0 ———————————— +5

If you answered in the positive, "supports genius energy" range in any of these areas, celebrate that! These are areas of your life that you can lean on to grow or stabilize your genius energy. We often put physical health on the back burner until something goes terribly wrong, and it's valuable to notice the ways in which your physical health is making a massive difference in your ability to thrive—far greater than it might seem. Note the role that you are playing in what is working well for you, biologically speaking. Sure, you may be getting great sleep, but it's likely because you are prioritizing it. Look at the ways in which you are already engaging in wise effort and double down on them.

If there are areas where your biology is depleting your genius energy—areas where you scored below zero—first, it's important to acknowledge that our current systems don't support our bodies in thriving. Have self-compassion that it is not your fault and that in order to be healthy in unhealthy environments, you just may need to be a deviant! If your energy is depleted and you have no idea what's going on (e.g., an undiagnosed chronic illness, hormonal/life changes), it can be hard to assess problems and solutions on your own. I recommend seeking support from a physician, and feel free to skip ahead to the Wise Effort with Your Body chapter of this book to explore this area further.

You also may want to take a look at how your inner psychology may be interacting with an unhealthy environment. Remember the three ways our genius gets misdirected? You may be **stuck in a story** that you are "special" and can get away with five drinks a night or that it doesn't matter if you put off that doctor's appointment another month. Or you may be **avoiding the discomfort** that comes with moving your body or scared to face your stress without using food to escape. You might be **holding too tightly** to a routine or schedule that doesn't allow for body care. Look at the areas where your sleep/eating/movement/illness/pain/substance use is depleting you and ask the same questions you explored in the last chapter:

- Am I running from discomfort?

- Am I holding on too tightly?

- Am I stuck in a story?

In the Wise Effort method, we will explore ways to shift to a more effective response. This will include working to design your environments to support you and opening up to the discomfort that comes with choosing wiser ways of eating, moving, resting, and caring for your body. More on that in the Wise Effort with Your Body chapter. In the interim, stay curious—taking note of how your energy is pushed around by your biology. No one has a healthy body or perfect health behaviors all the time. The goal here is to identify aspects of your biology that you can address to better support your genius energy.

Take my client Angelo, for example. Angelo, an engineer at a software company, experiences chronic back pain that interferes with his creativity and focus at work. It's hard to stay engaged when your back feels like it's on fire and you constantly need to shift positions. His back pain has worsened as his life has become more sedentary—he used to enjoy the risk of mountain biking in college but struggles to find time for it now with two kids, a forty-minute commute, and a demanding job. The less he moves, the more his back hurts, the more irritable he becomes, and the more snappish he is at work and home. Most evenings, he has a couple of beers to wind down but lacks the energy to get to the gym or go for a walk. Angelo is stuck in a vicious cycle of energy depletion, and his geniuses—engineering creative solutions and riding the edge of risk—have been lost in the mix. The good news? Just a few tweaks, like going to a doctor, exploring physical therapy, and finding a support team so he doesn't have to figure out pain management on his own might help. Swapping his beers for some forms of movement that get him out in nature again, even if it's not his dream mountain biking, could also be a step in the right direction. And redesigning his workspace to support more movement in his workday could help. It's going to take some engineering and risk-taking, but that is his genius!

Relationship Supporters and Depleters

Our relationships also have an enormous impact on how we feel and use our genius energy. We are tuning forks to the people who are around us—picking up on their moods, stress, and interests—and we have been since infancy. If your genius is being a visionary, a skeptic, or a helper, it's likely that your early attachments to caregivers shaped these aspects of your personality.[3] And your genius energy is still being impacted by relationships, no matter how old you are. Do you have people in your life who encourage you and help you recognize your potential? When you have those kinds of relationships, you may notice that you play a little bigger and feel more confident in your pursuits. The whole course of your day can shift when you are around a relationship supporter—and a depleter can tank your efforts in a hot second.

Depleters can cause self-doubt, lead you to hold back your genius, or lead you to unwise efforts.

The people around us (chosen and unchosen) are part of our environment—we interact with their energy, feed off it, feed into it, and can get depleted by it. If you are in relationships with people who scrutinize and criticize your every move, they might be squeezing your zest for life right out of you. But when you are in relationships with people who see you and cheer you on, there's nothing quite like the lift in energy you feel. Each of us is likely to have *many* people who energize us in different ways—not just one person who is all things to us. Just as with exercise and nutrition, it's wise to diversify your relationships and find the ones (plural!) that complement and optimize your genius energy.

Whenever I have a client who is waiting to find the "one person" who can provide them with everything—friendship, love, sex, and financial security—I remind them of the truth that no one person can support all our genius energies in every way. You might have one friend you reach out to when you need a motivational push to get out there and assert yourself and a different friend you turn to when you are sad and need to cry it out. There are even limits to what your spouse or romantic partner can provide. Maybe your partner provides comfort and security but not the adventure that you crave. You can seek out friendships that reinforce your wild side rather than depending on your partner to meet all your energetic needs. The best relationships complement your genius energy, build on it, celebrate it, and remind you how fabulous you are.

In chapter 10, you will get a chance to find ways to reenergize your relationships and design your Genius Advisory Board—a powerful exercise that will help you determine the kinds of relationships you want to build in your life to maximize your wise effort. For now, let's get curious about how your current relationships are impacting you.

Again, let's take a self-assessment of your relationships: Are they depleting or supporting your genius energy? In this exercise, we're considering general categories of relationships, and we'll get more specific about individual relationships in chapter 10. Mark an X along the line that best reflects where you land in each of these areas.

- **Immediate family:** Think about your relationships with your immediate family in general. How does interacting with them influence your genius energy?

    Depletes Genius Energy   **Supports Genius Energy**

    -5 ———————————— 0 ———————————— +5

- **Extended family:** How does your relationship with your extended family affect your ability to thrive?

    Depletes Genius Energy   **Supports Genius Energy**

    -5 ———————————— 0 ———————————— +5

- **Romantic relationship(s):** How does the dynamic in your romantic relationship(s) (if you have any) impact your ability to express your talents and strengths?

    Depletes Genius Energy   **Supports Genius Energy**

    -5 ———————————— 0 ———————————— +5

- **Work relationships:** How do your professional interactions and connections affect your energy and productivity?

    Depletes Genius Energy   **Supports Genius Energy**

    -5 ———————————— 0 ———————————— +5

- **Friendships:** Do your friendships energize you, uplift you, make you feel stronger? How do your friendships (or lack thereof) impact your ability to express your greatest strengths?

  Depletes Genius Energy   **Supports Genius Energy**

  -5 ———————————— 0 ———————————— +5

- **Online Relationships:** Do you have supportive online relationships? Are social networks draining your energy or fostering connection?

  Depletes Genius Energy   **Supports Genius Energy**

  -5 ———————————— 0 ———————————— +5

- **Community:** Do you interact with a greater community? Do your casual interactions feel positive and uplifting? How does your involvement in your community shape your overall energy and motivation?

  Depletes Genius Energy   **Supports Genius Energy**

  -5 ———————————— 0 ———————————— +5

Considering your answers, where are you strong in your relationships? Who amplifies your genius, and who depletes it? Are there rifts or drifts you'd like to repair? Any relationships you want more distance from? And how can you use your genius energy to support your relationships? Perhaps it's activating your inner dreamer to envision fresh, creative ways to bring some spice into a long-term relationship. Or maybe it's using your emotional sensitivity to recognize others who may be going through similar struggles and sharing your story with them. By leaning into these gifts, you can cultivate the connections and support that fuel you. As you will learn in the chapters ahead, building great relationships with wise effort takes getting curious, opening up, and focusing your energy on your values. Sophia is a perfect example of how this works.

Sofia was a genius at leadership and tended to be the chief organizer of her group of college friends. After her divorce, however, she realized that she was putting much more energy into her friendships than she was getting back. Her married friends rarely returned her texts or were too busy to meet up. She felt lonely and longed to rebuild her life. Over time, Sofia realized that being single in her midthirties was very different from being married. She saw that she needed to invest her energy in building new relationships instead of expecting her old ones to meet all of her needs. Her financial situation had also changed after she left her marriage, and she needed friends who understood that it wasn't feasible to go out for dinner and drinks every weekend. Sofia used her leadership skills to organize a hiking group for singles and discovered people who could share enjoyable and affordable experiences and relate to her new phase of life. They appreciated her genius at being bold and taking the lead, and she fed off their enthusiasm and openness to new experiences. It was a win-win—as genius energy exchange can be.

Workplace Supporters and Depleters

A lot of us want to engage in wiser effort at work because we spend so much time doing it. Maybe you want to be more efficient and productive, make an impact with your talents, or simply spend your days in a way that doesn't feel like a waste of your life. If you're feeling far from a genius at work, you're not alone.

According to Gallup's 2024 workplace satisfaction report, US employee engagement was at a ten-year low. Less than one-fourth of employees felt engaged in work, and 15 percent reported feeling "actively disengaged."[4] Engagement is a good proxy for genius energy. When you're engaged, you care about your work, go beyond simply meeting job requirements, feel driven to contribute, and take pride in what you do. You feel aligned with the overall success of your organization and eager to do what you do best. Do you feel engaged?

If not, there might be key factors depleting your genius energy. Your work environment—people, space, and culture—plays a huge role. If you feel a sense of autonomy, relatedness, and purpose, your genius is more likely to shine. But if you feel disconnected from coworkers and clients, face discrimination, or have no opportunities for advancement, your genius has no safe space to grow. Many jobs focus only on the results we deliver (money earned, tasks completed, targets met) and ignore the effort that goes into our work.

This isn't just about paid employment. If you're a homemaker, student, or in the exhausting process of looking for work, you also need to feel acknowledged for how hard you're working, even if it's not tied to a paycheck. When we aren't valued for our essential roles such as being a caregiver, volunteer, or homemaker creating a stable and loving home, it can leave us feeling less engaged and motivated.

Burnout is a syndrome where you feel exhausted, are negative about your work, and experience a sense of reduced professional efficacy. You just can't muster up the energy, desire, or genius to do your work well.[5] Dr. Christina Maslach, a psychologist at the University of California, Berkeley, described burnout as being "like a pickle."[6] Your genius can get pickled by the environment it's sitting in!

If you're dragging yourself to work, feeling increasingly detached from your job, or noticing a decline in the quality of your work, burnout could be creeping in. The worst part of being "pickled" by work is that you start to detach from your genius. You lose touch with your inner spark, spontaneity, and sense that you have something valuable to offer.

According to Maslach, we are burned out not because of something we are doing wrong but because of problematic work environments. Maslach identifies six key mismatches between employees and their workplace that can cause stress and exhaustion.⁷ Go down this list and note just how much your work is pickling you.

- **Workload:** Are you overwhelmed by your work or underresourced to meet the demands on you?

    Depletes Genius Energy   **Supports Genius Energy**

    -5 ————————————— 0 ————————————— +5

- **Autonomy:** Do you have control over how and when you approach your work? Does your workplace give you time to take care of your mental health, physical health, and family?

    Depletes Genius Energy   **Supports Genius Energy**

    -5 ————————————— 0 ————————————— +5

- **Reward:** Do you feel valued, well compensated, and appreciated at work?

    Depletes Genius Energy   **Supports Genius Energy**

    -5 ————————————— 0 ————————————— +5

- **Community:** Are your coworkers supportive? Do you look forward to seeing the people you work with and feel a sense of belonging?

    Depletes Genius Energy   **Supports Genius Energy**

    -5 ————————————— 0 ————————————— +5

- **Fairness:** Do you feel discriminated against? Does everyone in your workplace have equal opportunities for growth?

Depletes Genius Energy   **Supports Genius Energy**

-5 ———————————— 0 ———————————— +5

- **Values:** Does your work align with your personal values and purpose?

Depletes Genius Energy   **Supports Genius Energy**

-5 ———————————— 0 ———————————— +5

Where does your workplace support your genius energy? Where are mismatches depleting you? Few workplaces excel in all these areas, but if you are scoring low in a lot of these areas and you see little chance of things changing, it may be time to consider a new job. If leaving isn't an option due to financial constraints or other responsibilities, there are still ways you can practice wise effort in the workplace. We will explore those in chapter 12.

When you are doing right-fit work—work that is aligned with your genius and values—it will bring you energy even if it's stressful. I experienced this when I had my first child while serving as the clinical director of an intensive outpatient program for eating disorders. It was demanding work, but I loved it. I was constantly learning—how to effectively use psychodrama techniques, how to navigate insurance intricacies, how to manage a team—all under the guidance of a supervisor who genuinely cared about my well-being as a whole person. I was exhausted, but it was a "good stress" that stretched me and allowed me to use my genius. My emotional sensitivity helped me connect deeply with my team, while my persistence made me stick it out, especially for clients whose odds of recovery were quite low. I saw their genius energy, and I used mine to help them see it, too.

Some evenings, eager to get home to my baby, I'd pump breast milk in the car while driving, hoping the semitruck drivers wouldn't look down. I'd rush through the door to the comforting sight of my patient husband playing music or reading stories with our little one. It was a relief to have support at home—knowing my baby was cared for—and at work, where flexibility and right-fit work allowed me to share my genius energy. But even with all of that, I still fell into the trap of feeling like I was not doing enough.

That time in my life was some of the most demanding yet fulfilling work I've ever done; looking back, I now see that there was no way to do it all or live up to the expectations I was setting. I was in an incredibly privileged position to have great childcare and a healthy workplace, and it was still difficult. We need communities to support us if we are going to do effective work—people who share the load, workplaces that see us as whole people, and infrastructures to help working families. Although we are talking about the workplace here as a separate environment, it is inherently linked to your homelife and community. You need positive connections in the workplace and at home to support your genius energy if you want to use it to do good work at the office or in the home. If your workplace is crushing your genius energy, you need to get curious about what aspects of it you have the power to shift and where you can find more support. It might be that you need to open your mind to changing jobs, finding creative childcare solutions, or accessing the humility you need to admit you can't do it all at the same time. That will all take wise effort, which you will practice in the Open Up section of this book.

Life Circumstances Supporters and Depleters

When Giselle came to therapy, she wasn't just burned out from work—she felt as though she had lost her mojo entirely. Her genius for persuasion, which had made her an exceptional attorney, had turned inward, convincing her that she was broken for struggling to keep up with the demands of a high-powered job and motherhood. Her brilliance at producing high-quality work was driving her toward depletion in an environment where her efforts went under-recognized. A woman of color in a sea of white men, Giselle was swimming upstream.

On top of that, she was grieving and recovering from extreme life stress. In the past year, she had given birth to her second child; lost her mother to cancer; and moved across the country, thousands of miles away from her supportive siblings. It was no wonder her treadmill pace had slowed to a crawl. The badass mom and attorney she knew herself to be felt far away.

Sometimes what depletes our genius the most is uncontrollable life circumstances. Systemic barriers, like being overlooked, discounted, or devalued because of your race, gender, ability, sexuality, or other identity, can weigh you down. Or you might be reeling from a personal crisis—a natural disaster, a big move, a job loss, a breakup, or the death of a loved one—that has knocked you off your feet.

It's important to remember that loss, crisis, and even disasters are inevitable parts of life—70 percent of people will experience a traumatic event at some point in their lives.[8] If you're in the thick of it, feeling terrible is not only normal—it's warranted. (We'll explore this more in the Open Up Your Feelings chapter.)

How you respond to life circumstances can either restore or further deplete your genius energy. When life hits us hard, we are even more likely to fall into the three traps that deplete our genius—we get stuck in a story that we can't handle it or that it's our fault; we run away from our feelings; and we hold on too tightly to wishing things were different. To turn your energy around, you will need to practice getting curious, opening up, and focusing your energy. Don't worry; I'll walk you through the steps on how to do this in the Open Up section, like how Giselle and I walked together through her grief. First, Giselle became curious about her own self-stories about what it meant to be a good mother or effective attorney and the ways she was avoiding grieving. And then she opened up to another way of viewing her life, realizing that she could grieve while also expressing her genius at persuasion.

She began sharing her experiences with other women attorneys by crafting personal and inspiring articles for LinkedIn. One of her favorite pieces was an ode to her mom titled "Everything I Learned About the Power of Persuasion, I Learned from My Stay-at-Home Mom."

Through this process, Giselle's genius became a tool for connection and healing. Writing allowed her to feel closer to her mom, reclaim her spark at work, and persuade herself to take her grief and turn it toward helping other working moms trying to make it all work.

Now let's assess how your life circumstances impact your genius energy. Mark an X along the line that best reflects your experience in each area:

- **Major life transitions:** Are you recovering from—or still in the midst of—a crisis or traumatic event? Are you undergoing a major life transition like moving, switching careers, or becoming a parent? How is this life transition impacting your genius energy?

    Depletes Genius Energy   **Supports Genius Energy**

    -5 ——————————— 0 ——————————— +5

- **Grief:** Are you navigating a personal loss, such as the death of a loved one or the end of a relationship? How is this loss impacting your energy levels, talents, and skills?

    Depletes Genius Energy   **Supports Genius Energy**

    -5 ——————————— 0 ——————————— +5

- **Systemic barriers:** Do you face systemic barriers, such as discrimination or exclusion, that deplete your energy? How do barriers like lack of access to health care, job insecurity, lack of mental health support, or experiences of discrimination or marginalization impact your vitality and energy?

  Depletes Genius Energy   **Supports Genius Energy**

  -5 ————————————— 0 ————————————— +5

- **Safety and security:** Do you feel safe in your home, workplace, or community? Do concerns about safety impact your ability to express your talents and gifts?

  Depletes Genius Energy   **Supports Genius Energy**

  -5 ————————————— 0 ————————————— +5

- **Financial stability:** Do you have the financial resources to meet your needs? Are your finances a source of stress, limiting how and where you use your genius?

  Depletes Genius Energy   **Supports Genius Energy**

  -5 ————————————— 0 ————————————— +5

If you're scoring low in any area, give yourself permission to acknowledge what feels hard and overwhelming. It's not about "fixing" your circumstances—it's about approaching them with wise effort. You as an individual can't control systemic barriers or reverse personal losses, but you can get curious about how you might navigate them more effectively, which is what the remainder of this book is about.

This kind of acceptance can free up genius energy. What is under your control, and where you can make a difference?

Wisdom-Building Questions
I encourage you to reflect on the specifics of how your environment impacts your energy. Get out your Wise Effort Journal, title a page "The Impact of My Environment," and answer the following questions:

- Where in your biological environment do you see opportunities to make changes that could better support your energy?

- Are there relationships you're putting too much energy into or ones that could benefit more from your unique strengths and talents?

- What aspects of your work environment drain your energy the most, and where do you feel most inspired or energized?

- When you reflect on how your life circumstances are impacting your energy, how does this shape the way you view yourself and your struggles?

You should now have a pretty good sense of how your genius energy is impacted by your environment. What is out of your control, and what do you have power to change? Part of this process is defining for yourself how you want to show up in these circumstances—for example, do you want to stay present and connected? Maybe connecting with people who can relate to your struggle could help? Values like these can help you guide how you use your genius energy, which is where we will go next.

5
what are your values?

So far, we have spent a fair amount of time looking at your genius energy and how it becomes your problem. Now we come to the fun part. Your values are the compass that directs this powerful life force energy. They help your genius energy stay on track. When guided by the wisdom of your values, you will have the clarity and motivation to use your genius to tackle any challenge that comes your way. This is wise effort. Aligning your gifts and talents with your values will lead you from a one-star life to a life you can give a five-star Genius Review.

If you could live life fearlessly and freely and use your energy in the ways you want to, what would you do? Remember Michael from chapter 2, who wrote his Nightmare Review about leaving Vienna? Well, our work didn't end there. I asked him about his five-star Genius Review, and this is what he said:

> **Five Stars: Michael Living on His Own Terms**
> I'm living life on my terms. I only take on work projects that are a "fuck yes." I won't spend time on it if I'm not excited about it. And I no longer avoid pissing people off. Sometimes that means canceling things for a good reason, and for others, it's chasing down things that are meaningful to me. I will be the pain in your inbox if I really want it. A fearless review in the area of my health is that I am ready to go to the extremes. Some days, I have a challenging workout day; other days, I let myself do nothing, go sit in the sun with my friends, and use my time to enjoy Vienna in the summer.

Michael was on to something. Wise effort is not about being perfect; it's about coming alive, engaging with life meaningfully, finding vitality in the hopelessness of it all, and living out your Genius Review. In order to do this, you need to know where and how to direct your energy. What would a Genius Review life look like for you? You may be surprised that the things you are going after are not what you really want, and the ways you are acting are not how you really want to act. If you were to live life to the fullest, what would that be like? That's what you will figure out next.

What Brought You Here?

One of my favorite exercises, which I use to open my clinical trainings, is something I call "therapist musical chairs"—no small talk, only deep questions. I turn on music, and then I give these instructions: "Walk around the room, and when it stops, ask the person you are closest to, 'What is it that you care about that brought you here?'" It doesn't take much before people perk up, tear up, and feel close.

While leading this exercise in Sedona, Arizona, one night, I rang the bell, stopped, and found myself standing next to Dalya.

"What is it that you care about that brought you here?" I asked.

Dalya answered, "I care about refugees. I want to help them feel safe."

Later that week, Dalya shared that she had been born and raised in Baghdad, Iraq. "I was six months old when the Iran-Iraq War started in the 1980s," she said, "and I lived through two more wars before we escaped to Damascus in 2007. It took another two years before we arrived in the United States."

Dalya told me that her mom knitted to calm her nerves while the windows cracked from nearby bombings. As a child, she spent many days indoors playing board games when it was unsafe to go outside. When the shelling let up, Dalya and her friends would race to the rooftops to collect and trade shrapnel. She smiled with sad eyes, remembering what it was like to play during wartime.

For Dalya, the trauma only continued when she moved to the United States. She had trained as a microbiologist, but her degrees were void in the US, and she had to start from scratch. She was given a bill for $1,300 to pay off her plane ticket and was offered a job cleaning bathrooms in a hotel (which she declined despite the pressure to make money).

"How did you become a therapist?" I asked. Dalya explained that when she arrived in the US, her social workers learned that she spoke both English and Arabic and asked her to interpret sessions with other refugees. At first, the work was retraumatizing for Dalya, as she often had to interpret others' stories of war while processing her own. But as she continued, she found a new sense of purpose and energy. She had geniuses in determination and lightheartedness; even in the toughest situations, she could see possibility. Over the next few years, Dalya completed her master's in social work and became licensed as a therapist.

Toward the end of dinner, Dalya pulled out her phone and showed me pictures of her pool and front yard. She said, "I still don't fully feel at home here. I am not sure if I ever will. But I am grateful to have a safe place to live. And I'm determined for other refugees to feel safe also. It's painful, but it's possible."

In Dalya's story, you can feel the pulse of her genius (determination) and how she applied it to what she cares about: helping others, especially refugees. She values independence, play, industriousness, honor, compassion, and love, and you can hear how these values helped direct her genius energy toward starting a new life that is personally meaningful to her.

Values like these open our hearts and guide our genius energy in a direction that benefits not only us but everyone around us. Living in line with our values does not always make life easier. In fact, in many circumstances, it makes life more uncomfortable. However, our values ultimately help us generate more of what we really want in life and meet our core yearning for deep connection, feeling, and a sense of understanding, grounding, growth, and purpose.

Without values, your genius energy can run rampant or stay underground. But with values, your genius can be harnessed for the greater good. Values revitalize you when everything seems to fall apart and inspire you when you feel blocked or stagnant. Values channel your life force toward beneficial means. And when we collectively act on our values, we end up creating a more prosocial world.

What, Why, and How of Values

Many people have written about the "what" of living well, like goal setting, objectives, time optimization, and those "tiny habits" that stack up over time. Other self-help authors have written about the "why" of living well, encouraging us to look at the purpose behind our goals. I remember reading Stephen Covey's *The 7 Habits of Highly Effective People* in college. Covey encouraged readers to ask themselves about the why behind their climb, observing, "If the ladder is not leaning against the right wall, every step we take just gets us to the wrong place faster."[1]

What and why are important questions to ask when designing our lives, and values can help guide us in both. But values also add another important component: how. How do you want to move from Point A to Point B? How do you want to climb that ladder? With adventure or safety? With mindfulness or humor? By harming yourself or stepping on others along the way?

When your genius becomes a problem, it's often because your gifts and talents aren't aligned with your values. For example, if enthusiasm is your strength, without values you might overpower your teen when discussing their college choices. But when guided by values like respect or autonomy, you might step back a bit and give them space to come to their own informed decision. If you're highly organized, your values can help you approach an aging parent's health concerns with both efficiency and compassion. You have many talents and strengths (as you learned in chapter 1), and it's your values that channel them into meaningful action—so at the end of the day, you can feel proud.

Values help us describe how we want to be in the world and how we use our genius energy to get there. They aren't necessarily your strengths; they are how you want to show up in your strengths. For example,

Dalya's genius is determination in any situation, and she directs that by being of service (her value) to others. Here are a few examples of values to give you a sense of them, but I encourage you to make up your own. Values are very personal!

- **Being present:** Fully engaging in the current moment, giving undivided attention to the people and tasks at hand.

- **Being adventurous:** Embracing new experiences and challenges with enthusiasm and willingness to explore the unknown.

- **Being honest:** Communicating with transparency and integrity, staying true to your word and values.

- **Being courageous:** Facing fears and challenges head-on, taking action even when it feels uncomfortable or risky.

- **Being kind:** Offering compassion, understanding, and generosity to others in words and actions.

- **Being humorous:** Bringing joy and lightness to situations through wit and playfulness, helping others see the brighter side.

- **Being forgiving:** Letting go of grudges and resentments, allowing yourself and others the grace to move forward.

- **Being loyal:** Standing by others with steadfastness and reliability, honoring your commitments and relationships.

Notice that all of these values start with the word *being*. That is because values are ways of being; they are not static. They move and change with you depending on your context and how you want to act. What are the top principles you want to live by? If you aren't sure of your top few, hold that question as we move through some ways of defining values. I don't expect you to make a list of three core values, laminate them on a poster for your wall, and leave it at that. I want you to get a feel for what it means to live from your heart and use that to direct your genius energy. Your values are dynamic, evolving alongside you.

Values Help You Do Hard Things

Whether you have big goals like Dalya's of supporting war refugees or smaller goals like learning conversational Spanish, walking your dog daily, or improving your communication skills, your values provide the intrinsic motivation needed to stick with a task. They also give you the satisfaction of enjoying the process.

Years back, when I was in the library with my kids for story time, I overheard a mother and toddler debating about using the bathroom.

"Honey, you need to go now because we have a long drive home," the mother tried to reason.

The three-year-old looked at her, put out his hand, and demanded, "Where's my M&M?"

Many of us grew up getting "extrinsic rewards" like these. Whether it was good grades, "good girl" praise, or a handful of M&Ms, when you are extrinsically rewarded for a behavior, you will do it only when the extrinsic reward is present, not for the sake of the behavior itself. That young boy in the library was less concerned with the good feelings of growing up and developing competence and independence and more concerned with getting his M&Ms!

Values don't work like M&Ms. They are intrinsically rewarding, meaning you engage in them for their own sake. Sometimes people will notice that you are being kind or generous and offer you words of encouragement or praise, but not always. Sometimes you will disappoint people or be punished for living your values. When you are intrinsically rewarded, these pats on the back are not what drive you. Something deeper, something more consistent propels you forward.

Clarifying your values can help you navigate that tricky thing that happens when you are rewarded for doing what you love. Perhaps you've felt it when you start getting paid for work you'd do for free or when you post your workout on Strava. Suddenly what once motivated you from within feels driven by outside validation, losing some of its authenticity. Grounding yourself in your values can bring that genuine energy back to your efforts.

In a 2013 study published in the *Journal of Contextual Behavioral Science*, college students participated in online training meant to increase their academic performance using either goal setting or goal setting plus values exploration.[2] When the researchers asked the students to write out specific, measurable, achievable, relevant, and time-bound (SMART) goals, it had little impact on their grades at the end of the semester. However, students who set SMART goals *and* wrote about their personal reasons for caring about improving their GPA showed significant improvement in the semesters that followed.

Take a moment to reflect on yourself. What motivates you from the inside out? What are your top three values? Unlike willpower, when you apply values to your genius, your energy is endless.

Values Are a Process

Values are ongoing, unfolding ways of being with no end point. You will never graduate from being a loving parent or get to the end of being a generous friend, a creative writer, or a passionate lover. And although you can check the boxes of getting adequate sleep or hydrating your body, you will never finish caring for your body. How you express your values, though, changes as your context changes. Values are a process, but often their outcome is quite remarkable, making the seemingly impossible possible. As social activist adrienne maree brown writes in *Emergent Strategy: Shaping Change, Changing Worlds*, "Perhaps the most egregious thing we are taught is that we should just be really good at what's already possible, to leave the impossible alone."[3]

One of the ways I've learned about how to apply my values to my genius energy is by watching my kids play sports. As a psychologist, I am lucky to have psychologist friends who specialize in all sorts of helpful things. One of those friends, Liz Boyer, is a sports psychologist who has worked at the collegiate and Olympic levels. I called Liz one day when I was feeling lost on how to help my nine-year-old son with baseball. My genius of emotional sensitivity was picking up on his struggle, but I knew that my genius of persistence could backfire if not applied wisely.

Game after game, I would stand by the fence and watch him go up to the plate to bat, his hands gripping the bat and his face gripping harder. Then he would stand there, frozen, watching the ball whiz by. He'd never swing. "Three strikes—you're out!" the ump would shout.

The hardest part was the ride home, listening to him beat himself up. "I'm the worst person on the team and last in the lineup! I'm letting them all down! It's embarrassing! I don't want to do it anymore," he'd say, defeated.

My heart broke for my little guy. Do I let him quit? Do I push him to stay? I value teaching my kids grit but also not torturing them. What was the wise effort move here?

"It's so hard as a mom to watch your kid struggle," Liz said, "and this is a classic issue in baseball. It's a sport where even if you are a top major league player, you will get out 70 percent of the time. Think about that. If you had only a 30 percent chance of succeeding, would you not want to give up, too?

"He's focusing on the outcome—hitting the ball," Liz said. "You've got to get him to put his energy into something that he has more control over. How does he want to swing? How does he want to place his feet? And why is he playing baseball in the first place?"

Over the next few weeks, my son and I talked about why he wanted to learn baseball (to get better and play with his friends) and the processes he wanted to focus on (having an even swing and enjoying the game). With the attention off whether he hit the ball, he felt less stressed when at bat and significantly improved his game. I felt better, too, as I focused my genius energy toward my values. On the drive home, I empathized with my son about how hard it is to be at bat with everyone watching. I pointed out the progress I was seeing in his swing and was persistent in reminding him that no matter how he played, I loved him to pieces.

You can apply this same concept of "focusing on the process" to your struggles, whatever they may be. For example,

- **At work:** Perhaps you're working toward a promotion or managing a demanding project. Instead of fixating on the outcome—whether you get the promotion or the project succeeds—focus on how you approach your daily tasks. Are you showing up with creativity, organization, and collaboration? Are you using this opportunity to develop skills that matter to you?

- **In relationships:** Maybe you're navigating a difficult time with a partner or trying to deepen a friendship. Instead of worrying about whether the relationship will improve or survive, focus on the values you bring to it. Are you being compassionate, honest, and present? Are you making small efforts to connect, even in tough moments?

- **In health goals:** If you're trying to lose weight, run a marathon, or recover from an injury, shift your focus from the end goal to the daily practices that align with your values. Are you listening to your body, fueling it well, and showing up consistently for movement? Are you treating yourself with kindness along the way?

- **In creative pursuits:** Whether you're writing a book, painting a masterpiece, or learning a new skill, instead of obsessing over the final product, focus on the process. Are you showing up to create consistently? Are you embracing the joy and discovery in the act of doing?

By anchoring yourself in your values and focusing on the process rather than the outcome, you not only make the experience more meaningful but often discover that the outcomes you hoped for—or even better ones—naturally emerge.

Where to Find Your Values

When I'm in session with a client, I am on a values hunt. A client may be telling me about how they're jealous of their sister or the boxing class that's got them jazzed or how annoyed they are that their ex is late picking up the kids again, and while I am listening, I am pondering two key questions: 1) What brings you vitality? 2) What brings you pain?

These are the two tells when it comes to spotting values. If you were in my office, I'd be looking for the moments when you light up and lean forward on the couch; this is when I know we are on to something. And when your voice softens, you look down, or you change the subject, I can tell there's something painful but important showing up. As Debbie Sorensen and I describe in the *ACT Daily Journal*, "Values and pain are joined at the hip."[4]

That's what Daniel discovered when he was diagnosed with an uncommon aggressive cancer in his neck. As a military medic, Daniel's particular genius was his combination of sensitivity and vigilance. Working in the field, he had minutes, sometimes seconds, to figure out if his patient was fine, in a bit of trouble, or about to die. He often needed to make life-and-death decisions on insufficient data. But when he was diagnosed with cancer, this very genius was what tormented him. Daniel couldn't stop finding new subtle symptoms and worrying about all the possible adverse outcomes: *Am I dizzy? Did that CT scan show the nodes below my clavicle? What's that lump in my armpit?*

His worry was so all-consuming that some days, he called me between therapy sessions for extra coaching. His hypervigilance was especially on overdrive between tests. The days leading up to an MRI scan or blood test were excruciatingly full of uncertainty. So I was surprised when Daniel came into my office one day looking lighter.

"What happened to you?" I asked. "Something's shifted."

"It got really bad this weekend," he told me, opening up the journal he had been keeping. "Then this happened":

> May 24
>
> It's amazing how many days have passed since writing this gratitude list. But today was a peak day—truly one of the best I've ever had—with my daughter Athena out bouldering at Lizard's Mouth. Timeless. Nowhere else to be. Just the two of us, alone on the rock. She's incredible, and I'm so grateful. Lately, my thoughts have been shaded with sadness, like I might be leaving soon, but today was pure presence—minute after minute of total flow. We laid out a blanket at the edge of the crag, and then I headed for the rock face. Midroute, as I was reaching for a tough handhold, I glanced over at her. She was stretching for an impossible move and said, "Hi, Daddy." My heart nearly burst. It was life at its most life-y. We owned the entire Earth. If there was an alternate reality where this day did not happen, I feel like I would have never fully been alive.

Daniel touched something profound that day, an awake state that might have eluded him had he not been in such close proximity to his mortality. His values—his love for his child and the planet—channeled all of his genius sensitivity and vigilance toward being present. He wanted to live ALL of the moments. "Life at its most life-y" is an excellent way to describe our experience when we allow our values to carry us.

What Makes You Feel Alive?
Think about a recent time when you felt life at its most life-y. It could be a moment of awe, an upsurge of vitality, or a moment when it felt

good to be alive. Can you picture it? See if you can remember yourself in that moment as if you were peeking in a window. What was the setting? Who or what else was there? What were you doing? How were you holding your body? How were you breathing? Now imagine you could step into your body in that memory, hold the same posture, and feel the aliveness in your chest, your belly, and the palms of your hands. Breathe the way you breathed then. Enjoy this for a few moments—breathing your values in and out, amplifying them with your awareness.

Now, in your Wise Effort Journal, title a blank page "Life at Its Most Life-y" and draw what it felt like in your body. Perhaps it resembles an open, expansive spiral, like the one I introduced in chapter 1. Or maybe it resembles a flower that is opening or a person leaping across the page. Clients draw all sorts of things when I ask them to do this, and it's always inspiring to see on a page what your experience feels like inside. Life at its most life-y is you living your values and using your genius.

Next, consider what that life-y moment says about what you care most about and where you want to spend your time and energy. Whom do you want to be around? Or maybe it shows that you want to focus more on connecting with yourself, with nature, or with spirituality. Every day, look for those moments, no matter how small, when life feels most life-y. When you spot them, mentally highlight them. And for extra benefit, you can replay these life-y moments as you go to sleep at night. Instead of reviewing your worries or unfinished tasks, ask yourself, *When did I feel most alive today?* Be your own values highlighter and see if you can boil them down into something sweet to sleep on.

What Do You Regret?

Sometimes finding sweet, life-y moments can be hard because life's low points and regrets bog us down. If that's the case for you, please know that there is nothing wrong with you, and there is just as much opportunity to discover your values in your regrets as in your joys.

Regrets harbor potential untapped genius energy that, when released, can free you up to engage in the wisest form of effort—the effort of repair, amendments, new beginnings, or authenticity. Regrets tell you what type of person you want to be in the world, and they can be a wise guide in helping you make the shifts that, deep down, you know you need to make.

If you have been blocking your regrets, shoving them away in some attic of your mind, it's time to get curious and pull them out. All it takes is pausing to consider some simple but big questions. You don't have to fully answer these questions just yet. For now, read through them and notice what they stir up in your body.

- Looking back on your life, what do you wish you had done differently?

- Is there a moment in life where you wish you had been more bold, wild, or open to risk?

- Which relationships do you wish you had prioritized more?

- Have there been moments when you acted in ways that contradicted the essence of who you are?

"Regret makes us human, and regret makes us better," Daniel Pink said in his book *The Power of Regret*.[5] Pink has surveyed thousands of people and found that regret is one of our most commonly reported emotions, second only to love. In fact, 82 percent of people reported experiencing regret at least occasionally, and there are more similarities than differences in regrets across age, race, and gender.

When I interviewed Pink, he offered a solution for our regrets: Confront them. Think about them. And use them as clues.[6] He found that regrets typically fall into four main categories:

1. **Foundation regrets** are all the times we choose short-term gain over long-term benefits. We regret not saving money, not wearing sunscreen, or not exercising more.

2. **Boldness regrets** come from not stepping up, speaking out, or showing up in our lives. We regret not being true to ourselves and our dreams.

3. **Connection regrets** happen when we don't tend to relationships. We regret letting relationships drift or not repairing conflicts.

4. **Moral regrets** result from acting in ways that go against our beliefs and values. The most common are cheating, harming someone, being disloyal, or dishonoring authority.

Reading through these categories of regret, you can begin to see why we have them. At its root, regret teaches us to prepare for the future, be bold, connect with others, and be moral, and it functions to help us learn from our mistakes and grow.

In workshops, I'll often hand out blank note cards and ask the participants to write down at least one regret. Then I have them turn the note card over and write about the value this regret connects to. What is it that you care about that makes this regret so painful? In every regret is a hidden value. It's because you care that you have remorse.

If you regret not going to the dentist, maybe it's because you value taking care of your body. If you regret not attending graduate school, perhaps it's because you value intellectual growth. If you regret not repairing your relationship with your mom before she died, maybe it's because you value forgiveness, humility, and love.

At the workshop, we sit in a circle with our note cards and share what we wrote. "I value trust," said a participant who I know had had an affair. "I value self-respect," said a participant who had shared earlier that they were struggling with alcohol abuse. When you identify the value behind your regret, you can take the energy wasted on ruminating about the past and turn it toward action in the present. If you value trust, how can you act on that trust today? If you value self-respect, what does that look like in the here and now? Acting on your values helps you heal regret. Give yourself space to feel your regrets, but don't get stuck in them. We can't go back and fix the past, but we can heal from it and create a new future by how we respond in the present.

Opening Up

Eight months after my interview with Michael, he wrote me about how he was doing. This is what he said. When you live your values, you naturally will generate a Genius Review.

> My situation hasn't changed much, by which I mean that it's still drifting in the same direction. Today is one of my ON days—get up early, work out, eat healthy, then get to work (at 2 p.m.) and work until 8 p.m. It seems that I have many more ON days than I would like to, and things still keep piling up. BUT since our conversation in April, I have developed an ability to not feel guilty or under pressure all the time. And, for what it's worth and however long it will last, right now I'm exactly where I want to be. My health is still keeping me independent, I'm making enough money to pay my rent, I work with clients in a meaningful way, and I'm working on a video course and writing a book. Who knows if and where this will lead, but I shall be buggered if I'm not at least going to enjoy most of that ride. Oh yeah, also, Vienna is freaking cold in winter!
>
> Cowabunga,
>
> Michael

Wisdom-Building Questions

Take some time now to define the values that are present for you. Answer these questions under the title "What Are My Values?" in your Wise Effort Journal:

- What is your five-star, fearless Genius Review? If a year from now, you were to write a review of your life where you get what you really want, what would it say?

- Describe a time when life was the most life-y for you. What does it show you about what you care about most?

- What do you regret most, and what do your regrets tell you about what matters to you?

- Can you boil your top three values down into a few words?

- How might these values help you redirect your genius energy in a problem you are facing right now?

Practice Getting Curious

If all you remember after you close this book are the three main steps—Get Curious, Open Up, and Focus Your Energy—you will be well on your way to wise effort, but we've only just completed the first of those steps: Get Curious. You discovered that you have a genius energy inside you that has propelled you to do great things in life. It's your talents, strengths, what people admire in you, and what gives you energy. You also learned the ways that your genius can become your frenemy when you run from feelings, hold on too tightly, or get stuck in a story. You untangled a place where you are stuck and learned how context plays a role, and then you explored your values—what can redirect your genius when it gets off track.

Remember that bird stuck in the kitchen? It takes effort to find your way out. Getting the courage to turn around and do something different is uncomfortable. But it's what is needed to get yourself flying again. Your genius is your power; your values can help direct it; and in order to fly, you need to open those wings! That's why your next task is to open up your thoughts, feelings, and sense of self so that you can open up to change. When you do this, it takes the tangled energy of your struggle and transforms it into wise effort. If you draw this shift, what would it look like? Get out your Wise Effort Journal, title the page "Open Up," and sketch it out. Here's an example.

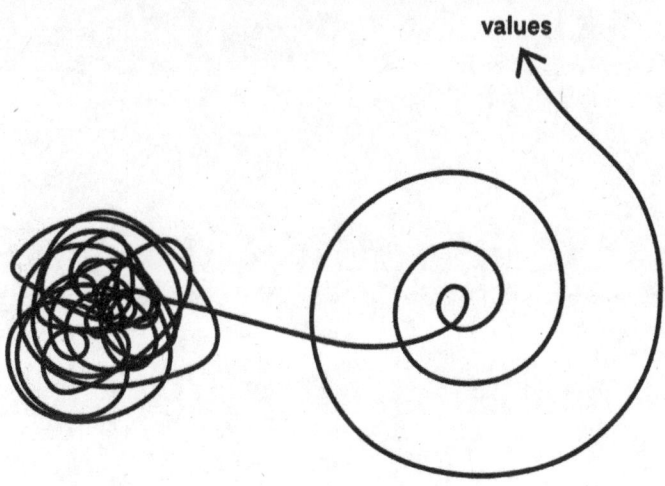

Opening your energy up to wise effort.

wise effort task #2

open up

You're the only one who knows when you're opening and when you're closing. You're the only one who knows when you're using things to protect yourself and keep your ego together and when you're opening and letting things fall apart, letting the world come in as it is—working with it rather than struggling against it. You're the only one who knows.

—Pema Chödrön

6

open up your mind

During the COVID-19 pandemic, a lot of people got pets—dogs, cats, hamsters—to keep them company. My neighbors got . . . a rooster. We live in a canyon where there's lots of land, and it's not unusual for neighbors to keep goats, horses, and worm farms. The rooster was a first. This rooster crowed at 6 a.m., as roosters are supposed to do, to greet the sun and welcome the day. It was a welcome new alarm clock in our neighborhood. The problem was that the rooster also crowed at random times all day—when I was recording an important podcast interview or webinar, when I was trying to meditate, when I was in session with clients. And it was not a sound you could exactly ignore. *Cock-a-doodle-doo!*

Our minds can be a lot like roosters in this way, crowing away all day long and distracting us from what we really want to focus on. Sometimes what they say is helpful and at the right time, like when we need to be reminded to meet a work deadline, solve a complex problem, or plan for the future. But other times, it really can feel like there is a rooster in there disrupting our peace.

Like a rooster, your mind might say unhelpful things, like when you are starting a new project and it criticizes every move or when you are trying to enjoy a nice moment and all your mind can think about is how it could be better or when it will end so you can get on to the next nice moment. What is your rooster mind crowing about right now? Is it helpful? Maybe it's not specific, well-formed thoughts that bother you but rather your mind jumping from one thing to the next. Regardless, you can't focus.

To channel our genius energy wisely, we need to learn how to work with our rooster minds. You may be thinking, *Just tell the* *neighbors to get rid of their &*^% rooster!* Sure, I could have done that, but I have equally noisy boys who throw balls in their yard. Plus, I want peace with our neighbors so I can call on them when I need their help. Trying to wrangle roosters opens up another level of problems. So does trying to fight your mind. As soon as you try to not think a thought, it rebounds—a phenomenon known in psychology as the ironic process theory.[1] Research has shown that when you try to suppress thoughts, especially emotionally charged thoughts, they become even more prominent.[2] This occurs because it's mentally demanding and your cognitive resources are stretched. You've likely experienced this when you try not to think about that thing you are really worried about, that hot person across the room, or how awkward you sound in a conversation. The thoughts just get louder and more distracting.

Another solution is to try to cover up the rooster sound with other sounds. I could have turned on white noise or pretty music. But that's problematic, too. I'd have to turn up the music until it was so loud that I'd drown out important sounds (like my clients talking), and the loud music would likely only remind me of—you guessed it—that darn rooster. Have you ever tried to cover a negative thought with a positive one or to distract yourself from your unwanted thoughts? I see this all the time with clients. "Just think positive" or "Don't think about it" is no match for your rooster mind. Plus, some of your unwanted thoughts may be important to examine. Even though they are painful, some of the thoughts you are trying to ignore need your attention.

But there's another option that isn't fighting the rooster mind or trying to distract from it: opening to it. Look, you can't get rid of your mind any more easily than I could get rid of my neighbor's rooster, but you can learn to work with it. Sometimes your mind has helpful things to say; other times, you need to let it crow away and focus your energy on what is important to you. Here are the five steps we will take in this chapter to open your mind so that you can use your values (not just your thoughts) to guide your genius:

1. Make space for your thoughts.

2. Question your thoughts.

3. Enter the paradox.

4. Savor what's good.

5. Trust your heart-mind.

Your brain is constantly producing thoughts, much like a rooster crows. Even at rest, the brain's default mode network generates spontaneous thoughts, causing your mind to wander to wonderful and not-so-wonderful places. Then, when you focus, your prefrontal cortex engages in deliberate thinking and planning. Both of these states are important—the wandering mind is where creativity happens, and the thinking and planning mind is where work gets done.

Your mind's capacity to use language and relate things conceptually is amazing. It allows you to fantasize, problem-solve, and make meaning of things. But there's a dark side to this because you can also anticipate painful events, relive terrible memories, compare yourself to others, and conjure up dreaded things that don't exist. Because your mind can relate abstract concepts, it can worry, make up stories, and talk you out of doing things that are good for you. Unless checked, your mind will lead you to put energy into all sorts of places that aren't aligned with your values.

Step 1. Make Space for Your Thoughts

To truly manifest your genius energy, you can't always listen to your mind. That's because when you are struggling, your mind isn't always the best at giving you advice. It's negative, it complains, it compares, it comes up with the worst-case scenario. Without space from our thoughts, we can't see them clearly, and it's hard to choose which thoughts are best aligned with our values. Our thoughts can really push our genius energy around if we let them.

Take my client Shana, for example. When I asked what she wanted to work on, she said she was tormented by thoughts about her ex-husband. She described him as narcissistic, demeaning, and emotionally detached.

"I'm standing there, handing my kids off to him," she said, "and all I can think about is how much I hate him. I keep replaying the time I had a horrible stomach flu, and he told me I was just being lazy. Then my mind spirals—what if he's saying the same thing to my boys when I'm not around? I get so lost in my head that I can't focus on helping my kids transition to his house."

Shana's thoughts were blocking her from using her genius at being an attuned and playful parent. When she was distracted by her thoughts, she had a hard time being the kind of mom she wanted to be. Some of her thoughts could have been true—her ex sounded like a real jerk[3]—but these thoughts weren't helping her parent her kids any better.

I handed Shana a piece of paper and asked her to write down all the thoughts she gets consumed by when she is transitioning her kids. "Let's get them out of your head and onto paper," I said. Here is what she wrote:

- I hate him.

- He's such a narcissist.

- I am a terrible mom.

- This is hard on my boys.

- I've screwed up my kids for life.

- It's my fault.

"We need to get you some space from these thoughts," I said. "Pick the one that distracts you the most and write it on the palm of your hand." She chose "I am a terrible mom" and winced as she wrote it.

"Now hold your palm right up to your face so the words *I am a terrible mom* are about an inch away from your eyes."

She held it up so that it almost touched her nose, and I continued, "What do you notice?"

She laughed. "All I can see is fuzzy words on a hand."

"Exactly!" I said. "You can't even see your thoughts clearly. Plus, how well can you be present for your kids' transition to their dad's when the thought is this close?"

"Not very well," she said.

Thoughts don't mean much unless you choose to believe them, and when you are so close to them, they can really blur your perspective. The next thing I had Shana do was slowly move her hand away from her face. "Move it far enough away that you can actually read the words," I instructed. "It's just a thought. When you have space from it, you can choose if you want to pay attention to it or not. You get to decide where you place your energy: on your judgmental thought or on your kids."

Try this exercise for yourself. Jot down some of the thoughts that get in the way of engaging in wise effort. Pick one that dominates your mind the most. When you are caught up in that thought, does it feel like a hand blocking your view? What does it block you from seeing or doing? How does it misdirect your genius energy? Can you imagine making some space from that thought, like a hand that is moving away from your face?

Notice that I'm not asking you to get rid of the thought or to write something positive on top of it. You may want to look at it from time to time. Your thought isn't good or bad; it's just a thought. You get to choose when, or if, it gets your full attention.

The most important thing to remember is that it's not your job to control your thoughts; it's your job to make space for them. With space, you have more choice in how you act.

Step 2. Question Your Thoughts

Now that you've got some distance from your thoughts, the next step is to start questioning them. When you question your thoughts, you can use your genius more flexibly. For example, instead of believing that her husband was always wrong, Shana started to ask herself four questions that support wise, compassionate speech:

1. Is it true?
2. Is it kind?
3. Is it helpful?
4. Is it the right time?

When she questioned her own thinking, she was more flexible in her responses. She knew she wanted to be a present and playful mom—that was her genius—and if her thoughts aligned with that, great. If not, she let them go.

Get curious. Ask yourself, *Hmm . . . is this thought actually true? Is this thought kind? Is this thought helpful? Is it a good time to think about this?* Because here's the thing—you can't believe every thought that pops into your head, and some of your thoughts can turn your genius energy into frenemies if you let them. That's because a lot of your thoughts weren't even yours to begin with.

Our thoughts are shaped by all kinds of factors—our evolution (we evolved a tendency toward negative thinking as a survival mechanism), our biology (some people are just naturally wired to be more self-critical), our upbringing, and our culture. If you grew up in a marginalized or oppressed group, you may have internalized toxic messages about your identity without even realizing it. If your caregivers were dismissive, punitive, or hypercritical, you might still hear their voices in your head. Shana shared that even though she and her ex are divorced, she can still hear him saying she's lazy and a bad mom. And after a while, she started to believe it.

Another reason to question your thoughts? They're often biased. Our brains rely on mental shortcuts to make quick decisions—but those shortcuts can be wildly inaccurate. Every day, we fall into these little cognitive traps without even noticing. Chances are, you've already fallen for a few today:

The empathy gap: We underestimate how much our emotional state influences our decisions. When we're calm, we assume that we'll handle a crisis rationally—but when stress hits, logic takes a back seat. Maybe right now, you're telling yourself you'll have no problem setting boundaries at work, but when the moment comes, guilt takes over and you say yes anyway.

The hard-easy effect: People tend to overestimate their ability to perform hard tasks and underestimate it for easy ones. Maybe you're feeling overconfident about tackling a complex project with little preparation, yet second-guessing your ability to complete a simple email without triple-checking it.

The law of triviality: We focus too much on minor details while ignoring bigger issues. Perhaps you're spending thirty minutes picking the perfect font for your presentation slides while avoiding the much harder task of structuring your actual presentation.

The default effect: We tend to stick with preset options, even when better alternatives exist. You might still be using the default ringtone on your phone, sticking with a mediocre insurance plan just because it was automatically selected, or eating at the same restaurant every Friday simply out of habit.

We all know what it feels like to be caught in a loop of unhelpful and questionable thoughts. While there's no definitive number of thoughts we have each day, science does confirm that the nature of our thinking shapes how we experience the world. Our thoughts subtly influence our perception of reality, impacting our mental health and overall well-being.

The common advice "Just think more positively" oversimplifies the complexity of how our minds work. Our thoughts are not entirely within our control. These biases feel like truth in the moment, which is exactly why you have to question them. No matter how convincing your thoughts sound, don't always take them as absolute truth. Especially those middle-of-the-night-worry thoughts.

A Pennsylvania State University study sheds light on the inaccuracy of many of your worries. Participants were asked to write down their worries and track whether they actually came true over ten days. The result? Researchers found that 91 percent of the participants' anxious thoughts never actually happened.[4] You might be thinking, *What if my worry is in that 9 percent?* Well, that's your negativity bias talking. The small percentage of worries that unfolded rarely did so as catastrophically as feared. In that study, more people had none of their worries come true than had any worries come true.

So the next time your mind starts spinning a story, take a step back and ask yourself, *Are you sure?*

Ask, *Are You Sure?*

Every day on the summer retreat at Plum Village Monastery, the sangha (community) takes an hour-long walking meditation. Single file, we move through the plum orchards and sunflower fields, headed nowhere very slowly. We walk around the lotus pond, children grabbing lotus leaves the size of their heads to hold up as umbrellas as adults of all ages carefully lift and lower their feet. On some retreats, there are over seven hundred people on these walks, and they can get a bit jammed up. You may walk only a few steps before stopping again. Along the walk are gathas (short phrases) written on flags, rocks, and wooden signs for us to contemplate. They say things like "Peace Is Every Step," "Breathe You Are Alive," "This Moment Is Full of Wonders," and "Enjoy Walking." The one gatha I found most helpful on these walks was "Are you sure?"

I'd be walking along, enjoying the breeze, watching my sons pick and eat plums, but it wouldn't be long before my mind would wander. *When are we going to get there? It's too hot. My kids are being too loud. That person in front of me is annoying. I forgot to respond to that email.* In these moments, I started saying the gatha to myself: *Are you sure?* This simple question interrupted my stream of thoughts and brought me back to what I was doing. This question isn't intended to strip away all uncertainty or stop any action but rather to remind us to invite curiosity about the accuracy of our thoughts. For you, this could look like the following:

Your mind: *I'll never be able to do it.*

You: Are you sure?

Your mind: *Everyone has to like me.*

You: Are you sure?

Your mind: *It's too late for me to change.*

You: Are you sure?

In addition to asking *Are you sure?*, here are three other questions you can ask yourself to interrupt your stream of thoughts. Give these a try and see what works best in opening up your mind.

1. Is there another way to see this situation?
2. Am I leaving something out?
3. Does this thought support my wisest efforts?

Question your thoughts often. You can't trust everything your mind tells you. But what you can trust is that many things can be true at once—which brings us to the next step.

Step 3. Enter the Paradox

Too often, we see the world as true or not true, right or wrong. You may think, *Either I succeed at this project or I'm a complete failure.* Or *Either I know what I'm doing or I shouldn't even try.* This type of dichotomous thinking prevents flexibility, stifles your willingness to experiment, and limits the creative ways you might apply your genius energy. It's hard to use your genius to innovate if you see things in such rigid, binary terms. Part of the reason we fall into inflexible thinking is that our brains are huge and metabolically expensive to run. Instead of calculating complexity, it's easier for your brain to give simple either/or answers. But this rarely benefits us.

For example, remember that rooster I mentioned at the start of this chapter? When I was stuck in thinking, *Either they get rid of that rooster or I am going to go nuts,* I was driving myself nuts. The solution was not either/or; I needed to use my emotional sensitivity to both embrace the rooster and take care of myself. I started using the rooster as my mindfulness bell to pause and ask, *Are you sure?* I learned to love the rooster, and every time it crowed during a webinar, I used it to illustrate a point. My persistence paid off. See, I'm even using this rooster as an example now, years after he moved on to the "happy farm" when another neighbor called the city about him. I kind of miss him.

So, to counter our mind's constricting tendency to think black-and-white, right and wrong, we need to enter the paradox of both/and thinking.

Paradoxes, by their very nature, hold seemingly opposite truths at the same time. For example, you can succeed at a task even if you fumble along the way. You can lack confidence and do things that are confidence building. When I train therapists, I like to tell them about a study that showed that therapists who experience moderate levels of self-doubt tend to be more effective in their work. This is because self-doubt can drive therapists to continually reflect on and improve their skills and avoid overconfidence. Remaining humble can lead to greater empathy and attentiveness to their clients' needs.[5]

Paradoxes are the creative, growth-oriented space that lies between two extremes. They are where the richness of life resides. Paradoxes are everywhere. Remember in physics when you learned that light is both a particle and a wave? Or in yoga when your teacher tells you to practice effort and surrender? Then there's the paradox of loving your career and loving being a parent. The two can coexist. Often it's our attempts to solve paradoxes that drain our energy. If you feel like you have to choose between exercise or getting your work done, you will constantly feel like you are falling short. But what if work-life balance is more of a Venn diagram with an overlapping middle? Your work can enhance your home life and vice versa; it can be a both/and.[6] That's entering the paradox.

Step 4. Savor What's Good

We have been talking a lot about how fighting unwanted thoughts may drain your genius energy. But what about the wanted thoughts—the experiences you want to remember? Turning your mind toward positive experiences is a powerful and intentional use of your genius energy. It not only might buffer negative experiences but also appears to change your brain on a deep biological level.

For example, my husband roasts our coffee every week. On Sunday mornings, our house smells like a roasting company, and his coffee is better than any I can get in town. When he first started roasting, each cup felt like a treasure. I sipped it like it was the best coffee I had ever had. I thanked him profusely. But, as with most good things, I experienced hedonic adaptation. I got used to it. Home-roasted coffee became the norm—just like that warm shower you take every day, the skyline view on your way home, or your cat's purr. As Rick Hanson often says, the human mind is "Velcro for the negative and Teflon for the positive."⁷ We have hundreds of positive moments in our day that we fail to appreciate.

But what if savoring those positive moments did more than just make us feel good? Research has suggested that our emotions—both positive and negative—can influence not only our psychological well-being but also our brain at a cellular level. Studies on mitochondria, the tiny powerhouses of our cells, have found that greater well-being is linked to increased energy production, while negative mood states can diminish it. Chronic stress may disrupt mitochondrial function, making it harder for our brain to process experiences in a balanced way. However, paying attention to and amplifying positive experiences may help restore this energy balance, improving both our mood and cognitive function. In fact, research has shown that when people cultivate positive emotions, their cellular energy levels increase, reinforcing the idea that mental habits shape not only our thoughts but also our biology.⁸

It may feel cliché, but there's sound science behind stopping to smell the roses (or, in my case, coffee). In one study, researchers handed out flyers that said "Life is uncertain" on a busy street. Those who received the flyer were much more likely to stop and smell a bouquet of roses than those who did not receive a reminder of uncertainty. Why? Because part of the reason we don't savor life's little joys is that we assume they will always be there . . . until they aren't. Recognizing the impermanence of things can awaken us to the richness of the present moment. Most of us don't like uncertainty (and our brains don't, either), but embracing it may actually sharpen our awareness of fleeting positive moments, making us more likely to cherish and enjoy them.

So how can we cultivate savoring in everyday life? Here are three simple strategies:

1. **Pause and notice:** Slow yourself down and take in the good. Whether it's appreciating the tree outside your window or the face of someone you love, appreciate something sweet and wonderful in the here and now.

2. **Remember impermanence:** Remind yourself that there will never be another moment exactly like this one. The flowers blooming on your morning walk will be different tomorrow. Pay attention to the changing nature of things, and use that awareness as motivation to savor them.

3. **Reflect on positive moments:** At the end of the day, take a few minutes to recall and write down a few positive moments you experienced. This can help rewire your brain to notice and savor them more often.

By integrating savoring into your daily life, you can counteract hedonic adaptation and make the most of the positive moments around you, even in the midst of uncertainty. And in doing so, you may not only uplift your mood but also support your brain's energy system—one cup of coffee, one deep breath, one fleeting moment at a time.

Step 5. Trust Your Heart-Mind

The final step in opening your mind is discovering another kind of mind, one where your thoughts don't reside at all: your heart-mind. While we often think of the mind as purely in the brain, many cultures view the heart as the seat of deeper, more intuitive wisdom. In Buddhism, this is called "chitta," or heart-mind, and in various cultures, the heart is considered the seat of the highest wisdom.[9] Your heart-mind connects to your values and is great to turn to when you need some guidance in how to use your genius energy. Should you say yes to another work project? Ask your heart-mind. Should you apologize to a friend? Ask your heart-mind. Should you take a walk or try to fit in one more hour of work? Ask your heart-mind.

Though this idea may seem more metaphorical than literal, even modern science has recognized the complex relationship between the heart and the brain. The heart has its own intrinsic nervous system with over forty thousand neurons, known as sensory neurites, that can sense, feel, learn, and remember. This means the heart functions somewhat independently of the cranial brain.[10] If you embrace this concept of heart-mind, it invites you to lead not just with rational thought but with a more integrated, compassionate wisdom that blends intellect with emotional depth.

From a spiritual perspective, your heart-mind is more than neurons; it's love-based wisdom. For example, you might have the thought *I can't handle this*, but if you act from your heart-mind, you'll find yourself handling it with grace and ease. You might think, *I might panic*, yet still step up and speak from your heart. Or you could think, *What if they don't like me?* but choose to reach out and connect anyway. The more you practice, the more you'll notice the difference between acting from your head and acting from your heart-mind. Your heart-mind houses your feelings and intuitions, that subtle knowing that you can't quite put your finger on. Often the heart-mind is a whisper, difficult to detect behind your loud thoughts. Listen for your heart or feel for it—often in your chest, belly, or places other than your head. Where do you feel yours right now?

This concept may be one of the biggest surprises and the most unexpected comforts on your wise effort path. The heart-mind is here for you, and you can trust its deep wisdom. It's a reprieve that you don't have to rely on your brain to figure it all out. If you don't quite have a sense of what your heart-mind is, in the next chapter, we will open up to your feelings that are related to this space.

Wisdom-Building Questions

Take some time to understand your relationship to your thoughts by reflecting on the following questions. Title this page in your Wise Effort Journal "Opening Up My Mind":

- What thoughts are getting in the way of using your genius the most? What thoughts block you from doing that thing you really want to do?

- What methods have you tried to get rid of your thoughts or change them? Has it worked in the short term? At what cost? Does it work in the long term?

- Write down an either/or thought that is blocking you from moving forward in life. Can you expand your mind to include both/and?

- What is a positive experience you have regularly that you want to savor? What genius energy do you have that can help you focus in this way?

- Write about your heart-mind. What is it saying about a struggle you're dealing with right now?

The essence of this chapter is that you can transform your relationship with your mind. You are not your thoughts, and you have more choice than you might realize about which ones deserve your attention. With cognitive flexibility, you gain greater agency over where and how you direct your genius energy. But what if it's not just your thoughts that are roadblocks to wise effort? What if painful feelings are getting in the way of you doing what you know in your heart you need to do? Or maybe your feelings have something important to tell you? Let's turn to that predicament next.

7

open up your feelings

Every few months, I spend the day sitting on the linoleum floor of the UCLA Stein Eye Institute. My husband, Craig, and I leave home at 5 a.m. to make his 7:30 a.m. appointment. The narrow hallways are packed with adults guiding their parents by the elbows; patients wearing eye patches, fresh from surgery; and elderly couples shuffling together, holding hands. Many of these patients have traveled farther than we have to seek treatment at the prestigious research university. There's no room to sit, and I prefer the floor anyway, so I stretch, catch up on emails, meditate, and listen to podcasts while my husband goes through hours of rigorous testing—a visual field test, an eye-pressure test, and that test where you read the letters from across the room with one eye covered.

It might sound odd, but I look forward to these trips. I appreciate the uninterrupted time spent catching up with Craig while inching along in bumper-to-bumper LA traffic. I feel youthful (the glaucoma division can do that for you), and it's a chance to act on my values of being loving, present, and patient.

I haven't always had this kind of attitude. A few years back, when my husband called me urgently to meet him in the kitchen, I thought he wanted to show me a red-tailed hawk—his favorite bird. I left my office and walked up the stone steps to find him seated at the table, appearing pale. He looked at me strangely, seeming to scan my face, and said, "Honey, I can't see part of your face. Your eye, part of your nose, it's just not there."

By the time we got into treatment at UCLA, Craig had already suffered severe vision loss. He could drive, work, and do most of his daily activities, but to see the whole picture—of my face, of a computer screen, or of a kid's pitched ball coming his way—he needed to tilt his head like a bird—a little right, then left, up, and down. Naturally, I panicked. Would he be able to keep working? Could he still play baseball with our kids? What did our future hold? To cope with these fears, I shut down, compartmentalized, got busy doing stuff, and ended the conversation quickly whenever family and friends asked how I was doing.

The worst part? I started avoiding looking at Craig when we talked. I hated how I felt when I saw him tilting his head. My emotional sensitivity picked up on the immensity of this loss. I felt a pain in the pit of my stomach and a tightening in my throat. *He can't see me the way he used to.*

Meanwhile, my husband (whose genius is patience, remember?) decided he'd better start practicing. At night, he would close his eyes and run his fingers along the wall as he walked from our bedroom down the stairs to the kitchen and back. He was opening up to the reality of what was happening for us as I was closing off.

When life pummels us, we always have a choice. We can run away, hold too tightly, or get stuck in the story (remember chapter 3?)—only to feel more defeated and scared. Or we can center ourselves and open up to feeling so we can remember our genius energy and assess how to use it wisely. And that's exactly what we're going to do here. Here are the six steps we will take to open up to feeling:

1. Center yourself.

2. Make room for what's hard.

3. Take care of your feeling.

4. Give it a name.

5. Ask, *What do I need?*

6. Act from your values.

The Gates of Grief

In struggling to cope with my husband's health changes, I turned to my bedside table of books for when things fall apart and found myself rereading Francis Weller's book *The Wild Edge of Sorrow*, where he walks readers through the Five Gates of Grief. The first gate is "Everything we love we will lose."[1] It's kind of horrible, isn't it? But true. We will lose our favorite dog and our twenty-twenty vision (if we ever had it). Our kids will grow up, and that beautiful tree that's blooming on your morning commute will drop its purple flowers. But does that mean we shouldn't get a dog or admire the tree? Of course not. Closing off to Craig was doubling my loss. Plus, it blocked me from the sweetness of how he was patiently and effortfully tilting his head to look at my face. He hadn't worked that hard to see me since we were dating!

Whether it's grief you are feeling or another difficult emotion, it's opening up to it and walking through its gate that will allow you to engage your wisest efforts. All humans have a difficult gate they are walking through at any given moment in time, and you can use your gifts and talents, your inner genius, to get through it.

I turned my persistence toward attending medical appointments, keeping copious notes, and asking his surgeon lots of questions so Craig didn't have to. I used my emotional sensitivity to find solace in the sweet moments. There's excellent coffee around UCLA and a really fun taco place called Pinches. It feels good to hold hands like an old married couple while we walk the hallways of the Stein building. And every time my husband calls me to look at a hawk, I use my emotional sensitivity to remember how important it is to say yes. Say yes to life. Everything we love we will lose, and someday, and not too far off, we will all be shuffling along.

Why We Close Off

It's natural to want to turn away from your feelings. We close off because it hurts to stay open, and we don't know how to take care of our feelings. Most of us were taught some very unhelpful messaging about emotions. Maybe as a kid, you were encouraged to get rid of "bad" feelings quickly, taught that some feelings like anger or fear are even *dangerous*. Or you were fed the lie that you are supposed to feel good all the time and that if you aren't happy, there's something wrong with you. Our emotional literacy and emotion regulation skills developed in the context of our culture and upbringing. Some feelings were more acceptable to express than others in your family or at school. Maybe it was okay to be cheery and optimistic but not to be *too* excited. That looks bad. Or maybe it was okay to be sad, but not for too long. That's weak. You may have learned that some feelings are too much for others to handle. Perhaps no one told you this directly, but it was modeled to you in the way you saw your dad cry only once or twice or how your mom expressed her anger only by layering on the guilt or slamming doors with no explanation.

As a result, we don't always know what to do when feelings show up. We are afraid they will hurt us or overwhelm others. We worry that we can't interpret them or they are too confusing. And so we sometimes act in really unwise ways. As you can see from my story about Craig, if you can't open up to feelings, you can't use your genius when you need it most.

Step 1. Center Yourself

Before I could face the intense feelings I was having about my husband and use my genius energy to help him, I needed to find some ground in the groundlessness of it all. Strong emotions can hijack our nervous system, sending us into panic, impulsive action, or shutdown. Our genius energy gets off track—going either into overdrive or underground. To build resilience and use your energy wisely, you need a strong foundation—a stable center to act from. As you will read, there are plenty of ways to find your center—you can ground with the breath, through nature, through spirituality, and in community.[2] To be resilient is to know these resources and access them readily when you need them. Before I offer you a plethora of ideas, first check in with yourself. What resources do you already have inside you, around you, and in your community that you lean on to center yourself? How do you find your ground when it feels like there is no ground to stand on?

A key point here: I don't want you to use these centering strategies to control or get rid of your feelings. I am not saying, "Take a deep breath and breathe away your fears." What happens if you take a deep breath and your fears don't go away? *Oh no! Tigers above, tigers below.* Or what if your sadness is a sign that you care? Do we really want to breathe it away? Of course not! I want you to find strength, inner stillness, and stability to stay with your feelings *longer*. Long enough that you can respond with wisdom. Instead of trying to control the spin, you can discover your center in it. The centering practice below may be useful when

- Your energy is frantic and scattered.
- Your energy is hijacked by conflict or disagreement.
- You are distracted by unhelpful thoughts.
- You are afraid of your emotions or engulfed in them.
- You feel pulled in many directions.

I'll share ideas on how to center yourself, drawn from the science of nervous system regulation, the deep well of contemplative practice, and the lived wisdom of hundreds of clients who teach me daily what we need to do to get grounded. Don't be overwhelmed by the variety of these techniques. Try a few from each list and see which ones sink in for you. My hope is that you'll find a few useful and become familiar with them so that you have them when you need them.

Center with the Breath

Attentive breathing has been a trusted practice for centuries, with countless breathwork techniques available to explore.

- To center your attention, try mindful breathing. Bring awareness to your natural breath—simply observing each inhale and exhale as it flows through your body for five to ten minutes.

- To slow yourself down, try deep breathing, with a slightly longer exhale than inhale. Counting helps focus the mind. *Breathing in, 1, 2, 3, 4 . . . Breathing out, 1, 2, 3, 4, 5.* When you breathe slowly and deeply, it activates the vagus nerve, the longest cranial nerve, which runs from your brain stem through your heart and to your gut. Remarkably, about 80 percent of the vagus nerve's signals flow upward from the gut to the brain, sending messages of safety—that it's okay to rest, to connect.[3] Five or so minutes of slow breathing can also offer a form of "deep rest" where the body starts to restore and repair itself at the cellular level.[4]

- To increase energy and boost mood, try Wim Hof breathing: breathe rapidly for thirty breaths, then exhale and hold your breath at the bottom as long as possible. This method has been associated with positive daily mood and stress resilience by increasing oxygen saturation and influencing the autonomic nervous system.[5]

If breathing exercises aren't your thing or make things worse, that's okay! There are plenty of other centering skills to choose from.

Ground with Intense Sensations

Sometimes the best thing to do when faced with a strong emotion is to meet it with other strong physical sensations. Using heat and cold, breath retention, and high-intensity exercise can bring you back to the present moment. Acute, high-intensity stress (also called hormesis) prepares your body for future stressors and has been associated with cellular resilience and improved mood. You can ground yourself with intense short-term hermetic stressors like these:

- Take a cold shower. The shock of cold water boosts norepinephrine levels, which enhance mood and focus.[6]

- Dunk your face in cold water. This triggers the mammalian dive reflex, slowing your heart rate and shifting your body out of fight-or-flight mode.[7]

- Experience an orgasm, sex, or sensual pleasure. Few experiences ground you more fully in the present moment.[8]

- Do some jumping jacks, push-ups, or a short sprint. High-intensity interval training (HITT) boosts mood and stresses your cells in ways that build resilience.[9]

Hold On to Something Solid

When you are overwhelmed, it can be stabilizing to make physical contact with something solid. When you place your hand on a sturdy wall, press your feet against the floor, or hold something tightly in your palm, it can help anchor you in the present moment.

- Imagine roots growing from your feet into the center of the Earth like a tree.

- Hold tightly to a special rock, shell, or piece of jewelry.

- Lie on the ground. Surrender to gravity and let your body be supported.

- Place one hand on your belly and the other on your heart and breathe.

- Rub your hands together and place them over your eyes. Go inside yourself.

Center with Sound

Sound is a simple way to engage your body's natural relaxation response and balance your threat and drive systems. Certain types of sound (especially low-frequency and binaural beats) can stimulate the vagus nerve and balance the nervous system.[10] What music soothes you? Whose voice helps you feel at ease? What about nature sounds?

- Create a playlist of centering music. Include songs that are meaningful to you or that have a soothing beat or voice. Give it a creative title that you will want to click on and share! (My go-to playlist is called "Losing my Sh*t.")

- Listen to sounds of birds, wind, rain, waves in nature.

- Make your own sound—try a long, low humming sound on your exhale or singing. These activate your vagus nerve with the vibration of your vocal cords.

Move Your Body

When you're having a strong feeling, sometimes the worst advice is to just "sit with it." Physical activity metabolizes stress hormones like cortisol and adrenaline while triggering the release of endorphins, your body's natural stress relievers. And if you can move outside, even better. Time in green spaces improves cognitive function, enhances emotional resilience, and restores balance to the nervous system. Try one of these:

- Take a walk at sunrise or sunset to soak in the regulating effects of morning and evening light.

- Shake or dance it out! A quick full-body shake can help reset your nervous system.

- Hang from a tree, flow through a few sun salutations, or walk barefoot in the grass to reconnect with the Earth.

- Tap your fingertips under your eyes, at your temples, on your forehead, and across your jaw. Rhythmic tapping like this on acupressure points has been associated with reduced stress hormones.

Choose a Mantra

Many spiritual traditions use short phrases, prayers, or chants to center the mind and heart. In Sanskrit, *mantra* comes from *manas* (mind) and *tra* (tool), meaning a tool for the mind—something that centers and stabilizes you. At Plum Village Monastery, I learned the simple mantra "Breathing in, I have arrived; breathing out, I am home" as a tool to use when I needed to find my center. Another was the walking mantra "yes" with one step, "yes" with another. "Thank you" with one step, "thank you" with the next.

It's important to understand that simply repeating an affirmation doesn't automatically transform your entire life. I prefer mantras that are not pie-in-the-sky promises—such as "May I be rich and happy all the time"—but rather remind me of what's already true or help me open my heart. Like the one I was taught to say in Catholic school to the person behind me in the pew: "Peace be with you."

The power of mantras and prayer doesn't hinge on belonging to a particular faith. Visualize the energy of the words entering your whole being. The sound of prayer and mantra create soothing vibrations that can activate the vagus nerve, balancing your nervous system.[11] Plus, they naturally slow your breath to an ideal rhythm—about five to six seconds in, five to six seconds out[12]—giving you a three-in-one benefit: slower breathing, grounding words, and a calming sound.

Do you have a favorite prayer, poem, saying, or mantra that grounds you? Or maybe you want to create your own? Here are a few favorite mantras to try:

- I can handle this.

- Just this moment.

- I am here now.

- I allow things to be as they are.

Center with Others
Strong emotions like shame, sadness, or fear can lead us to withdraw from others. Counteract the urge to isolate, and reach out for connection. You can borrow other people's centering energy.

- Leave a voice memo for someone and ask them to leave a voice memo back. The sound of a human voice is even better than text.

- Hold someone's hand; ask for a hug; go get a foot rub or massage.

- Focus your attention on a kind face or take note of everyday acts of kindness.

- Go to spaces where there's a grounding vibe—like your favorite bookstore, park, coffee shop, or yoga studio.

On those long days when my husband was undergoing multiple eye surgeries at UCLA, I would walk to the botanical gardens hidden in the center of the city campus. Walking along the redwood-lined path, smelling the earthy pine scent, and experiencing the quiet were a break from the medical building's chemical odors and constant beeping. My senses were so open, I felt everything more intensely, and it was good to be in that garden and let my feelings physically move through my body. Sometimes I'd cry; other times, I'd run my hands along the trees' rough bark or look for a dropped pine cone to hold tightly. The Earth is amazing in its ability to relieve and carry some of the heaviness of life.

The key is to have a variety of centering practices that you can readily draw on as resources when you feel off-kilter. You can do these practices ten times a day or a hundred—and every time you do, you strengthen your ability to do it again. Pick a few from the list above and experiment with them today. Centering will help as you move on to the next step.

Step 2. Make Room for What's Hard

It's hard to have a big heart. Sometimes you don't want to have to deal with what you are feeling. But when you block off your feelings, you also block your genius energy. When I stopped running away from my fear about my husband going blind, I intuitively knew what to do: use my emotional sensitivity to look at him and love him. Then use my persistence to do what needed to get done—get him the best treatment possible. In order to do this, I needed to make room for what was hard. Feelings like fear, sadness, anger, and embarrassment often go hand in hand with living values like compassion, adventure, bravery, honesty, and love.

Let's practice making room for difficult feelings right now. Research has shown that using imagery to mentally walk through a situation before facing it can help you follow through when the moment arrives. Your brain and body don't fully distinguish between what's imagined and what's real—so by rehearsing now, you're laying the groundwork to be able to do this again when a difficult feeling shows up.

Think of something you've been wanting to do but keep avoiding because of discomfort or something that is challenging for you right now. Maybe it's speaking up in a meeting, reaching out to someone you miss, saying no to something that drains you, or connecting with someone you love. There's a wise move you want to make or something you want to let go of and a big feeling that is getting in the way.

Hold it in your mind for a moment. This is something that matters to you.

Now imagine yourself right at the edge of the moment when your feeling gets intense—before you take that step, when your emotion gets strong. What emotions arise?

- Where do you feel it in your body? Is it tightness in your chest? A buzzing in your head? An uneasiness in your stomach?

- If you could outline it with a Sharpie, where would its edges be?

- What color would it be?

- Does it have a texture? A weight? A movement?

- Maybe there's hesitation. Maybe your heart speeds up. Maybe there's a pull to turn away.

Let all of that be there—without pushing it away. This is part of the experience. Instead of fighting the feeling, make room for it.

Stay with it for a moment. Exhale in and around the feeling, making room for it. Let go of the struggle to fix it or get rid of it. Just be with it. Open, allow, let go of tension or holding. You can make space for this hard thing. Take one more exhale and gently return to the present.

The more you practice being with emotions, the more flexible you will become with them. If you can have an emotion without running away from it, there are all sorts of things you can do with your genius energy, including caring for yourself.

Step 3. Take Care of Your Feeling

It may come instinctively to you to take care of others when they are hurting. But it might not be second nature to offer yourself the same kind of support when you are hurting. It certainly wasn't for Daniel, the rock climber with cancer.

I noticed that when Daniel talked about his cancer in session, he would hold the side of his neck that *didn't* harbor his surgery scar. I watched him do it for a few sessions before I pointed it out: "What are you avoiding?" He told me touching his scar made him think that he was going to die and leave his kids.

"I even avoid touching my neck in the shower," he said. Here was a medic who could handle life-and-death situations in warlike environments but couldn't touch his own neck. Of course, it wasn't his neck he was avoiding; it was his fear that came with it.

I moved to sit with Daniel on the couch, next to the side he avoided. I looked at his scar up close—it was a quarter inch wide, traveling from his ear down to his collarbone. Anyone would be terrified to bear the history that had led to a mark like that. I looked at it for a while; then, moving closer, I asked if I could touch it. He nodded. I placed my palm against his skin and waited for his body to relax a little. I told him I was sending warmth and kindness to his scar and to his fear. Then I asked him if he could do the same thing—put his hand on his neck and offer himself care and kindness. Daniel hesitantly placed his palm across the surgery scar.

The whole experience was beautiful to witness. When Daniel allowed in some compassion from me and eventually himself, he transformed his aversion into something to be honored. Daniel recently told me that he still touches that scar in the shower every day and now uses his genius of sensitivity and vigilance to check whether everything feels okay. Some days, it's harder than others, but he knows from his medical training that he needs his genius vigilance to touch his neck to check for any cancer growth, and with self-compassion, he can also take care of his fear with the same sensitivity he'd offer to a wounded soldier in the field.

Compassion excludes no one, including the parts of yourself you shy away from or don't like. Unlike self-criticism, which depletes your energy, self-compassion encourages you to pursue growth and change—not out of a sense of inadequacy but from a place of care for your inherent goodness. And there are over two thousand studies demonstrating its effectiveness.[13]

Caring for your feelings isn't so different from how you care for others. You can place a hand where you feel the emotion in your body—physical touch releases oxytocin, a hormone that calms and soothes. You can say to yourself, *I'm here for you, no matter what*. Offer yourself gentle touch, kind words, and patience.

Try it right now. What happens when you place your hand where you hurt and wish yourself well?

This is another practice you can do ten or one hundred times a day, and every time you do it, you'll get better at it. It's uncomfortable to take off our armor and expose our vulnerabilities. Yet that is where the healing happens. Take care of your feelings and let others help you. Then give them a name.

Step 4. Give It a Name

In Vipassana meditation, there's a practice called "labeling," where meditators silently note their experiences: "bored," "angry," "afraid," "itchy." They sit in silence, and their only task is to notice and name what is happening: "Feeling sleepy," "Unpleasant sensation in my hip," "Irritation rising."

This simple act does a few powerful things. First, it develops your observer self—you realize that you are experiencing anger, but you are not anger itself. Second, it reveals the impermanence of emotions. If you feel irritated one moment, you might feel ease the next. If you watch something long enough, you can't help but notice it change.

Try it right now. Pause and name what you're feeling. Maybe "I feel anxious. There's a tightness in my chest." Or "I feel calm. My breath is steady." Just observe. Where do you feel it in your body? Is it shifting? Are there other sensations you didn't notice before? Can you let them be as they are? Changing and moving?

Neuroscientist Matthew Lieberman found that naming emotions helps regulate them.[14] In MRI scans, when participants looked at distressing images, their brain's fear center (the amygdala) lit up. But when they named their emotion, the activity in their amygdala decreased, while the brain's emotion-regulating center (ventrolateral prefrontal cortex) became more active.

In other words, naming emotions engages the newer, wiser parts of your brain and can help tone down the threat system that makes you reactive.

Different cultures name and express emotions in unique ways. I was amused when a German client of mine once was describing a nemesis at work and told me she was feeling "schadenfreude"—the pleasure of seeing someone else fail.

You don't have to get the label exactly right. There's no "correct" way to name what you feel. The point is to put words to what's happening inside you. Because when you can name what you feel, it's like pulling a blanket back from what you have been hiding under. You see it more clearly, and you can let others in to see it, too.

Like when I told Craig, "I'm sad you don't see me the same way you used to."

Or when Daniel told me, "I'm afraid of what will happen to my kids if I die."

Once you name your emotions, you can start to have a conversation with them. Have you ever asked your stress, grief, or joy, *What do you need?* When you know what your feelings need, you can better direct your genius energy toward just that.

Step 5. Ask, *What Do You Need?*

A few years back, I participated in a powerful workshop called Feeding Your Demons led by Lama Tsultrim Allione.[15] Lama Tsultrim, the first American woman ordained as a Tibetan Buddhist nun, adapted this practice from the eleventh-century Tibetan meditation practice of chöd. We were guided through a visualization, imagining a difficult emotion or struggle as a personified demon standing before us and asking it three key questions:

1. What do you want?

2. What do you really need?

3. How will you feel when you get what you need?

Workshop participants described their "inner demons" vividly—guilt appeared as a black knight with a hole in his chest, grief showed up as a reddish-brown monster sitting in a pit of mud, and in my case, my anxiety was a woman wearing a pencil skirt and heels with knotted hair. What followed was transformative.

First, we asked our inner demons of anxiety, stress, sadness, and guilt what they wanted. They answered superficially, saying things like "Gobs of money," "To rip someone's head off," "Endless praise," "To be left alone," or, in my case, "Chocolate." But when asked the second question, *What do you really need?*, their answers shifted to deeper desires: "Forgiveness," "The freedom to exist," "Space to be heard," or simply "Love."

There's a difference between wants and needs. What our emotions (or inner demons in this exercise) may want us to do is flee or numb out, but that is not what's under the want, which satisfies a deeper attachment need for soothing, security, or compassion. Next, we asked our inner demons how they would feel if they received what they truly needed. They said things like "Peaceful," "Accepted," and "Free."

Then the true shift and the most unusual part (if this isn't sounding unusual already) occurred when we imagined turning what it would feel if it got what it actually needed into a nectar we fed to our inner demon, literally letting the demon drink it until it was completely satisfied. People imagined feeding the demon a golden nectar of acceptance, pure white light of healing, or a cool, soothing liquid of ease. And then, when it got what it really needed, the final step was to transform the demon into an ally. The participants reported that they morphed into wise women, animal spirits, or, in my case, a caring older therapist.

If this sounds off-the-charts odd, there's actually some science behind it. In 2022, Eve Ekman, a leading researcher in the area of emotions at University of California, San Francisco (UCSF) and colleagues at the Greater Good Science Center did a waitlist-controlled trial of the Feeding Your Demons practice with sixty participants. In their qualitative analysis, the participants said that the exercise of feeding their inner demons reframed their relationship with distressing emotions, helping them gain greater self-compassion and acceptance.[16]

Every emotion, even those we demonize, has a function. We wouldn't have evolved feelings if they didn't have some kind of message to offer. They motivate us to protect ourselves and connect with one another. When you listen to your emotions and give them what they really need, not what they appear to want, they transform into an ally. When Daniel asked his fear, "What do you really need?," his fear answered that it needed him to spend more time with his kids while he was still alive and build community that would support them if he died. Now he had something worthwhile to direct his energy toward besides worrying about his neck.

Emotions are not really inner demons; they are signals that you can choose to listen to and tend to. And when you dialogue with them, you may discover that they often point to your fundamental yearnings (to connect with others, to make sense of things, to feel deeply, to be oriented, to have purpose, to develop competence).

So ask your feeling what it needs, not just what it wants, and then use your values to guide your genius energy toward that.

Step 6. Act from Your Values

Remember that whatever you're feeling, you can always act on your values. Your pain points to what you care about. Turning emotions into values-based action not only helps you make positive changes in your life, it builds your resilience to stress. I've seen this firsthand as an instructor for a climate resilience research project spanning eight University of California campuses and led by stress expert Elissa Epel.

Being a college student today is incredibly daunting. On top of figuring out midterms, dating, and how to do their own laundry, students feel the burden of our world's problems on their shoulders. When we asked students in our climate resilience class to complete the prompt "When I think about the condition of the planet, I feel . . . ," they named emotions like apathy, anger, frustration, fear, anxiety, and hopelessness. Of course they did. They were not alone—a 2021 study of ten thousand youths (ages sixteen to twenty-five) across ten countries found the following:

- 59 percent were very or extremely worried about climate change.

- 75 percent said the future feels frightening.

- 83 percent believe people have failed to care for the planet.[17]

In our course, we teach students to center themselves, name their emotions, and care for their feelings—just as you've practiced here. But, as importantly, we help them channel their values into action. For their final projects, students use their talents to create change: launching a climate podcast for Gen Z listeners, starting a clothing repurposing program, or organizing campuswide meditation sits. The initial results from the course showed reduced climate distress; increased confidence in addressing climate issues; and lower levels of depression, anxiety, and stress.[18]

Whether you're stressed about work or about the state of the planet, you can turn that energy around by asking,

- What does this feeling tell me I care about?

- How can I use my gifts, talents, and strengths to act on that care?

Your feelings can teach you what cause is worth helping, what problem is worth solving, and what message is worth articulating. Open up to them, then act from your heart.

Wisdom-Building Questions

To help you practice opening to your feelings, reflect on the following questions. Title this page in your Wise Effort Journal "Opening Up to Feelings":

- What did you learn (or not learn) about emotions growing up?

- What feelings are hardest for you to feel?

- What centers you?

- What are you feeling right now? Can you name it? What does it need?

- What do your feelings tell you about what you care most about?

- If your feelings are your biggest teacher, what are they teaching you right now?

To choose wise effort, you need to be willing to feel. In this chapter, you have taken the time to practice opening to your feelings. We've also explored how your thoughts and feelings are something you observe but not all of who you are. The next question we will open up to is, who are you? That's what we will tackle next as we open up your sense of self.

8
open up your wise self

Every year, I attend professional conferences, but they aren't always the most comfortable environment for me. I'm mostly a homebody, and there have been more than a few nights when I've left my hotel room in sweatpants, hoping no one sees me sneaking back with takeout for dinner. It takes courage to muster up the energy to attend, but I do it because it supports my professional values.

One year, I attended a breakout session on self-compassion, a topic that was right up my alley. When I saw the founder of a well-known publishing house alone at a table, I directed my genius for persistence and sat next to him. I knew this could be the perfect chance to pitch some of my ideas about *Wise Effort*. I didn't have a chance to say one word to him before the workshop started with a visualization exercise: "Think about your earliest memory of shame. Something that sticks with you even now."

I was quickly transported back to a memory of being seventeen and knee-deep in bulimia, driving home from school. I had gained back my weight from anorexia, and on the outside, everyone thought I was doing great. But I was far from it. On my way home most days, I would stop at the gas station and buy stacks of Reese's Peanut Butter Cups, a box of oatmeal cookies, and a pint of Ben and Jerry's. I would open the wrappers in the car at a local park and eat everything I never allowed myself to eat. This was the one hour out of my day when I escaped from the pressure to perform and rebelled against all my mind's rules. No one would ever see me, so I told myself it didn't count.

In this memory that came to me during the conference, the next thing I saw was me on my knees, purging in the dank and dingy park bathroom. I heard a mother's and little girl's voices as they entered the stall next to me. I froze. The little girl, maybe three or four years old, peeked under the stall and saw me kneeling there. Then came the shameful part—the mother sharply said, "That's disgusting!" and pulled her daughter back. I believed those words were about me. *I am disgusting*. Now, don't get me wrong: kneeling on the bathroom floor in a public park is pretty disgusting. But there is a difference between *doing* disgusting things and *believing you are* disgusting at your core. This story—that I was disgusting—and the feelings of shame that came with it stuck with me for decades, even after I recovered, until that day in the hotel conference room.

The workshop leaders told us, "Now turn to the person next to you and tell them what you saw. Their job is to practice listening with compassion."

Gulp.

I didn't sit at that specific table to share my most shameful memory. I was there to land a book deal. The professional part of me was horrified, but the teenager part of me wanted help. It all came spilling out. I told the publisher my whole gross story, including how disgusting and ashamed I felt.

Here was the surprising thing—he wasn't grossed out at all. The publisher looked at me with gentle, wise, and understanding eyes. He saw my shameful parts, but he didn't look at me like I was gross. He looked at me like I was a human.

Next, the workshop presenters asked us to switch roles. This was my chance to offer some compassion back. The publisher told me his most shameful story, one he had carried around for decades and had allowed to define him. I could see how horrible he thought it was and how hard it was to tell me. All I could feel was openhearted toward him. He wasn't horrible at all: he, too, was human.

For a moment, we were not therapists, authors, or professionals but two humans sharing our human experience. After the workshop, I felt a lightness, a freedom from my "I am disgusting" story. Sure, I don't love the memory, but I no longer have such a visceral reaction to that part of me.

Now, here's the clincher: as we were packing up to leave the room, the publisher turned to me and said, "You know, Diana, I think you could write a really good book on self-compassion." And that is how my second book, *The Self-Compassion Daily Journal*, came about.[1] I needed to write that book in order to write this one, because without compassion for yourself, it's hard to choose wise effort.

We spend much of our lives believing stories about who we are and who we are not. You may think you are a superstar in some settings but feel like a real moron in others. You feel in control of your life one minute but completely confused the next. When you step into your Wise Self, you tap into a much more expansive self. You know what to do and who you really are. And when you know that, you can step into the most powerful form of your genius energy.

So what does it mean to be wise, and how do we grow wiser? Or maybe wisdom is something we already have? Or something that's all around us? Let's explore the concept of wisdom a little more. These are the six steps on the path we will take together:

1. Remember that you are already wise.

2. Ask, *Who am I?*

3. Let go of your story.

4. Find your many bodies.

5. Expand your sense of self.

6. Act with compassion.

Step 1: Remember That You Are Already Wise

Think about a time when you were facing a challenge or needed to make an important decision. How did you attempt to come to a wise answer?

Maybe you took long walks on the beach. Perhaps you checked in with your gut. Maybe you hashed it out with your best friend, sought advice from a wise mentor, or wrote about it in your journal. Or maybe you took it to your guitar, talked to someone who had passed, or prayed to a higher power. Your wisdom is deep within you, but it also extends beyond you.

If you came to a wise answer, it's likely you drew upon what the Berlin Wisdom Paradigm describes as the five criteria for wisdom.[2] Pull out your Wise Effort Journal and list your answers to these questions under the heading "I Am Already Wise." Choose a current problem or struggle. How could you use your wisdom to help direct your energy?

Factual knowledge: What do you already know from books, podcasts, media, education, and lifelong learning that can help you with this problem?

Procedural knowledge: What genius qualities can you bring to this situation? Could your emotional intelligence, creative talents, character strengths, interests, or personality be helpful?

Lifespan contextualism: How will your response impact you and others ten, twenty, or thirty years down the road?

Value relativism: Are there perspectives you have not considered or given yourself a chance to understand?

Awareness of uncertainty: Remind yourself that everything changes and there are many paths you can take. What do you know to be true about uncertainty and change?

To grow wiser, you need to be intentional about it. Folks who practice being open to experiences, emotional regulation, and reflective thinking score higher on measures of wisdom.[3] You may think that older equals wiser, but that's not always the case. My twelve-year-old son often asks better questions than I do at almost four times his age. We can all name some very psychologically rigid and unwise people who are older than we are. Being smart also isn't the same as being wise. You likely know some pretty clever people, and they aren't always the ones you would trust with your big life decisions. To be wise, you need both wit (cleverness, problem-solving skills, and procedural and factual knowledge) and virtue (compassion, kindness, and values).[4]

Our wisdom extends beyond the boundaries of our individual brains, encompassing the bodies we inhabit, the environments we engage with, and the social connections that shape our thoughts.[5] In *Indigenous Sustainable Wisdom,* Darcia Narvaez and colleagues wrote that wisdom is learned "through exploration rather than being told."[6] A textbook can't tell you when it's time to put your dog to sleep or what to say to your friend when she tells you she is getting a divorce. And an app can't decide when it's right to lean in for a kiss. Your wisdom is in the DNA from your ancestors, the tree outside your bedroom window, your morning stretch, the uneasiness in your tummy, and the gathering of your community. I feel wise when I step outside barefoot under the night sky when I can't sleep. The stars can put any problem into perspective. And I feel wise when I notice my heartbeat picking up in anticipation of a bold move and then decide to follow through. Your wisdom is in so many places. It's in the Post-it notes you use to organize your thoughts, in the hand gestures you use to show your thinking, and in someone's kind eyes as you tell them your story.

I see our wisdom as including the wisdom of our emotions, our bodies, our ancestors, our learning history, the wise world around us, and even the mystical. Wisdom is about discernment—"the wisdom to know the difference." It is about knowing that many truths can coexist at once. And when you use this wisdom to channel your genius energy, you tap into something big and powerful: wise effort.

Do you see how broad and deep your wisdom is and why it is so important in directing your genius energy? Even though that's the case, wisdom is not always easy to access. One way to get there is to start questioning the very nature of who you are. To fully manifest your genius, you need to know that your Wise Self is bigger than just you.

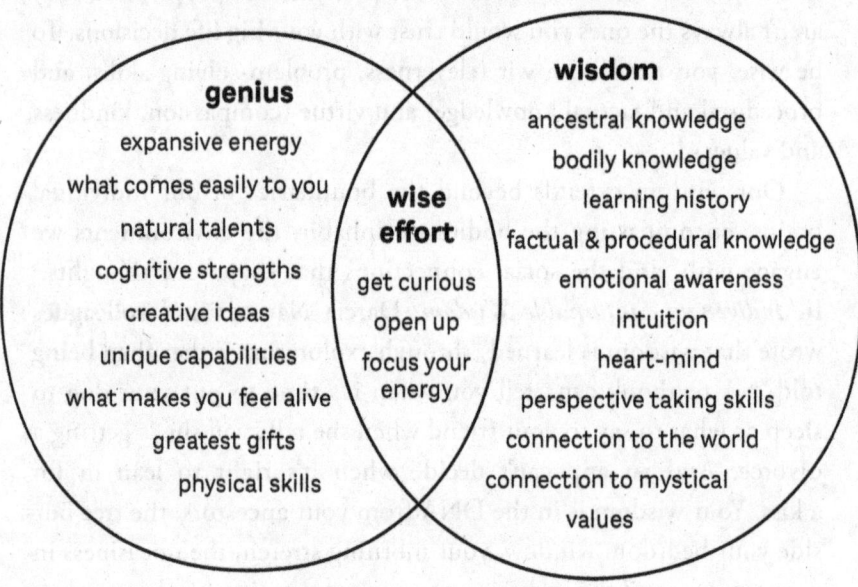

Wise Effort happens in the place where wisdom meets genius energy.

Step 2. Ask, *Who Am I?*

Have you ever asked yourself, *Who am I?* Like, who is this person you call you? Try this: point to yourself. What would you point to? If you grew up with an individualistic perspective, you likely wouldn't point to a tree or clouds in the sky. You'd probably point to your chest.

This question is another of those Zen koans. And it's a great one to use to open up your sense of self a bit. We think we are our physical body, our appearance, what we do for a living, or the content of our thoughts or feelings. Clients will tell me, "I am the type of person who just can't get over things" or "I am too anxious to do that" or "I am just a bad picker when it comes to relationships." What stories do you tell yourself about who you are? How long have these stories been around? Do you let these stories shape what you do and don't do?

In ACT, we call this attachment to self-story "self-ing," and it's considered a behavior, something you are doing. We create narrow and inflexible stories about ourselves and let them define who we are without ever really looking at them. These stories may have developed for a good reason, often to protect you, and it's beneficial to have compassion for their origins. But are they really all of you? Do these stories capture the whole of who you are?

In workshops, I'll often pair up participants and have them play with this question. One member of the pair asks the other the question "Who are you?" over and over again, without commenting in response. At first, the person answering might say things like "I am a therapist," "I am a son," "I am a tennis player," or even "I am the oatmeal I ate for breakfast." But after about twenty rounds, we get to the good stuff. Responses shift to things like "I am space," "I am love," "I am you," or "I am all." After being asked enough times, "Who are you?," you will start to feel it—you aren't just the person whose chest you point to. You are so much more.

Psychology has long wrestled with this question, too: *Who are you?* Carl Jung described a self that unifies many parts of you—the social mask you wear; your repressed shadow parts; your inner masculine and feminine; and your many unconscious archetypes, like a rebel, a warrior, and a hero. In modern psychology, researcher Paul Gilbert of compassion focused therapy (CFT) has expanded on Jung's ideas to add an evolutionary lens. He says we have "many selves" that match our evolutionary drive to avoid threats, seek resources, and belong. We might have a fearful self, an angry self, a competitive self, and a compassionate self, each reflecting different emotions, motives, or responses.[7] Joseph Ciarrochi of process-based therapy calls these selves "self-as-shield" and "self-as-prize." We develop them for a reason—to shield us from life's pain and help us obtain prized resources. This isn't far from Richard Schwartz's work in the area of internal family systems (IFS); he describes us as having many "parts," each playing an important role in our inner life. We have no "bad parts"; we just need a Wise Self to help them get along.⁸

Across cultures and disciplines, one theme remains: you are not just one thing. You are an interchange of experiences, emotions, and interconnections. Whether framed as archetypes, parts, ancestral wisdom, or interwoven identities, the self is both personal and collective, ever-changing yet deeply rooted in something greater than itself.

Let's play with this question of *Who are you?* a bit to make this concept more tangible and personal to you. Open your Wise Effort Journal, title the page "Who Am I Really?," and answer this prompt as many times as you can until you feel a perspective shift. Include roles, positive characteristics, negative self-judgments, or anything else that comes to mind.⁹

I am _____.

Now look at your list. Does it encompass all of who you are? Is anything missing? You'll likely soon realize that there is no way to describe the whole of who you are in a list like this. You are complex, dynamic, and ever-changing depending on context. Are there times when you aren't a good tennis player, and are you really always funny? Plus, what happens when you let these roles define you?

If we aren't careful, your *I am* and *I am not* statements might organize your life. That bike trip you want to go on with friends? *No, sorry, I can't. I'm too slow.* Or that relationship you might want to end: *I can't because I can't be alone.* These are the stories that misdirect our genius energy.

So how can we move out of these small selves into our wiser, more flexible sense of Self?

Step 3. Let Go of Your Story

A Wise Self can hold many truths at once. It's flexible, not fixed, and allows you to change in different contexts. These definitions of you aren't always true, and they don't fully define you. Self-stories like this, when they are held too tightly, limit your genius energy. Go down the list of *I am* statements you made, one at a time, and loosen them up. Add the disclaimer *sometimes*. I am bad at math *sometimes*. I am a good cook *sometimes*. I am nice *sometimes*. You get the point. All of this depends on the situation. None of these stories about you is always true. The only real constant here is this:

I am.

Write down those two words. They are the simplest definition of your Wise Self. You just *are*. You are not the roles you temporarily play, your skill sets, the stories people tell about you, or your ever-changing body.

Pick a few stories that you tend to get stuck in about yourself. Choose ones that hold you back from taking risks, lead you to play small, or prevent you from putting your genius energy where you long to put it. For example, maybe you are fantastic at gathering information and creating strategic plans, but you have a story that you could never be an operations manager because you are not smart enough. Or maybe you are a genius at positivity, empathy, and organization, but you have a story that you could never be a life coach because you are too bad at setting boundaries. Your self-stories are holding your genius energy back. We need to loosen them up! Now answer these statements in your Wise Effort Journal under the title "Let Go of My Story":

- If I were to get flexible with the story that I am _____, I would _____.

- If I were to let go of the story that I can't _____, I would _____.

- If I were to see that it's just a story that I have to _____, I would _____.

Here are some more examples to get you started:

- If I were to get flexible with the story that I am out of shape, I would go running.

- If I were to let go of the story that I always know what people are thinking, I would listen better.

- If I were to see that it's just a story that it has to be perfect, I'd start painting.

No matter what story you tell yourself about who you are and what you are capable of, it isn't always true. That's because it's just a story and we can choose to believe it or not, prove it wrong, or add a different ending. Be on the lookout for inflexible statements that start with "I am," "I always," "I have to," "I'll never," or "I can't." And when you spot one, loosen it up by adding the disclaimer *sometimes*. Extra credit if you watch out for rigid stories you hold about other people, too, like "They are," "They always," "They have to," "They never," or "They can't." These stories might be keeping you from seeing people as who they truly are, from building deeper relationships, or from forgiving.

Loosening up the story frees your Wise Self to step in and give your genius energy some direction.

Step 4. Find Your Many Bodies

When Thich Nhat Hanh traveled with his group of monastics, he assigned everyone a "Second Body" (another monastic) to look after in the airport. Is your Second Body lost? Still in the bathroom? Do they need help with their bags?

Sometimes we need to rely on others to make sure we head the right direction in life. Your Second Bodies have helped you hash out major life decisions, supported you through school, and been a force for positive change in your life.

One of my Second Bodies in the past year has been Trudy Goodman. She's in LA, so we connect with each other on Zoom, do a quick check-in, then mute ourselves and get to work writing our books. Sometimes meditation teacher Jack Kornfield (Trudy's husband) will walk by in the background in his bathrobe, which is cute. We unmute to say we are grabbing a bowl of cereal, need an eye break, or need to read part of what we wrote, but most of the time, we stay dialed in and focused. Trudy has ADHD and says that I help her with her samadhi (concentration), and writing makes me anxious, so having Trudy's easygoing and playful presence makes it much more palatable.

This highlights a phenomenon in social psychology called the Köhler effect, where you perform better working with others than working alone, particularly if you are paired with someone who is more skilled or capable. It is especially helpful in situations where a task involves physical or mental endurance. Not only do you perform better, but challenges appear less daunting. For example, research has shown that when you are standing at a hill with a good friend, you perceive it to be 10 to 20 percent less steep than when you are standing there alone.[10]

Whether writing, working out, or creating art, start thinking about who your Second Bodies are. Expanding your Wise Self to include others in this way makes your efforts feel so much less effortful but also enhances your performance. We are better writers, more creative thinkers, and more powerful change makers when we collaborate with our Second Bodies.

Who are your Second Bodies? We think "I" climbed that mountain. Or "I" got that degree. But we never accomplish anything without the help of others. Think about the many bodies that got you here.

As interpersonal neurobiologist Dan Siegel explains it, "There is a Me and a We, and there is a MWe."[11] We need to keep our genius energy on track.

Step 5. Expand Your Sense of Self

By now, you're probably getting a sense of just how expansive your Wise Self really is—it's BIG. Another way to connect with it is by noticing moments that bring a sense of awe—those experiences that shift your perspective and remind you that you're part of something larger. You may have felt this when you saw a shooting star, stood at the top of a mountain, or got caught up in the collective energy of a packed stadium. In moments like these, the usual noise of your mind fades, your sense of self softens, and you feel more connected—to the world, to others, and to something beyond yourself.

Psychologist Dacher Keltner describes awe as a powerful force that helps us step outside ourselves and even makes us more cooperative and compassionate.[12] It's a reminder that we're not just individuals navigating life alone but part of a much bigger, interwoven experience.

So the next time you find yourself in a moment that takes your breath away—pause. Your Wise Self is what is noticing this.

Feeling that you are part of a greater whole seems to quiet the brain's default mode network (DMN)—the area associated with self-referential thinking and rumination—while increasing connectivity between the regions of the brain responsible for attention, compassion, and emotion regulation.[13]

Another avenue to feeling spacious, albeit still mired in politics and legality, is plant medicine. Psychedelics such as psilocybin (found in magic mushrooms) also influence the DMN, effectively "dimming" the activity in this network. When the DMN quiets down, people can experience a profound sense of unity and belonging—with community, the Earth, the universe, or even God.[14]

I've seen firsthand the incredible shifts that can happen for clients during well-guided psychedelic journeys. They often describe feelings of deep connection, clarity, and an enhanced ability to see themselves and their struggles with a new perspective. Of course, the jury is still out on for whom this approach works best, and it's not a path to take lightly. When I spoke with Brian Pilecki, a leader in the area of psychedelic-assisted therapy research, he suggested that working with a well-trained ACT therapist can help integrate and enhance the psychological flexibility gained from a psychedelic experience.[15] The preparation and integration sessions are as important as the journey itself. If you're considering a journey, set and setting are also essential. I encourage you to find a well-trained professional and to read about the subject beforehand.[16] Michael Pollan's *How to Change Your Mind* is a great place to start.[17]

Other ways you might explore this expanded self include meditation, spiritual practices, and breathwork. There are lots of modalities to get you there, and the most important thing is to know that it's always there waiting for you. When do you feel an expansive sense of self? Not only do these practices help you zoom out from whatever struggle you're in, they almost always inspire you to do meaningful things with your genius energy.

Step 6. Act with Compassion

There's no better place to put your genius energy than toward acts of compassion. No matter what your talents and skills are, there is likely a living being out there that can benefit from them. And when you offer compassion, it energizes you right back. It is a renewable resource. Unlike empathy, which is feeling someone else's pain directly, compassion does not drain you—it sustains you because you are doing something about it. Compassion is being moved by the pain of others and acting on your natural desire to help.

Humans evolved to be compassionate. It's what bonds us to our families, drives us to protect the vulnerable, and unites us in times of crisis.[18]

Compassion flows three ways:[19]

1. Toward others—offering kindness and support to those in need.

2. Toward us—treating ourselves with the same care we give others.

3. From others—being open to receiving compassion when we need it.

Often one of these flows feels harder than the others.[20] Maybe you hesitate to offer compassion because you worry that it will make others dependent on you. Or perhaps you resist receiving compassion because you equate it with weakness. But are these fears true?

Fears of compassion can make you less resilient to life's stressors.[21] Marcela Matos and her colleagues at the Center for Research in Neuropsychology and Cognitive Behavioral Intervention (CINEICC) collected data from over four thousand participants across twenty-one countries and found that compassion is associated with greater mental health and feelings of social connectedness during times of adversity. When we open our hearts and allow an exchange of energy, compassion doesn't drain us; it sustains us.

Now let's take a look at your flow of compassion. How could you use your genius energy to support others in need? How could you use your genius energy to support yourself? And how could you use your genius energy to allow kindness in from others who want to help? Compassion is never one-sided—it's a flow of our Wise Self.

Wisdom-Building Questions
Cultivate a stronger, more holistic sense of self by reflecting on the following questions. Title this page in your Wise Effort Journal "Opening Up My Wise Self":

- What's a story that is holding you back from using your genius energy wisely? If you were to let it go, what would you do that you aren't doing now?

- What would you tell your younger self if you could go back and visit them in their struggle? What does your older self tell you about your struggles now?

- Who are your Second Bodies? Who supports you? Which ancestors can you draw on when you need strength?

- What are your fears about giving, receiving, or offering compassion to yourself?

- How can you use your genius(es) to offer compassion to others?

Your Wise Self is a compassionate self. If I were to ask you the question I posed at the beginning of the chapter one more time—*Who are you?*—maybe now you could come to a simple, powerful answer: you are love. We all are.

9
open up to change

At his first job after rehab, Kelly worked at a group home for people with intellectual disabilities, where he earned four dollars an hour. He would help the residents get up, shower, dress, and eat before they attended their work simulation programs. His days started early, and before work, he made an effort to mentally prepare for the day ahead. In those early days of recovery from heroin, pharmaceuticals, alcohol, and cocaine, Kelly held on to daily practices in the face of a mind that most days believed that it was all for naught. In the dark mornings before work, Kelly would write on yellow Post-it notes, "If just for today, if I could not hurt anyone. If I could just do my job, that would be pretty great. God, help me remember that today." He focused on the things he could do: get up in the morning and go to work. Write on a Post-it note. Sit a few minutes in the quiet dark. Pray for the grace not to break anything. Those faithful practices carried him when belief was nowhere to be found.

And then the unthinkable happened.

First he achieved two years of sobriety, then three. At age thirty, a high school dropout, Kelly went to community college and eventually got into a PhD program at the University of Nevada, Reno, with Steven Hayes as his mentor. Together, with the help of many others, they created ACT. He went on to serve as the founding president of the Association for Contextual Behavioral Science and to publish over ninety research papers and eleven books.

When he came to teach a small seminar for my PhD program, Kelly shared his story with us and his staunch belief in possibility. Sure, probabilities may be low. The odds of Kelly Wilson recovering from drug addiction and becoming a prominent psychologist were incredibly slim, much like the odds I faced in recovering from anorexia and writing this book for you.[1] But what Kelly taught our little room of budding psychologists was to be interested less in probabilities and more in possibilities when it comes to behavior. As he described to me a decade later in an interview, "When I sit with someone, I assume that there is something possible for them, no matter how dark it is, no matter what the circumstances are."[2] This was his gift, and it saved him and inspired hundreds of thousands, including me, to learn ACT.

Remember, you, too, have gifts. You have the power to use your genius energy to do incredible things when you focus it with wise effort. For Kelly, that meant transforming his struggle into a treatment approach that has spread worldwide, but it doesn't have to be that grand. As Kelly demonstrated, changing your behavior starts with small steps, things you can do right away. It can be as small as choosing not to open the news app when you wake up in the middle of the night with a racing mind and grabbing a calming book instead. When you focus on the things that you can do and are faithful to your daily wise effort practice, you can make a good life.

Here are the six steps we will take when working toward change:

1. Radically accept.

2. See the choice point.

3. Try something different.

4. Use wise effort skills.

5. Develop wise habits.

6. Do it again.

Step 1. Radically Accept

In order to make a change, you first have to accept where you are. Whether you're stuck in a habit that drains your energy or facing a major life shift, the reality is that you can't move forward while resisting what already exists. Radical acceptance isn't about liking or approving of something; it's about dropping the struggle against reality so you can use your energy in a way that actually helps.

Think about how much time and effort go into wishing things were different. Wishing you hadn't made a mistake, wishing someone else would change, wishing life were easier. That energy could be going toward something meaningful—something you actually have control over. Radical acceptance is what frees up that energy.

A common misconception about acceptance is that it means being passive, giving up, or tolerating things that aren't okay. But acceptance has nothing to do with resignation. It means acknowledging reality—including your thoughts, emotions, and circumstances—without immediately trying to fix, avoid, or control it. It doesn't mean staying in harmful situations or allowing mistreatment. It means being honest with yourself about what's happening so you can respond wisely instead of reacting out of denial or frustration.

When you stop fighting reality, you free yourself to take action that actually matters. It's a paradox—you can both accept what is and make changes toward what can be. At first, this might bring up emotions like sadness, fear, or disappointment. But on the other side are clarity, peace, and the freedom to move forward.

If the word *acceptance* doesn't sit right with you, try a different one: *allowing*, *acknowledging*, *opening*, or *making space*. The idea is the same—stop wasting energy on what can't be changed and use it where it counts.

Here's a way to explore this for yourself. Fill in the blanks:

- When I radically accept _____, it frees me to _____.

Here are some examples to get you started:

- When I radically accept **my mistakes**, it frees me to **try again with courage.**
- When I radically accept **my anxiety**, it frees me to **take action despite my discomfort.**
- When I radically accept **that someone I love may not change**, it frees me to **focus on how I show up in the relationship.**

Radical acceptance is a practice, not a one-time deal. You accept, and then you fall back into not accepting, and you accept again. Every time you accept, you widen your zone of flexibility.

Think about something that is bothering you that you are struggling to accept, and practice radical acceptance. Here's how:

With your body: Uncross your arms, open your palms, soften your forehead, and smile with your eyes.

With your mind: Say silently to yourself, *I can allow. I can open. I can be with this.*

With your behavior: Choose an action that demonstrates your acceptance. Sometimes you need your behavior to guide your mind and body in a different direction.

As Tara Brach, author of *Radical Acceptance*, puts it, "The boundary to what we can accept is the boundary to our freedom."[3]

Step 2. See the Choice Point

A choice point is the moment when you become aware of a decision between two paths:

Move toward your values: turning your genius energy toward what matters to you in your heart.

Move away from your values: running away from discomfort, staying stuck in a story, holding on too tightly.

The term "choice points" was coined by ACT researchers Anne Bailey, Joseph Ciarrochi, and Russ Harris.[4] Choice points are moments of awareness when you recognize your ability to choose how to respond rather than automatically reacting based on fear, habit, or emotional discomfort. By noticing these moments, you can get untangled from your struggle and can best direct your genius energy. It looks and feels like this:

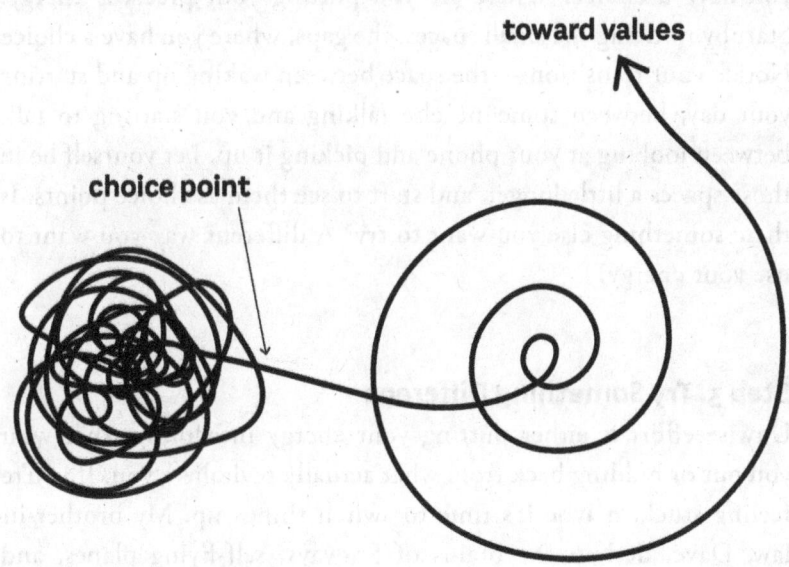

A choice point on the wise effort journey.

Sometimes the choice is to do nothing at all. Have you ever surfed an urge? Let your tears flow? Other times, the choice is to put your energy into turning the semitruck of your life around. You need lots of space for that! You apply for that job, schedule that follow-up doctor's appointment you've been avoiding, or send that anxiety-provoking email. All of this requires you to radically accept and see the choice point. Are you facing any choice points right now? Do you anticipate choice points later today? This week?

In Tibetan Buddhism, this space of transition is referred to as the "bardo."[5] "Bardo" translates as intermediate state, and it's the interval between any significant transition—between life and death, between waking and sleeping, when the sun is just rising, or when you walk in the door at the end of your day. In *How We Live Is How We Die*, Pema Chödrön calls this space "being in the gap."[6] We are always at a choice point—in the gap. Every moment is in transition to something, and we get to decide how we show up in it.

Every moment we wake up to is a choice point. Even right now, you have a choice. Where are you putting your precious energy? Start by noticing the small spaces, the gaps, where you have a choice. Notice your transitions—the space between waking up and starting your day, between someone else talking and you starting to talk, between looking at your phone and picking it up. Let yourself be in those spaces a little longer, and start to see them as choice points. Is there something else you want to try? A different way you want to use your energy?

Step 3. Try Something Different

Unwise effort is either putting your energy into things that wear you out or holding back from what actually revitalizes you. If you're feeling stuck, maybe it's time to switch things up. My brother-in-law, Dave, designs the brains of Segways, self-flying planes, and land-mine-detecting military robots. He told me that of all the features he ever created, his favorite was the "get unstuck" button.

He programmed this button for those moments when a robot finds itself trapped in an impossible situation with no way out. Once activated, the robot tries every behavior in its repertoire—Jump! Hit your head against the wall! Do a backflip! Crawl! Eventually it finds its way out. Dave says this approach works much better than programming a robot to "think their way out." If they do that, they tend to get more stuck.

The same may be true for you. Sometimes thinking your way out of your problem won't help. Instead you need to behave your way out of it. This is a fundamental principle in the science of evolution. To improve and change, first we need variation: do something different. Then we need to select what works and retain it. You may not know exactly what to do, but when you stop doing what's not working and try something new, you are on to something. You give up on your automatic, unwise habit of running away, holding on too tightly, or getting stuck in a story and explore other possibilities instead. Your own version of doing backflips, crawling, or jumping might look like pausing before you send that defensive email or getting up early on a Friday morning to call a friend, write, swim, or have sex with your partner. Variation is a good thing.

Opportunities for variation happen multiple times a day. They show up in the gaps, the choice points. You can choose something different in small ways (like choosing to go to happy hour instead of pushing yourself to work an extra hour) or big ways (like choosing to disappoint people, leave your marriage, or change jobs). Choosing new behaviors expands your zone of possibility. This is how you evolve. And who doesn't want to do that?

Let's try an exercise to help you become familiar with this process. Grab your Wise Effort Journal and title the page "Do Something Different." In the center of the page, write a few words describing a choice point. This could be a choice point around the struggle you defined at the start of this book. For example, you could write, "The moment I get home from work and want to drink," "Not sure if I should say yes to the work trip," or "Feeling hurt in my friendship and wondering if I should say something." Then, underneath the choice point, write a few values and the genius energy that can help you out. For example:

Choice point: Wondering if I should insist that my aging dad stop driving

Geniuses: Imagining the future, emotional intelligence

Values: Action, authenticity, loyalty

Now, for getting unstuck, remember that there are hundreds of ways to practice wise effort skills, live your values, and use your genius. Instead of thinking you have just one option, I want you to open your mind to think about many options, like that robot Dave designed. I like to call this a *brainstorm of possibility*. Write down as many different new ways that you can use your wise effort skills as you can think of. To refresh your memory, a table of the skills is provided in the Additional Resources section.

Here is an example of someone caring for an aging parent who has dug in his heels. Her brainstorm looked like this (the wise effort skills are in bold):

Brainstorm of Possibility

- Take some **centering** breaths on my drive over to visit him.

- Open to feeling and **make space for feeling** guilt, resentment, and fear, and remind myself I hurt because I care.

- Imagine the future when my dad is gone and use those **values** to help guide me in how I want to act.

- Ask myself, *Am I sure?* every time I start catastrophizing.

- Focus on **savoring** the unexpected things that go well.

- **Use my genius** for verbal organization and write out a script for what I want to say next time he dings the car.

- **Use my genius** of empathy to understand how he feels.

- **Use my genius** of action to research drivers for seniors.

- Remember I have **Second Bodies** (and if I don't, hire a therapist who specializes in geriatric care).

- Remember that I, too, am growing older. What kind of **wise ancestor** do I want to be?

You are creating options here, ways you can use wise effort skills to turn your spiral of genius energy in the right direction. Now that you have your brainstorm of possibilities, let's make them happen.

Step 4. Use Wise Effort Skills

I hit the get-unstuck button at the end of my first year in the PhD program for the Eating and Weight Concerns Lab at the University of Colorado Boulder. With the promise of three hundred days of sunshine, hiking trails, and a highly regarded adviser, I started the program in a firm place in my recovery. However, I wasn't prepared for the intense striving and competition that doctoral programs often breed. I quickly lost sight of my purpose, and my genius energy of persistence got caught up in pushing my way to the top of my class. My frenemy, relentless self-drive, was back.

At the end of my first year, I relapsed again. But this time, I wasn't purging in a park bathroom; it was in the bathroom of the Muenzinger Psychology Building, one floor up from where I was seeing clients. I was mired in shame, afraid to tell anyone—especially my clinical adviser—about what was happening. Our stories keep us stuck ("I am researching eating disorders; I can't have one"). Driving home from the lab one day, I stopped at a gas station for candy and caught my image in the mirror. I had swollen salivary glands, bloodshot eyes, and thick makeup covering the bags under them. *Who am I?* The face I saw looking back at me wasn't just my face—it was me when I was seventeen, the face of my clients, the face of anyone who has struggled with addiction. It was the face of my father, my grandmother, and my future if I didn't turn this energy around. My Wise Self was poking through, waking up.

Looking into my eyes in yet another gross setting, I knew what I needed to do. I remember walking in the door and handing the bag of Reese's Peanut Butter Cups and melting ice cream to my husband. "I need your help," I said. "My frenemy is back."

I am ever grateful to have married such a patient man. "I'm here," he said.

It takes a lot of bravery to choose wise effort, especially when you are so off track from your values. Sometimes pressing the get-unstuck button seems both impossible and necessary. I took a leave from my PhD program, fearing that my career, and everything I had worked for, was over. I opened to the feelings of humiliation, panic, and uncertainty that came with letting go. And I used my emotional sensitivity and persistence to do it with grace.

Pause here. Where have you steered off track from your values? What is the brave move you need to make? Is there a get-unstuck button you need to press?

The week I left my PhD program, I knew I needed a reset, so I enrolled in the Eldorado Mountain Yoga Ashram for teacher training. My primary teacher was Ananda, meaning "divine love" in Sanskrit. She worked at Home Depot by day and served at the ashram in the afternoons and on weekends. Ananda was full-bodied and soft-spirited and could effortlessly fold into Sukhasana (cross-legged pose) or hold Warrior 3 with the steadiness of an oak. She looked right at me and knew what I needed.

In yoga, it's customary to receive a mantra from your teacher as part of your Sadhana (forty days of spiritual practice). Ever the eager

PhD student, I was ready for a complex Sanskrit phrase that would take the FULL forty days to memorize. You know, something to impress my family and friends when they asked me the dreaded question of what I was doing with my free time. But Ananda saw right through my ambition. She didn't care about that. She was invested in giving me something that would help. She handed me a simple rosewood mala—a string of 108 beads—and gave me my mantra: "Ham Sa," which translates as "I am."

My instruction was to repeat the two sounds silently, just to myself—"Ham" on the inhale and "Sa" on the exhale for 108 breaths. It wasn't fancy or impressive, but it worked—it centered me and helped me apply my genius energy of persistence where I really needed it. I'd use it when I wobbled in my standing poses or in my recovery and when I got my courage up to ask my adviser if I could come back to school the following year. I went on to study acceptance- and awareness-based interventions for bulimia. But this time, I didn't do it to be impressive. I did it because I was genuinely curious and wanted to give back what had been so freely given to me. No matter what situation you are in, there's an opportunity to use wise effort skills and get your genius energy pointed in the right direction again.

Step 5. Develop Wise Habits

With practice, wise effort will become easier over time. Eventually it will become a wise habit to get curious, open up, and focus your energy toward what matters most. One difference between wise and unwise habits is that unwise habits are circular. They go around and around, staying the same or getting more rigid over time. Wise habits, by contrast, open up your energy toward broader, more flexible ways of being. Wise habits get more spacious with use. Wise habits let energy flow freely; they support your growth, your evolution.

The most effective way to form habits isn't about "breaking bad habits" but about building new, meaningful ones. You create pathways that elevate your life.

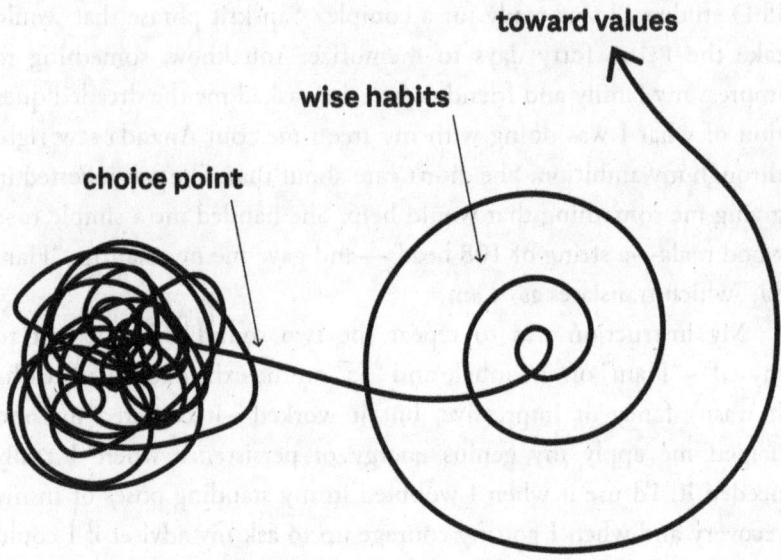

Wise habits are intrinsic to wise effort.

Before we go on to describe wise habits, I want to offer a quick disclaimer: the kind of habits I'm talking about here aren't just about putting your shoes by the door so you are more likely to go for a run. We are talking about something bigger. Wise habits are noticing the choice points, when you have strayed from who you want to be in the world, and choosing wise effort instead. They are about making wise, bold, brave moves that can feel hard. For example:

- Someone asks you to add another thing to your list of to-dos, and you check in with your heart-mind before you answer. You feel relief when you say no.

- You catch your mind ruminating about feeling left out and step back from your thoughts long enough to reach out and connect. It feels good to be brave.

- You're driving away after fighting with your partner, and you turn around to apologize. This is how you want to act.

There's a science to what you are doing here—you are noticing the choice point, using your wise effort skills, and experiencing the reward of acting from your heart.

Behavioral scientists describe habits as loops with three key parts—a cue, a behavior, and a reward.[7] The cue is what prompts you; the behavior is what you do; and the reward reinforces the behavior, making it easier to repeat. To develop wise habits, start by noticing choice points—these are cues to choose your wise effort skills. Then choose a wise effort skill from your brainstorm of possibility. The intrinsic reward is the good feelings that come with acting wisely.

Here's an example of a wise habit:

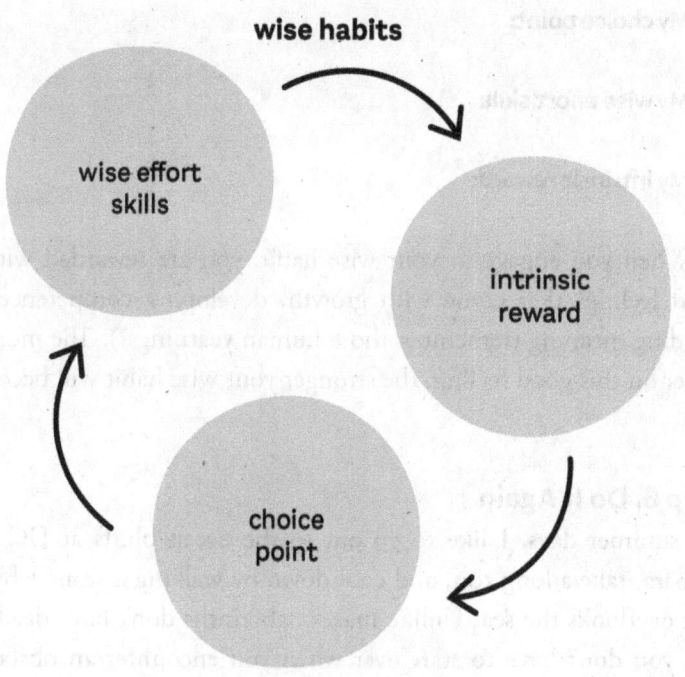

Three steps you can take to cultivate wise habits.

Choice point: You are procrastinating on an important work project because you really want to do a great job.

Wise effort skills: You open up to feeling and name your experience—*I am feeling anxious*—and you open up to your Wise Self by offering yourself compassion—*Of course I am anxious; this is a big deal. Everyone feels anxious about things they care about.* Then you act on your values and open your computer.

Intrinsic reward: You start your work and feel empowered and proud that you didn't run away. You get your work DONE.

Now it's your turn. Try mapping out your own wise habit using these principles:

My choice point:

My wise effort skill:

My intrinsic reward:

When you engage in your wise habit, you are rewarded with the good feelings that come with growth, developing competence, and building meaning (remember those human yearnings?). The more you linger on this good feeling, the stronger your wise habit will become.

Step 6. Do It Again

On summer days, I like to go out to the ocean bluffs at UC Santa Barbara, take a long run, and cool down by walking a stone labyrinth that overlooks the sea. Unlike mazes, labyrinths don't have dead ends, and you don't have to start over when you encounter an obstacle or wrong turn. The twists and turns, which seem like lapses, are part of the process. Sometimes I'll walk through the labyrinth and find myself on the edge of it again, far from the center; other times, it's a beeline to the middle. No matter where I am, I know where I am going. This is what wise effort looks and feels like—a spiral, a wonderful twisty mystery, a journey toward home.

I relapsed countless times before achieving steady recovery from disordered eating, and from time to time, my persistence can run away from me. But now I spot it sooner and know what to do when it happens—I get curious; open up; and focus my energy toward my values of creating beauty and intimacy and being of service. Lapses are a normal part of the human experience; they're literally built into our psychological models of change: precontemplation, contemplation, preparation, action, maintenance, and . . . relapse.[8]

When you do lapse, see it as a knock on your door, inviting you to remember your values. Get curious—what is happening here? Open up—what are you willing to feel? Focus your energy—what do you need to do? Then do it. You can do this ten times a day or one hundred times a day, and every time you do, you are choosing wise effort.

Wisdom-Building Questions

To get in the habit of using your genius energy wisely, reflect on the following questions. Title this page in your Wise Effort Journal "Open Up to Change":

- What are you willing to radically accept so you can have more freedom from your current struggle?

- What is something new you'd like to try today from your brainstorm of possibility?

- How can your genius help you make the changes you want to make around your struggle?

- What is one wise habit you would like to establish to help you with this change?

- What do lapses look like for you? What do you want to do when they happen?

Practice Opening Up

You now understand the three tasks of Wise Effort:

1. **Get Curious:** Tune in to what is keeping you stuck and how your genius is playing a part in it.

2. **Open Up:** Welcome your feelings, get to know your mind, and meet the many parts of your whole self.

3. **Focus Your Energy:** When confronted with a choice, move in the direction of your values.

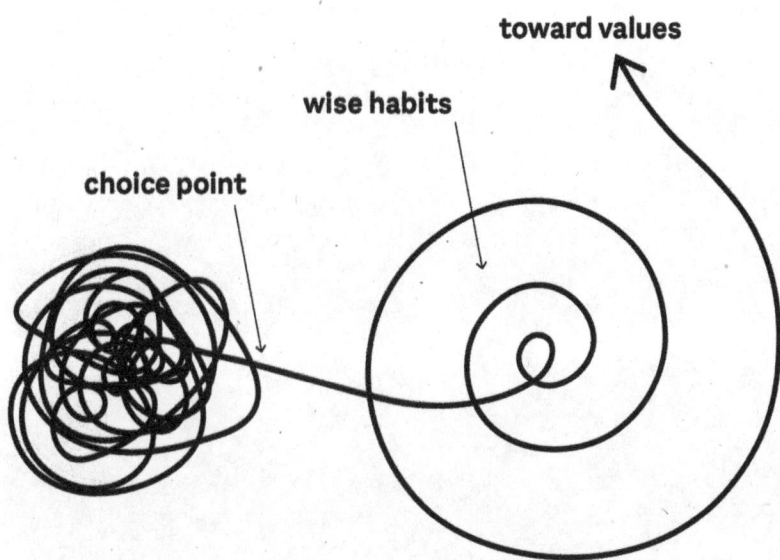

The Wise Effort Method: Get Curious, Open Up, Focus Your Energy.

The Wise Effort method can be applied to pretty much any area of your life that is important to you. In the chapters ahead, you will explore how to focus your energy in your relationships, in your body, at work, with your creativity, and in your community. You now have a path and a method to follow. It all comes back to these steps. Your final task is to put them into practice.

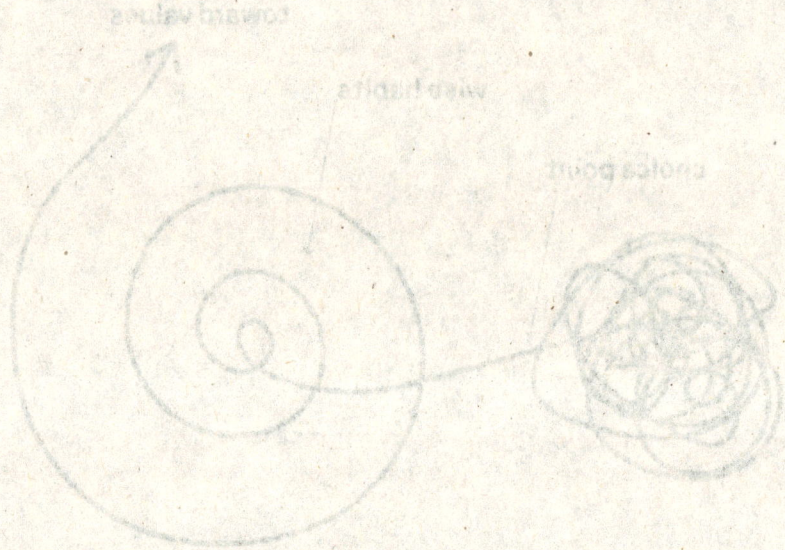

wise effort task #3

focus your energy

This beginning has been quietly forming
Waiting until you were ready to emerge.

—John O'Donohue

10
wise effort in relationships

Robert Waldinger's TED Talk "What Makes a Good Life: Lessons from the Longest Study on Happiness" has over forty-seven million views, and there's a good reason. You feel energized in his presence.[1] Waldinger, who is both a Harvard psychiatrist and a Zen priest, is the fourth director of the Harvard Study of Adult Development, which for over eighty-five years has been following two generations of 724 families that began as a cohort of male Harvard students and inner-city residents. Since the 1940s, the researchers have asked these participants about their daily lives and well-being. Questions like these:

- Whom can you really count on to be dependable when you need help?

- How often do you feel lonely?

- What is the secret to aging well?

When I asked Waldinger about the secret to a long, healthy, and happy life, he replied, "I would say being engaged in activities you love with people you care about and who care about you."[2]

The Harvard Study data is rich, showing that having strong relationships is a better predictor of health than money, fame, or success. The health of your relationships at age fifty is a better predictor of your physical health at age eighty than your cholesterol levels. The study also showed that a lack of connected relationships is toxic. People who were more isolated than they wanted to be were less happy, their health declined earlier in midlife, their brain function declined sooner, and they lived shorter lives than those who were not lonely.[3]

What the Harvard Study shows is that it's not the number of connections you have or the type of connections that matters; it's the *quality* of those relationships. If you have two good friends and don't feel lonely, you are better off than if you have ten friends and feel disconnected.

Healthy relationships are at the heart of a good life. You can apply your wise effort skills to any relationship challenge—whether it's lack of friends, fraught family relationships, or marriages that have lost their spark. You invest your energy in relationships because you recognize that they are your true wealth.

Get Curious About Your Relationship Map

When your connections are strong, you feel at your best. They provide you with security, growth, emotional closeness, shared experiences, romantic intimacy, help, and fun.[4] Do you have someone to call when things fall apart? Someone who is genuinely happy for your success? Someone who pushes you to do hard things? We need those people to depend on. Let's get curious about the relationships you have and the ones you may want to strengthen.

What's most important to building strong relationships is how *you* show up in them. Are you using your genius in your relationships? Are you aligning your genius energy with your values?

I once had a conversation with relationship expert Dr. Ann Kelley on her *Therapist Uncensored* podcast about that classic experience of fighting with our partners in the kitchen.[5] I asked Ann, "What do you need in that moment when you're fighting with your wife?" Her answer? "To be understood." This gave a clue to her values—Ann values seeking understanding in relationships. It also gave a road map of what she *could* do in this moment of struggle. She could see her frustration as a choice point and act on that value—in other words, use her genius in emotional intelligence to seek to understand her wife instead of trying to get her wife to understand her! We can live our values in any relationship we are in, whether the other person is a positive energizer or an energy depleter.

Let's get curious about how you want to use your energy in your relationships.

Create Your Relationship Energy Map

1. Get out your Wise Effort Journal and title the page "My Relationship Energy Map." Draw a spiral of energy at the center of the page and write "Me" in the middle.

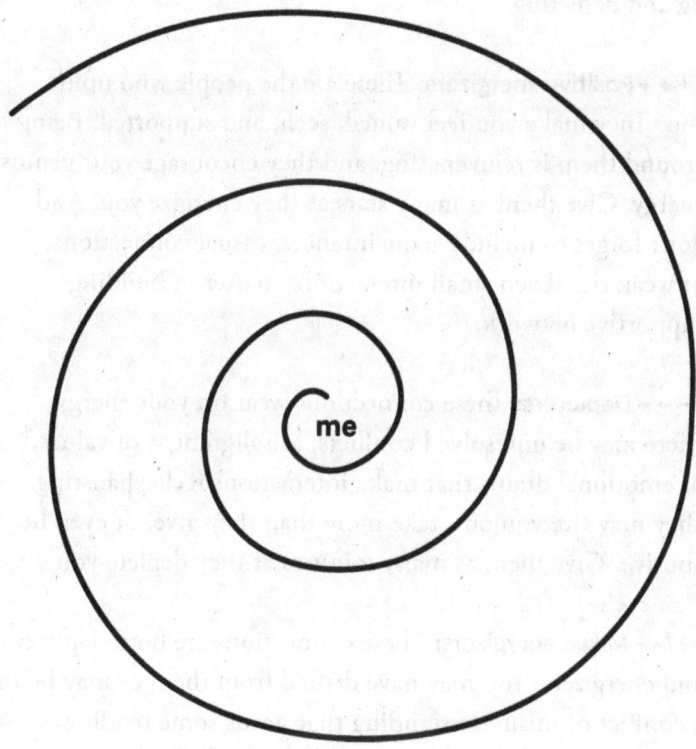

Create your relationship map.

2. Pick five to ten relationships that influence your energy. Put the initials of these connections around the spiral—friends, family members, colleagues, acquaintances, pets, even organizations or communities that influence your energy.

3. Position them based on impact on your energy—closer to the center means they have a strong influence (both positive and negative); farther away means they have less impact.

Categorize Your Relationships

Use the following symbols to represent the nature of each connection. You can use more than one symbol for a relationship if it is both energizing and depleting.

> **+ + + + Positive energizers:** These are the people who uplift you. They make you feel valued, seen, and supported. Being around them is rejuvenating, and they encourage your genius energy. Give them as many stars as they energize you. And don't forget to include acquaintances, casual connections, or weak ties. Even small interactions matter in building a supportive network.
>
> **– – – – Depleters:** These connections wear on your energy. There may be unresolved conflicts, misalignment of values, or emotional drains that make interactions feel exhausting. They may tire you out, take more than they give, or even be abusive. Give them as many minuses as they deplete you.
>
> **++/– – Mixed energizers:** These connections are both depleters and energizers. You may have drifted from them or may be in a conflict or misunderstanding that needs some tending.

Direct Your Relationship Energy

If you want someone closer in your life, draw an arrow moving them toward the center. If you need to create more energetic distance, draw an arrow pointing outward.

Take a look at your map. Are there a lot more arrows pointing inward, toward you? This may be a sign that you crave more connection. Or maybe there are a lot of arrows pointing outward, away from you? This may be a sign that you need to put some effort into setting boundaries with people. How many depleters versus energizers do you have in your life? If you have a lot of mixed energizers, that's okay, too. Your wise effort skills can help clear up any energetic rifts.

Reenergize Your Relationship Ecosystem

Your next step is to actively reshape your relationship landscape—without "needing" others to change.

Strengthen the Positive Energizers

Usually, positive energizers bring out your genius energy, not only because it feels good to be around them but also because you feel safe to be yourself around them. You can show your flaws and still feel loved for who you are. The biggest energizers want the best for you, challenge you to step up your game, appreciate your unique gifts, and accept you as you are.

Look at the positive energizers on your spiral. Which of these relationships do you want to deepen, spend more time on, or prioritize? Pick one to work with and write that person's name in your Wise Effort Journal, then answer the following questions:

- What values do you want to bring to this relationship? Do you want to be understanding or maybe adventurous, kind, honest, or vulnerable? Are you acting in line with those values?

- Are there thoughts and feelings that block you from fully expressing yourself and connecting in this relationship?

- Does your genius ever become your problem in this relationship? Are there ways you are putting in too much energy or holding back? How?

- Are you being a positive energizer in this relationship? How can you offer your genius energy? Are there interests, talents, and gifts you can share with this person? Brainstorm some possibilities that would strengthen your connection.

Defuse from the Depleters

Some relationship depleters are so toxic that you need to end the relationship altogether. But that is not always possible—we have to work with them, coparent with them, or spend holidays with them because they are connected to other values we care about. When that is the case, depleters can feel even more depleting when you give them your energy by acting out of alignment with your values. Complaining, comparing, and ruminating about how depleting they are will only deplete you more. Save your energy for clarifying your boundaries, aligning yourself with positive energizers that can support you, and showing up with dignity.

Pick one of your most depleting relationships. Write that person's name in your Wise Effort Journal and answer the following questions:

- What centering practices could help you feel more grounded around that person?

- What are you feeling in this relationship? What do these feelings need? How can you care for these feelings?

- Independent of how the depleting person shows up, how do you want to show up? What are your values in this relationship? Are you aligned with them?

- Has your genius become your problem in this relationship? How?

- Is there something you want to radically accept about this relationship?

- Are there choice points in your interactions with that person where you could choose a wiser response?

- Remember your Wise Self. Can you see that this depleting person suffers, too?

Reclaiming your energy in these relationships can be as small as noticing when you are gossiping about them and choosing to put your mental energy toward what you want to grow instead. Or seeking to understand their perspective instead of insisting on being right. Or maybe it's breaking some mental rules about what a relationship "should" look like, as Giulia Preziuso, author of *It's Your Mother's Fault*, does. She allots seventeen minutes of one-on-one time when she visits her mom. After having been estranged for ten years, seventeen minutes feels like a behavioral stretch, and setting that limit allows her to stay in the relationship without being completely depleted by it.

Sort Out the Mixed Energizers

For the folks who are both depleting and energizing, there's likely some repair or adjusting of roles needed to improve these relationships. You can be an energetic drawbridge—letting it down when needed and pulling it back to recharge. Write the name of a mixed energizer in your Wise Effort Journal and answer these questions:

- Are you stuck in a story, holding too tightly, or avoiding discomfort with this relationship?

- Can you see that they may be doing the same? Have compassion for both of you.

- Do you need to tune up your values in these relationships? What would help you be more aligned?

- Is there something that you would benefit from radically accepting about this relationship?

- Is there a wise change that you could make that might improve this relationship?

Every ecosystem is an exchange of energy, including your relational one. As you begin to shift your energy in this space and act more from your values, you just might find that other people shift, too. But don't count on it! Take pride in focusing on what you have power over—how you use your energy. Then double down on the people who amplify your genius.

Design Your Genius Advisory Board

Now that you have a clearer sense of the relationships you want to strengthen and some values that will support that, let's make what I call your Genius Advisory Board. Your Genius Advisory Board members are the positive energizers whom you can consult when making a big decision, lean on for support, and offer your genius back. Your Genius Advisory Board might include the following:

- People who have a genius for keeping you motivated to move your body and stay physically healthy

- People who have a genius for assertiveness and help you set boundaries

- People who have a genius for humor and help you laugh at yourself

- People who have a genius for risk-taking and push you out of your comfort zone

- People who have a genius for emotional awareness—they won't freak out when you are anxious and can be with you when you are sad

- People who don't compete with you but rather welcome and celebrate your genius

Look at your relationship map and write "My Genuis Advisory Board" in your Wise Effort Journal. Make a list of three to five people to put on your board. Are there some people you would like to have on your board but don't have a strong enough relationship with yet? Add them, too.

Or maybe there are people you want to have on your list but whom you have drifted from or have a rift with. We'll talk about how to strengthen those relationships next, but first, design your board. Then, one by one, reach out to them. Tell them that you are working on the Wise Effort method and you would like them to be part of your Genius Advisory Board. Tell them why you chose them (what genius do you see in them?) and how you would like to be there for them in return. You may even choose to meet with these people on a regular basis.

There are few things that make you feel stronger than having a board of geniuses to exchange energy with. That's because *mattering* to others makes us feel seen, valued, and connected.[6] It reinforces our sense of purpose, reminds us that we are needed, and strengthens our resilience in the face of challenges. When we know we matter, we're more likely to show up authentically, take meaningful risks, and invest in the people and projects that give our lives depth. Feeling like we matter isn't just a nice bonus—it's a core psychological need that fuels our capacity for wise effort. So create a board of people who matter to you, and make yourself matter to others by showing up and offering your genius energy freely.

Open Up to Courageous Conversations

Even the positively energizing relationships in your life aren't always easy to navigate. We may want to connect with others, but we fear being rejected or making mistakes. Or we put our best foot forward, use all our great communication skills, and still don't get what we hoped for. We hurt in relationships because we care a lot about them. But when we run away from our feelings, hold on too tightly, or get stuck in a story, it makes the pain so much worse. Your genius becomes your problem when you overuse your energy to try to control another person or underuse your energy and are inauthentic.

Remember that bird stuck in the kitchen? Trying to fix, control, or set another person "right" will lead you to hit your head against the window. It just doesn't work. This is what Stephen Rollnick, cofounder of motivational interviewing, calls "the righting reflex."[7] When you are setting someone "right," you aren't really listening to them, and they will feel it. It's a real relationship killer. What can you do instead? Put your energy toward connection.

In couples therapy, I often instruct partners to sit across from each other, and while one partner starts talking about their problem, the other partner must listen and reflect back what they hear. Often the person talking can get only a few sentences out before the "listener" jumps in with a defense or correction to set them "right." It usually takes a few tries, with me intervening and saying, "Hang on, let's try that again. Can you really listen, with your whole heart, and reflect back what you hear?" When they finally do it—validate their partner—you can see their partner's nervous system start to relax. *Finally, you heard me.*

It starts with *opening up*—to listening, feeling, and showing up with care. Here's how:

- **Center yourself:** Find your footing first. Take a few slow breaths, go for a walk before you talk, or say your mantra a few times. Make sure you are stable and centered before you open up. Especially if you are in a conflict or entering a difficult conversation.

- **Open your mind and really listen:** Step back from your own thoughts for a moment and take in what the other person is saying. Instead of planning your response, focus on *understanding*. Try reflecting their words back: "So what I hear you saying is . . . ," but don't assume you've got it all right. Ask questions. Get curious.

- **Open to what they're feeling:** Pay attention to their tone, their body language, and what's underneath their words. Name the emotion: "It sounds like you're really worried about . . ." or "That makes sense—you have every right to feel frustrated." Sometimes just feeling *seen* is enough to shift a conversation.

- **Open up your Wise Self to compassion:** Can you see that they are hurting, too? Let them know you care, even in small ways. A simple "I'm here for you" or a softer tone can make all the difference. You don't need to fix anything—just *being present* is powerful.

- **Open your actions to show you care:** Listen for what they need, then put your energy there. Maybe touching their arm, a few words of encouragement, or handling a small task to ease their load. Or maybe it's something bigger—an apology, an acknowledgment, or a real change in behavior.

Opening up to connection shifts your energy from fixing, advising, or defending to seeing, hearing, and honoring the other person.

Opening up deepens great relationships, but it's just as important when things are rocky and you're working toward repair.

Open Up and Forgive

Sometimes the relationships that are most depleting to us are the ones with people who have harmed us. Although not every harm needs to be forgiven, there are some resentments that eat away at us, draining our energy and keeping us stuck. Forgiveness is not condoning what has been done but rather opening up to the pain of it so that you can allow the wound to heal. You may never "move on," but instead you use wise effort to direct your energy toward healing the parts of you that need love, compassion, and support.

When Amy told me that her husband had had an affair, I took a piece of paper, drew a large heart on it, and showed it to her. First I crumpled the paper up, and then I smoothed it back out.

"Sometimes in relationships, we hurt each other," I said, "and we can work through it, smoothing over the wounds and getting back to something like we were before." Then I took the heart and tore it a third of the way down. "But sometimes," I continued, "there are deeper tears—things that can't just be smoothed out or put back together the way they were." I held the torn paper carefully. "The rip will always be there, but you can learn to hold it differently. Instead of trying to force it back together or throwing it away, you accept it for what it is—a heart that's been through a lot."

What about you? Who has crumpled your heart? Any rips? Forgiving someone who has hurt us can't be rushed or forced. It's a process that unfolds in its own time. And forgiving doesn't mean we forget what happened or ignore the harm that was done.

After many months of individual and couples counseling, Amy chose to stay with her husband. I recommended a couples retreat with Terry Real, author of *Us: Getting Past You and Me to Build a More Loving Relationship*.[8] There, her husband focused on using wise speech to validate Amy's feelings without becoming defensive and

Amy worked on openly expressing her hurt. She told him, honestly, that she loved him and also that if he ever cheated again, she'd leave for good. Forgiveness is a paradox, a practice of both/and thinking, a willingness to move forward, and a clear boundary.

Sometimes with clients, I'll refer to past resentments as "Voldemort," the dark figure from *Harry Potter*, the one we dare not name. The more we avoid saying their name, the more they have power over us. This happens a lot in family estrangements, which are more common than we think. Over a quarter of individuals have cut off contact with a family member, and this becomes like a wound that never heals. Your dad, brother, or sister becomes Voldemort, the name that no one will speak. It's chronic stress, with some people reporting that they think about it every day but feel like they can't do anything about it, and it has ripple effects on the entire family system. Research in family estrangements has shown that often it isn't just one thing that ends a relationship. Called the "volcanic effect," there's often an accumulation of crossed boundaries that erupt at some point.[9] But just because you don't have contact with someone doesn't mean you can't forgive them. You can still work toward forgiveness, even if you choose to never see that person again or limit your contact.

To forgive is to say it out loud, to call out the name, hurt, or betrayal that you fear speaking. You do this because that wound deserves your attention and needs your compassion. You don't have to excuse what someone did or even invite them into your life, but when you forgive them, you let go of the tension and stress that weigh you down. As writer Anne Lamott puts it, "Forgiveness is giving up all hope of having had a better past."[10] Forgiveness doesn't erase what happened, but it can feel like letting go of a fist that's been tightly clenched. It frees up your energy. Often forgiveness also comes with grace—you see the other person, and yourself, with a bit more perspective. You open to your Wise Self and feel compassion, seeing that the person who hurt you was struggling, too. They were acting from a place of their own pain or lack of skill. And maybe you were as well.

If the wise effort move for you is to forgive, you might say or write something like *You hurt me. And I imagine you hurt, too. I forgive you, and I forgive myself. I set us both free.* You don't have to share this directly with the person; that's not necessarily the point. The point is to transform your relationship with them in your heart so you can say "Voldemort" all you want. Sure, you will have a twinge of pain, but your fear won't control you anymore.

Use The Wise Effort Method to Reconnect

Whether you are struggling in a relationship or just want to deepen the ones you have, you can use the Wise Effort method—get curious, open up, and focus your energy—to reconnect. First remember your values. Then open up to the difficult feelings that come with relationships—fear, sadness, irritation, even rage—open up to connection and compassion and hold space for the imperfections that come with being human. Remember that we all yearn to belong, to feel safe, and to be seen. Notice the choice points. When you see one, focus your energy toward your values. Reconnect, forgive, or set that boundary you need to set. This will be hard, but it will also bring relief. That's how you know it's wise effort.

Be a Genius Friend

Remember that Genius Review you wrote at the beginning of this book? For a truly Genius Life, you need people who care about you and people you care for. With wise effort, you can become an energizer to others, let go of resentments that are weighing you down, and aim your genius energy toward connection. Don't let your genius become your problem. If your genius is reliability, how can you be a reliable friend but also reliable to yourself? If your genius is being the social glue, how can you connect people while also being the glue to your inner world? Use your genius wisely, and you will be healthier, happier, and more fulfilled because of it.

Patti and Helena, Besties for over Thirty Years
On Saturday mornings, Helena and Patti go for a walk on the path that runs along the shoreline of Santa Barbara. Being early birds, they like to meet before breakfast and walk and talk before sharing a latte and scone. When they were in their thirties and elementary school teachers, they "power walked" while gossiping about faculty-room drama and stressing about back-to-school. In their forties, they walked and worried about their kids, their marriages, and their finances, ditching the scones for bagels with fat-free cream cheese. When Patti got divorced, they walked, cried, and made a plan. And when Helena's daughter attempted suicide, they walked, cried, and made another plan. In their fifties, their walks became spottier as Helena retired to paint, write, and travel while Patti kept up the meaningful but challenging work of teaching. In their sixties, their walks slowed when Patti developed a health condition that caused her to lose sight in one eye. Some days, there were no walks at all, just coffee and bagels.

But now, in their seventies, Patti and Helena have picked up the pace again. They've brought back the power walk and ditched anything fat-free. They aim for gluten-free, brag about their grandchildren, and still worry about their children. My mom, Helena, tells Patti that she worries about me working too hard in writing this book, and Patti tells her the same thing she did thirty years ago: it will be okay. Walking and talking through the decades, Patti and Helena have been besties and are healthier and happier because of it. They validate each other, don't need to fix each other, and give each other grace. They've been late, said the wrong thing, and gotten in tiffs, but somehow they keep coming back to walk. That's what wise relationships can do for you.

11

wise effort with your body

When I asked my client Jazmin if she remembered ever enjoying being in her body, she told me about being five years old and playing in the park around the corner from her apartment. She loved flipping upside down on the crossbar to hang from her knees. But by the time she was eight, she had grown larger and taller than other girls in her class. She felt awkward in her skin.

Jazmin shared that she dreaded junior high gym class, when she had to change in the dressing room and hide her developing chest. And she hated wearing shorts that showed her cellulite. Embarrassed and confused by her body changes during puberty, Jazmin started avoiding sports, hiding under baggy clothes, and turning to her math work instead. It just felt better to be in her head than in her body.

It wasn't just her physical body that confused Jazmin. It was also her emotional body. When her parents divorced, Jazmin felt a void, a pit in her stomach, when she came home to an empty house after school. It felt like hunger, but it wouldn't go away no matter how much she ate. She remembered standing at the fridge with her spoon hitting the bottom of the ice-cream tub, feeling empty and stuffed at the same time. When she came to work with me at age thirty-six, Jazmin struggled with binge eating and said she hated her body. We had some work to do, and it started with getting curious—what is happening inside your body? What does it really need? These same questions are where you will start, too.

Most of us long for a better relationship with our body. Maybe you want to eat better but find it hard to make changes. Or you can't seem to get yourself off the couch to exercise. Perhaps you judge your body as too old, too fat, too small, too awkward, too _____ (fill in your blank here) and let these thoughts limit what you do physically. Maybe you are so focused on looking a certain way that you have become disembodied. Or perhaps you spend so much time in your head, analyzing, problem-solving, and getting your work done, that you forget about your body altogether.

Your body has its own genius—an incredible ability to maintain balance, heal itself, and adapt to internal and external challenges. It operates complex systems like hormones and blood sugar, fights off infections, and repairs cell damage, all while adjusting to the rhythms of your daily life. An endocrinologist once told me she'd rather fly a 747 with no training than try to run a pancreas—it's that complex and amazing.

In this chapter, you will explore how getting curious, opening up, and focusing the energy of your body can be a powerful source of vitality. When you respond to your body's signals—honoring its intuition and nourishing it with food, rest, movement, and pleasure—you will unlock a tremendous energetic force.

Get Curious About Your Body's Signals

A wise relationship with your body is an embodied one. Embodiment means inhabiting your body, understanding and responding to physical sensations, and expressing yourself physically. It gives you an authentic, powerful presence.

Think about people you've met who seem truly "embodied"—the way they confidently walk into a room, dance with their eyes closed, or intuitively place a hand on their chest when something moves them deeply. It's a grounded confidence, a connection between body and mind. When do you feel most embodied? Is it during a workout, tossing a football with your kids, or laughing with friends? It might show up in moments of strength, creativity, or connection—doing physical labor, being outside, moving to music, or having sex. Embodiment isn't just physical; it's how you inhabit your life. Do you feel like you are "in" your body? Are you aware of what's happening inside you?

Embodiment begins with curiosity—specifically, getting curious about your body's signals. For my client Jazmin, this meant taking time to listen. Early in our work together, I asked her to write a letter from her body to herself: If your body could tell you what it's been like to be your body, what would it say? What would your stomach say? Your thighs? Your eyes? And what would these body parts say they need from you?

Try this for yourself. Open your Wise Effort Journal and title a page "A Letter from My Body." Then let your body speak. What has it endured? What does it long for? Are there parts of you that feel neglected, exhausted, or unappreciated? Are there parts that you've criticized that might be asking for compassion? Perhaps, like Jazmin's, your body simply wants to move in a different way.

Here's an excerpt from Jazmin's letter: "I want to swim, swing, have sex, jiggle, be moved. You judge me, berate me, criticize me—and I'm tired of it! Give me a break and let me play a little."

Once you've written your letter, read it to yourself. Let your body's message sink in. If you feel inspired, write a response—one of understanding, kindness, and commitment to treating your body differently.

The next step in embodiment is developing *interoception*—the ability to sense what's happening inside your body. This internal awareness includes noticing your heartbeat, breath, hunger, and fatigue. But interoception isn't just a body-awareness tool; it's a life-awareness tool. Research links it to improved mental health, more mindful eating habits, and better decision-making.[1]

Even in high-stakes environments, interoception plays a critical role. Stock-market traders with stronger awareness of their heartbeat make better trades and earn more money.[2] Even therapists who can better sense their own physiological changes can better detect and respond to client distress.[3]

My doctoral research focused on interoceptive awareness of appetite signals—helping individuals struggling with eating and weight concerns reconnect with their hunger and fullness cues.[4] It's fascinating, and a little heartbreaking, that we have to relearn something that came so naturally to us as kids. But it's not surprising when you consider how much our modern environment pulls us away from our bodies.

For example, Jazmin noticed that she tended to overeat while at her computer. She felt the most checked out of her body while working. And she isn't alone in this. Linda Stone, a former Microsoft executive, coined the term *screen apnea* to describe the phenomenon that we tend to breathe more shallowly or even hold our breath when using screens.[5] Stone did some kitchen-table science (not randomized or controlled) on the topic and found that 80 percent of the colleagues and friends she tested had shallow or suspended breathing while working on a screen. The clincher? Those 20 percent who didn't show screen apnea were folks who tended to be pretty embodied—dancers, singers, a triathlete, and a cellist. Since screens are an unavoidable part of life, the wise response isn't to resist them but to create reminders to stay present in your body. Something as simple as a Post-it note on your screen saying *Breathe* or *Check in* can help you look up, take a deep breath, and reconnect with yourself. Or you could write the acronym HEART. It covers a lot of the bases of interoception:

Hunger: Am I hungry or full?

Emotion: What emotions do I feel in my body right now?

Activity: Is my body craving physical movement?

Rest: Am I tired or low on energy?

Tension: Do I notice stress, pain, or tightness anywhere?

HEART is a quick mental check-in that helps you scan your body for its most essential signals: hunger, movement, emotions, fatigue, or stress. From there, you can respond with whatever meets the need—a snack, a stretch, a nap, a phone call to a friend, or some self-massage.

Your body is always talking to you. What is it saying? Do you need a big sigh? To release some tension in your neck? To head outside for a walk? Try HEART right now. When you open to your body's sensations, you also open to its intuition. Maybe your body is whispering something bigger than just the need for a rest—it's telling you it's time to take a different life path.

Open Up to Intuition

Intuition is a felt sense, a nudge, that gives you clues about a situation, decision, or person. For years, during my struggles with disordered eating, I wasn't just disconnected from my body's physical signals—I had also shut down my inner knowing. I cut myself off from what I wanted, longed for, knew in my heart was true for me. In my recovery journey, and in my work with clients, I've found that when we start listening to our bodies, we hear more than just *I'm hungry* or *I'm tired*. We begin to receive deeper messages:

- I need to say no to this, even though everyone is telling me to say yes.

- Something feels off.

- I'm being pulled toward something new.

Tuning into my body's wisdom has guided some of my biggest life decisions. It nudged me to say yes to a first date with my husband. It encouraged me to lead retreats, even when I wasn't sure I was ready. It shapes how I parent my kids. But learning to trust this knowing didn't happen overnight. I had to consciously open up to my body and practice listening.

Over the years, I've developed a simple way to access my intuition: checking in for a whole-body yes or a whole-body no when making decisions.

A *whole-body yes* feels expansive, clear, even energizing. A *whole-body no*, on the other hand, comes with tension—I feel it in my clenched stomach or tight shoulders. I've learned the hard way that when I override a whole-body no, I pay the price later. I am stuck in things I don't really want to do, and it depletes my energy.

But intuition doesn't have to work alone. Once you check in with your body, you can cross-reference it with other sources of wisdom:

Second Bodies: Get perspective from people who know you well.

Experts and evidence: Seek guidance from those with experience or research in the area.

Problem-solving mind: Use logic and critical thinking to analyze the situation.

When these sources align with your body's knowing, you can trust that you're making a wise, informed decision.

Science has a complicated relationship with intuition. Some researchers warn that while intuition can be fast and efficient, it's also prone to biases and errors—especially in complex situations requiring careful analysis.[6] But that doesn't mean we should dismiss it entirely.

Rather, we can view intuition as a powerful decision-making tool when balanced with wisdom. Like any skill, it improves with practice and reflection. So before making a choice, pause and ask yourself,

- Is this a whole-body yes?

- Is this a whole-body no?

Then, give yourself the space to settle into a wise answer. The more you strengthen this connection, the more intuition can guide not just your decisions but also how you eat, move, rest, and experience pleasure. Let's explore that next.

Open Up to Your Body's Needs

Countless wellness programs tell you what, when, and how much to eat, exercise, or sleep. Although many of these are helpful to get you started, wise effort is about customizing your own plan to fit your values and your unique body.

Open Up to Wise Eating

Wise eating begins with getting curious about your eating patterns. Notice when you are hungry, when you are full, and when you are using food to run away from discomfort. For example, I gave Jazmin the following assignment: "If you are eating at the refrigerator, sit down," restating the title of one of my favorite books by Geneen Roth.[7] "Pay attention. What is happening there? What are you feeling? Are you really hungry, or is it something else?"

I had Jazmin start tracking how hungry she was before eating on a scale from 0–10 and how full she was when she stopped, with the goal of not getting too hungry or too full. With appetite awareness training, she began to get better at telling the difference between loneliness and hunger. She also tracked which foods worked best for her body and began using a biometric device that monitored how food and stress affected her body. Oatmeal with walnuts for breakfast gave her sustained energy. Cheerios made her crash. Eating earlier in the evening helped her get a better night's sleep, and swapping snacking for a quick walk around the block increased her heart-rate variability and gave her the stress relief she was looking for at work. She started incorporating more whole foods and cooking for herself. She ditched fake diet products and felt more in control and at peace with food.

Foundational in this work is exploring your eating values. What matters to you about food and eating? Remember that values offer a deeper intrinsic motivation for change than a scale or diet plan can. Get out your Wise Effort Journal, title a page "My Eating Values," and answer the following questions:

- When have you felt the best about your eating habits?

- What types of food give you sustained energy? What eating habits work well for you?

- What do you regret when it comes to your relationship with food?

- How does the way you eat impact other important domains of your life, like focus at work, energy to play with your kids, or social life?

- Does how you eat link to other values, like caring for our planet?

- What three words best describe how you want to be in your relationship with food?

Finally, start to notice the *choice points*. When do you tend to engage in unwise eating? Is it when you're stressed, lonely, or celebrating? By becoming aware of these moments, you create space to choose differently—aligning your actions with your values. Is there a genius energy that you can use here, too? Maybe it's applying your talent for planning out the home-cooked meals you want to make this month. Or your genius for gathering people together for a themed potluck. Or your gift for aesthetics to set a beautiful table to sit down at without your phone and practice mindful eating. Notice the choice point, use your genius, and enjoy the rewards that come with eating in a way that works for your unique genius body.

When you do, your eating may naturally shift. Remember that eating is about so much more than just the food on your plate. We read "eating contemplations" at our dinner table most nights to remember to be mindful of our food and the people we are eating with. I encourage you to remember them, too: *This food is the gift of the whole universe: the Earth, the sky, the universe, numerous living beings, and* *much hard, loving work.*⁸ When we are aware of this interconnection, we can't help but eat wisely.

Open Up to Wise Movement

Many of us struggle to get in the amount of movement our bodies need, and it's not because we don't know that exercise is good for us. If simply listing the benefits of exercise worked, more than 25 percent of Americans would meet the CDC guidelines for physical activity.⁹ Needless to say, most of us don't.

When Katy Bowman, a biomechanist, and I asked our audiences for reasons why they don't move their bodies, they shared all sorts of things like "I have too much work and too many family responsibilities" and "I keep comparing myself to people in my exercise class." In our book *I Know I Should Exercise But . . . : 44 Reasons We Don't Move and How to Get Over Them*,¹⁰ Katy and I grouped these reasons in seven main categories. As you read through them, see which ones you relate to most:

1. You are not motivated.

2. You don't have enough time.

3. You are embarrassed.

4. It's uncomfortable.

5. You are stuck on your screens.

6. Your environment makes it impossible.

7. Other people won't move with you.

To overcome these barriers, we suggest that once again, you start with values. Sure, movement is good for your heart and lungs and mental health, but what's the bigger why behind moving your body?

What values could you lean on when these excuses show up? Get out your Wise Effort Journal, title a page "My Movement Values," and answer these questions for yourself:

- Why is moving your body important to you?

- How does movement impact the important domains of your life? Are you a more patient parent when you get in a morning walk? More creative at work when you take a yoga class at lunch?

- When does movement bring you more vitality, making life feel more life-y?

- Are there any physical activities you regret not trying or that you want to bring back?

- What types of movement bring you the most vitality? When do you feel at your best moving your body?

Next, look at some of the barriers to movement that are in the list above. How might opening to feeling, opening your mind, or opening your sense of self help you live out these values? Maybe it's welcoming your feeling of awkwardness as you try a new exercise class or asking yourself, *Are you sure?* when your mind comes up with all sorts of reasons why you don't have time for a walk. And don't forget to practice self-compassion: strong-arming yourself into moving more will only make you want to move less. Finally, support your wise habits by engineering your environment to be movement rich. A few small tweaks to your context (sitting on an exercise ball at work or using a standing desk, setting up walking meetings, or scheduling movement during part of your lunch break) can help.

For Jazmin, that meant introducing more movement into her day. She started by walking to the park early in the morning before anyone was there and tried hanging from the crossbars again, as she had when she was a kid. Could she build the strength to cross a few? Jazmin also joined the YMCA to swim and started making friends with the regulars. As she moved more, she felt more energy, confidence, and connection. And she started respecting her body's need to rest, too.

Open Up to Rest

Every body—all sizes, colors, abilities, gender expressions, and ages—deserves to rest. As Tricia Hersey writes in *Rest Is Resistance: A Manifesto*, "Rest saved my life. This is my truth. I don't need anyone else to verify this, nor do I need complicated theories to support what I know to be true in my heart, my body, and my spirit."[11]

As you did with eating and movement, take some time to explore how rest relates to your values. In your Wise Effort Journal, title a page "My Values Around Rest" and answer these questions:

- How would prioritizing rest affect other areas of your life, such as work, relationships, or creativity?

- Looking back, are there times in your life when you wish you had rested more?

- What does rest mean to you?

- What types of rest leave you with the most energy and vitality?

- Are there ways you are seeking rest that aren't really restorative?

Next, get curious about how much rest your body needs. Pay attention to its natural rhythms—the times when your energy and focus are high and when they dip. These ultradian rhythms (*ultra* meaning "many" and *dia* meaning "day") occur multiple times throughout the day, signaling when your body needs a break.[12] Get curious about the times of day you have a natural lull and see it as a choice point. What if, instead of reaching for another cup of coffee or a sugary snack during an ultradian dip, you opted for a deeper rest? Not all rest is created equal, and it's important to distinguish between junk-food rest—activities that feel restful but don't truly replenish your energy—and deep rest, which restores you at a cellular level. Research has suggested that practices like meditation, prayer, visualization, yoga nidra, and slow breathing go far beyond passive relaxation, conferring profound physiological and psychological benefits.[13] These techniques can lower stress hormones, soothe the nervous system, and even support cellular health, potentially slowing aging. Incorporate at least ten to twenty minutes of deep rest into each day if you can. Not only will rest restore your energy, it's also a chance to pause and enjoy your life.

Open Up to Pleasure

Enjoying the pleasure of being in your body is just as important as caring for it. Whether it's the pleasure of climbing into bed with clean sheets, relaxing with a good book, taking time to savor your morning coffee, or indulging in great sex, there are many good feelings and sensations to enjoy. So, get curious and ask yourself, *Am I experiencing enough pleasure?* If you aren't, it's time to get curious. Get out your Wise Effort Journal and title a page "Opening Up to Pleasure":

- What are the most pleasurable parts of your day right now?

- Where are you spending your time and energy in ways that don't truly bring you pleasure?

- What self-stories block you from prioritizing pleasure? Do you believe you don't deserve it? Do you feel like you must earn pleasure?

- Where and with whom do you feel the freest to experience pleasure?

If you immediately thought of sex when I mentioned pleasure, that's a great place to get curious, too. Are you getting the kind of sex you want? What do you want more of? What feels painful, boring, or obligatory? What feels exciting, playful, or connecting? The same psychological barriers that keep us from taking care of our bodies can block us from having fulfilling erotic experiences.

- We run from discomfort. Sensuality can be embarrassing, vulnerable, hard to initiate.

- We hold too tight to things being a certain way. We are stuck in a stale routine, expectations about our partner, or the outcome.

- We get stuck in our heads. We are caught up in thoughts about our body image, are worried about our performance, or think too much about what our partner thinks.

> If you aren't careful, you just might end up in your Nightmare Sex Review:
>
> *They held back, didn't let go, were so focused on looking good, it never really felt that good.*
>
> *It was boring, uninspired, the same ol' same ol'. Seen this before.*
>
> *It felt obligatory, like they were so focused on getting somewhere, they were never really present.*

To engage wise effort in the bedroom, consider ways you can apply your genius to sex and sensuality. Get out your Wise Effort Journal and title a page "My Sexual Genius." Explore some of these questions:

- What are your sexual interests?

- What types of sensual experiences are you most drawn to?

- How can you amp up your emotional intelligence, communication skills, and empathy in your sex life?

- Are there ways you can bring more eroticism into your day?

- Where are you holding your sexual genius back?

There are so many ways to ignite your genius for sexual energy. Remember that the key to making a wise change is trying something different—anything different! Could you use your genius for throwing great dinner parties and include some questions from Esther Perel's conversation card game *Where Should We Begin?*[14] Or explore your artistic talents by adding some nude figure drawing? Maybe you could use your design genius to set up a sensory-rich bedroom with massage oils, candles, and soft textures? Or your musical talents to create a playlist that turns you on? For some great tips on how to increase your sexual pleasure, I recommend Emily Nagoski's book *Come As You Are*.[15] And for ideas about how to turn pleasure into power, I recommend adrienne maree brown's *Pleasure Activism: The Politics of Feeling Good*.[16]

Yes, Yes, Thank You, Thank You

To have good sex and more pleasure, you need to be open—physically, emotionally, spiritually, and mentally.

Try using this mantra whenever you notice pleasure or sexual energy in your day:

Yes, yes, thank you, thank you.
Yes, this is what it feels like to be alive, to be human, to be riding the current of pleasurable energy.
Yes to the way the breeze feels on my skin.
Thank you for this body and the way it moves.
Yes to conversations that spark something in me.
Thank you to this moment, just as it is.

This openness will translate into the bedroom. It also makes it easier to say yes to discomfort, yes to awkward sounds, thank you to weirdness, and yes to the unknown.

Sex isn't just about performance; it's about being receptive to the entire erotic personal and interpersonal experience. Keep one eye on what is happening in your body and one eye on what is happening with others. This is engaging your Wise Self in the bedroom. The point here is that we can open up to feeling pleasure. Whether it's experiencing the big O, curling up with a blanket and a good show, or accomplishing a physical challenge, spend some time taking in the good by practicing the art of savoring (go back to chapter 7 for more on this concept).

There are hundreds of ways to engage in pleasure. Whatever floats your boat—a quickie, a sunrise bike ride, or a rosewater facial—every body needs some daily joy. So use your genius energy to level up your pleasure!

A Whole-Body Yes

We were born connected to our bodies, inhabiting them fully, trusting them, and using them to communicate and experience pleasure. At some point in life, for a variety of reasons, many of us lose this loving connection and our ability to inhabit our bodies fully. Now is your chance to reclaim the energy that comes with being embodied. You can use wise effort to care for your body and enjoy this lifelong, ever-changing adventure. Listen for the whole-body yes, and your genius body will show you the way.

12

wise effort at work

Most of us spend a lot of time working—whether it's for compensation in a workplace or uncompensated at home—so we shouldn't allow our work to be one-dimensional. It's one of the most important things we do. When it's going well, our work can be a place where we can explore our creative purpose, fulfill social needs, and express our genius energy in ways that make a positive difference beyond just us. But a lot of times, our work feels lackluster, exhausting, or even soul draining.

If the latter is the case for you, consider that maybe you haven't given yourself enough power to change the way you are in it or permission to leave and find more fulfilling work. With wise effort, you can make big changes in your work life if needed—or fine-tune something that's pretty good into something that is GREAT. Either way, every human, including you, has the right to feel good about what they do.

In this chapter, we'll take a deeper look at whatever you call work in your life. We'll explore how to approach it, whether to change it, or whether it's time to pursue something entirely different.

Get Curious About Your Work Genius

My first job was in the pen department at an office supply store. It was there that I learned two things about myself: I don't do well with idle time, and I'm great at connecting with strangers. I was using my genius for sure when helping a stressed-out bride pick out the perfect pen for her invitations or when persisting in learning all the types of mechanical pencil lead—did you know 0.3 mm is best for technical drawing, but 0.9 mm is best for sketching? Well, now you do!

No matter what job you're in, your genius energy wants to shine through. My occupation has taken many turns since then, but there's been a through line—with each position I've held, I've learned more about my genius energy: how it gets off track and where it best thrives.

What about you? How well is your genius energy being expressed in the workplace? Pull out your Wise Effort Journal, title a page "My Work Genius," and answer the following questions as they relate to work:

- **Interests:** What excites you at work? Do you have enough freedom to explore your interests in the workplace?

- **Personality:** Do you feel energized working independently, collaborating with others, or balancing the two? Do you thrive with structure and routine, or do you prefer variety and spontaneity? Does your work fit your temperament?

- **Talents:** What do you do best, and what type of work comes easily to you? Are you using those skills now?

- **Emotional intelligence:** What social skills, empathy, or self-awareness do you contribute? Are you using your emotional intelligence at work?

- **Character strengths:** What virtues guide you in the workplace? Is your moral code or character a match for your team or workplace culture?

In organizational psychology, matching your interests and strengths to your job is called "job sculpting."[1] When work matches your deeply embedded interests, it leads to greater job satisfaction, improved performance, and reduced turnover.[2] In fact, employees who use their strengths daily are six times more likely to be engaged at work than those who do not.[3] Whether your gift is in being highly analytical, self-sufficient, loyal, a harmonizer, or a natural leader, you can express it in a multitude of situations in the workplace. Look for opportunities to offer your genius energy. Often we hide our authentic gifts because we are afraid they will be judged, we don't want to stand out, or we don't value them ourselves. Remember your fundamental dignity and good nature, put them out there, and start looking for them in others, too. When you encourage others to express their genius, there is a synergetic energy exchange that will make your collective work better.

If you're in a leadership position, recognizing and naming genius energy is one of the most powerful tools you have to boost morale and transform workplace culture. Be specific when you see it, and build teams around it. Complementary genius energy strengthens a team—for example, pairing a big-picture brainstormer with a detail-oriented executor or matching a visionary strategist with a grounded problem-solver makes for great synergy.

As we explored in chapter 4, when there's a big mismatch between you and your workplace, it can lead to burnout—a syndrome characterized by exhaustion, detachment, and decreased performance. Go back to chapter 4 and look at your mismatches. What is draining your energy the most? Being overworked, underinspired, or disconnected from a work community? Or maybe the combination of life stress and work stress colliding?

Here's the clincher: it's how you relate to these stressors that might be having the biggest impact on your energy. Stress research has shown that stress itself is not necessarily what is so taxing; rather, how we hold our stress, interpret it, and respond to it determines its impact on our well-being. Seeing the stressors at work as a challenge (*Bring it on, work deadline! This is an opportunity to apply my genius!*) rather than a threat (*I'm never going to get this done. Work stress is killing me*) leads to better physiological responses, including reduced cortisol levels and improved cardiovascular health.[4]

There's a more nuanced approach to burnout than just changing your position or job. Look at how you are using your precious energy at work. Is there a way you can shift to a challenge mindset? Can you recharge by soaking up small moments of good? Linger a little longer on your achievements when you complete something rather than just moving on to the next thing, and open up to Second Bodies who can help you share the load? No job, even the most solo one, is done in isolation. Connecting to a greater community (even if it's online or a conversation with a customer) can boost your energy. Let's take a look at how the ways you are relating to your experience at work may be playing a role in your energy drain.

When Your Genius Becomes Your Work Problem

Many of us are drawn to work that allows us to use our natural talents and strengths. But sometimes this genius energy can get away from us and leave us drained. We may overuse it—pushing ourselves relentlessly, refusing to take breaks, insisting that there's only one right way (our way) to do things. Or we may underuse it—holding back our ideas, doubting our abilities, and keeping our genius small.

When working in academia, for example, I often see brilliant researchers become so hyperfocused on their narrow line of research that they can't see beyond their theoretical model. Sure, they are great at creating theories, but when they don't integrate others' ideas, their work becomes increasingly rigid and exclusionary over time. Similarly, when training therapists, I often see that their genius for validating clients' feelings leads them too far into the realm of offering emotional support and holding back advice on how to change. They become so focused on empathy that they hesitate to take an active role in using their therapeutic genius to guide clients toward making meaningful changes.

Remember, too much or too little of any genius can leave you imbalanced. Are you overplaying some of your strengths or underplaying others? Do you hold back your talents in the workplace because you're afraid of standing out or disappointing people or because you doubt whether your genius is even a genius at all?

Much of my early career followed this pattern: I was so tuned in to what people wanted from me that I lost sight of what I wanted for myself. I wouldn't ask for what I needed because I feared disappointing others. Over the years, I developed the practice of "one eye in and one eye out." The best way to balance my emotional sensitivity is to keep one eye on my own needs and the other eye on the needs of those around me. By toggling back and forth between the world outside and the world inside, I keep my emotional sensitivity in the zone of wise effort.

Where has your genius energy gotten off track in the workplace? Where is it being overused, underused, or misdirected? Maybe you're avoiding discomfort by people-pleasing instead of showing up authentically. Or perhaps you're clinging too tightly to expectations, ignoring your whole-body no and saying yes to things you don't truly want. Let's take a deeper look at why. Remember the three reasons why our genius gets misdirected, and answer these questions in your Wise Effort Journal under the title "When My Genius Becomes My Work Problem":

- **Are you running from the discomfort of taking risks or disappointing people?** What discomfort are you currently avoiding at work? How might facing it help you grow? What's the worst that could happen if you disappointed someone? What's the best that could happen?

- **Are you holding on too tightly?** What expectations—yours or others'—are you gripping too tightly? Are you pursuing a goal because you genuinely want it or because you feel that you *should* want it? What would happen if you let go of control in one area of your work and allowed more spontaneity?

- **Are you stuck in a story?** What's the story you've been telling yourself about your work and abilities? Where did this belief come from, and is it actually true? If you could write your inner narrative, what would it sound like? Could you be telling a different story to support you in your work life?

To get out of these traps, you need motivation and inner fortitude to face what is hard and change course. And the best way to develop those qualities is to double down on your work values. Deeper clarity about your values will help you avoid misdirecting your genius energy in the workplace.

Get Curious About Values

At Plum Village Monastery, every retreatant signs up for working meditation where you practice mindfulness with daily chores. The monastics start the sessions with intention setting. Whether you're washing pots, picking vegetables, or setting up meditation cushions, you are to ask yourself, *What are the overarching values I want to bring to this work?*

You even set intentions before doing toilet-cleaning meditation—the one job I avoided signing up for year after year until my friend Lucia asked me to join her.

"Come clean toilets with me! It's the best. You're in and out quick. No one wants to do it, but it's actually pretty easy."

I liked Lucia. She was from Spain, and our sons had been playing a lot of Ping-Pong together. I thought, *Maybe if I join this working group, we can become friends, too.*

So I followed Lucia and joined the toilet-cleaning meditation. "What is your intention in cleaning toilets?" the nun leading our group asked.

It may sound odd with a task as icky as cleaning public toilets, but reflecting on your values can help transform the yuck factor. Everyone's intention was different:

- *For years, others have cleaned toilets for me. This is my way of giving back.*

- *I want to become more comfortable with discomfort.*

- *I want to create a clean, welcoming space for the children and families who come here.*

I thought about mine. My intention was to connect—to new friends and to myself. I had spent a lot of time in bathrooms alone, harming myself and away from my values. This was my chance to turn that energy around.

It turned out Lucia was right. That working meditation was the best thing I did all week at the monastery. We carried wheelbarrows full of disgusting trash to the dumpsters, but we sang songs while we worked and made those bathrooms sparkling clean for families to brush their teeth. Most importantly, we lived our values of giving back, being with discomfort, and connection. You never know why someone does the work they do, but if you scratch the surface, you just might find some treasure in their intention.

Your values are the heartbeat of meaningful work.[5] Values not only drive what you put your energy into but are also the engine for why you've chosen that work in the first place and how you show up. Get honest with yourself and start looking at your values in the workplace. What is the bigger, overarching reason you want to work? Are you living that reason now? Are there ways you can bring wise effort to what you do? When you achieve that, you are practicing wise livelihood—a powerful way to be at work.

Open Up to Choice Points at Work

Choice points aren't always dramatic, quit-your-job-and-move-to-Costa Rica choices (though sometimes they are). More often they're small but powerful opportunities to adjust, realign, or reclaim a little more of your energy. Take Jane, for example.

Jane, like many of us, had had enough of the mounting disconnect, polarity, and widening disparities within our politics, society, and culture. At the same time, she was massively overwhelmed by the task of managing her family restaurant while caring for two young children. It all felt too hard, draining, and grim. She wanted to get through, sure, but she also wanted to be part of the solution, especially as a white woman in a position of privilege.

Jane's particular genius had been passed on to her by her grandmother, also named Jane: the gift of gathering people around a table for meaningful conversation, fantastic food, and healthy dialogue—all were welcome. Jane felt energized by the idea of bringing women together over her love of food and hosting, creating a space for open and respectful conversations. It took courage to tell her parents she would leave the family restaurant where she had worked for over a decade and even more courage to start her own business, the Communal Table. It was a choice point—she knew she had something to offer, and there was a need in the community for her genius. It began with a few small gatherings at community gardens, artists' studios, and open spaces and grew into regular sold-out events.

The concept was simple: Jane would cook an incredible meal from locally sourced ingredients, then gather women to discuss vulnerable and universal topics such as self-care, finances, pleasure, and creativity. Jane curated and asked questions like "How have you experienced grief, and what have you learned from it?" And she always kept a few seats open for people who didn't have the financial resources to pay. Since she started, she's hosted almost a hundred of these events and recently was acknowledged for her work by chef Alice Waters, who is known as an originator of farm-to-table cooking. It takes a lot of effort for Jane to put these events together—from the physical effort of making the meals to the psychological effort of holding the space with vulnerability and authenticity. But whenever she does, she leaves full and reenergized because of it.

Let's take a closer look at what's weighing you down at work—and where you might be able to intervene with wiser effort. Try this five-part exercise that I adapted from the book *The Stress Prescription* by Elissa Epel. Open your Wise Effort Journal and title this exercise "Choice Points at Work":

1. **Write down everything that's draining your energy at work.**
   Be honest. Big or small, if it's weighing on you, put it on the list. (If it helps, look back at the mismatches from

chapter 4: overwhelming workload, lack of autonomy, lack of community, unfairness, lack of appreciation, or misalignment with your values.)

2. **Circle the things you have the power to change.** Some of your stressors are set in stone, but not all of them. Where do you have agency to make a shift? Where could you ask for support, set boundaries, or take action?

3. **Underline anything you could eliminate.** Are there tasks you could delegate, taper off, or say no to? Sometimes stress comes from doing things we don't actually need to do.

4. **Put a box around anything important but unchangeable.** These are the stressors you don't have control over—at least not directly.

5. **Look at what you circled and underlined**—these are your choice points. This is where wise effort comes in. Making changes won't always be easy. It means facing discomfort, stepping into your power, and sometimes taking risks. But you have the skills for this.

For the things you can change:

Open up to feeling: Name what emotions come up when you think about making this change. Are you afraid of judgment? Embarrassed about how things have played out? Acknowledge those feelings instead of pushing them down. Take care of yourself, offer some compassion, and center yourself in your values before you act.

Open your mind: Stress gives us tunnel vision. When we're overwhelmed at work, our minds shrink down to the immediate problem, making it feel inescapable. But pause for a second and ask yourself, *Are you sure?* Are you sure this will be a disaster? Are you sure you'll fail? Are you sure you know exactly how this will go? Keep your mind open to the possibility that you don't really know.

For the things you can't change:

Open yourself: You don't have to carry the hard stuff alone. Find some Second Bodies to lean on who get it—colleagues, mentors, friends in your field—to support your work. Choose people who want the best for you but also who aren't afraid to give you some feedback. But be wise in whom you share your vulnerabilities with, especially if they are related to your work. Use your wise mind to choose people who are positive energizers.

Open your behavior: Radical acceptance isn't passive—it's an active choice. Try filling in this sentence: When I accept _____, it frees me to _____. Maybe accepting a difficult boss frees you to stop seeking validation that won't come. Maybe accepting that your job is temporary frees you to stop stressing about every little thing. Or maybe accepting that this job is a dead end will allow you to get out sooner rather than later. Unclench a little. See how it feels.

Open up to your genius: Are there better places to use your genius energy? If you are in a job that is unchangeable and making you miserable, it's probably time to find better work that treats your values, skills, and genius with respect. Start looking at a brainstorm of possibilities. Are there places where you could live your genius and your values? Yes, there are! It might take some patience, flexibility, creativity, and support, but don't give up on the possibility that work could be better.

Focus Your Work Energy

Even work that seems solitary is rarely done in isolation. We humans need each other—for feedback, for emotional support, and to refine our craft. Malcolm Gladwell's ten-thousand-hour rule, which suggests that mastery requires ten thousand hours of practice, falls short if those hours lack purposeful guidance and feedback. With wise effort at work, you can better lean on others, embrace diverse perspectives, and work with integrity. And when you do, you'll feel it. You won't feel trapped. Work won't suck. Instead, you'll take pride in what you do and find great satisfaction in doing it well. That's the kind of work you deserve. If you're already doing work you love, you're fortunate! Use wise effort to level up your genius energy. And if you're not in work that fulfills you—and have the privilege and freedom to change it—go after what makes your heart sing. Don't stay stuck; let your work evolve with you. We need your voice, your talents, and the impact only you can make with your genius energy. Remember that this energy is a renewable resource. Learning to direct it wisely can transform not only your day-to-day interactions but potentially your entire career.

Maria Turns a Love for Dogs into Perfect Pup

Before launching Perfect Pup, a concierge pet-sitting service, Maria slogged through forty hours a week as a paralegal. She spent her days at a computer editing documents for demanding attorneys and feeling unnoticed and undervalued. She was a genius at administration and communication, but the only feedback she received was critical. She woke up with dread each morning, counting down the days until her next vacation. Her job drained her life force.

In therapy, Maria talked a lot about her volunteer job at the pet shelter. She shared about an older dog named Wobble with three legs and how she had found a perfect place for him at a coastal ranch. She teared up, smiled, and leaned in while discussing helping these animals.

"Some days, I feel like a hero," she told me in one session. "With a phone in my hand looking for placements and an abandoned dog at my feet, I feel like I matter. Volunteering also helps me with the parts of me that my mom couldn't care for when she was drinking. It's like I'm giving them what I never got and getting it back in return." Maria's values and strengths in working with animals were clear. This raised the question for her: Why not turn her love of animals into a paid job? She was thrilled at this idea but also plagued by self-doubt, fears of financial insecurity, and self-stories about her business ownership capabilities.

We worked in therapy to get more flexible with these issues and started to form a plan. It started as a side gig with a few clients a month, but eventually Maria grew a part-time pet-sitting job into a full-time business. She quit her toxic job at the firm and used her administrative genius to start a newsletter and figure out liability insurance. Maria applied her genius in communication to win over even the pickiest pet owners, easily charming celebrities who named their pets after designer bags. Most importantly, Maria loved the animals she cared for; she was living her values, and the pet owners loved her for it in return. She now spends her days driving between multimillion-dollar homes and the dog shelter. Some of her time is paid, some is volunteered, and all of it feels well spent.

Work Wisely

No matter what work you do, you can enrich it by living your values, staying open, and being wise about how you use your energy. Doing this makes *what* you do for a living less critical and puts more priority on *how* you engage with your work. The world needs your unique genius, so put it to good use. You may never fully see the impact of your efforts, but never underestimate how far they can spread. Simply witnessing someone fully engaged in their work is enough to inspire others to do the same. Imagine if we all did that—wouldn't the world be a much more vibrant, joyful place?

13
wise effort in creativity

The first question book coach Jennie Nash asks her clients is "Why do you want to write this book?" The most common answers aren't "I want notoriety" or "I want to make a lot of money." Instead, it's usually some version of "I don't want to die without doing this thing I have always wanted to do." Creative expression is literally about life and death. The second most common answer is that people want to raise their voice and claim their stories. They want to speak out. They want to express their innermost beliefs and yearnings. It's a shout into the void. In other words, creative expression is BIG.

Many of us feel an energetic pull deep in our gut to create something. It could be something you share with others, like writing a book, singing in front of an audience, or painting a piece of art that gets hung in a gallery, or it could be personal and just for you, like hauling out that box of watercolor tubes you bought years ago to try to capture the sunset from your porch. This pull is our genius energy looking for a way to be expressed. But all too often, the paint tubes sit perfectly plump and untouched alongside your equally untouched copy of *The Artist's Way*. And maybe it's because of how much it means to us that we both hold on too tightly to it and tell ourselves a story about why we aren't good enough to pull it off.

Underuse of your genius energy when it comes to creativity often manifests as playing small, holding back, and never touching that guitar at the back of your closet—not because you don't value it but because you've blocked yourself from doing it. It can show up as you not singing in church because you think you can't hold a tune or even refusing to wear those red shorts you love because you think they make you look fat or you fear you might stand out too much. But wait! Creativity wants to stand out.

Overuse of your genius energy also undermines your creative voice. You overcite other people's work, overprepare, overpractice, and cling tightly to a story that you need to be an expert (with another degree or a few more years of practice) before you can express yourself. And the saddest form of misuse of your genius in creative expression? It's putting it off altogether.

In this chapter, we're going to dive into the realm of creativity and discuss some ways you can redirect your genius energy to satisfy your creative urges.

Get Curious About Creative Contexts

Many of us live in environments that devalue creative pursuits and put them in the category of "afterschool electives" alongside the other important things deemed "extra," like physical activity and life skills. We put the art history department in the basements of our universities and leave them unfunded. We don't pay comedians, dancers, teachers, journalists, or street performers well, even though they open our eyes, make our hearts sing, and inspire us to shift our perspective in just a few minutes' time. So why should we value that creative genius in ourselves?

One of the reasons so many of us get stuck creatively is because we have to create the context to support it all on our own, starting with our own beliefs and mindset. We have to feel that we are psychologically safe to create. A supportive atmosphere frees you to express yourself, take risks, and collaborate openly. If your household is constantly frustrated with your painting-supply mess, your neighbors are banging on the walls when you drum, or you are the only person of color in your adult ballet class, you may feel limited in freely expressing yourself. Finding environments where you feel safe enough to step out of the box is essential. Where are the spaces you feel freest to express yourself? If you don't have any, I encourage you to start looking for some.

Often creative expression allows you to live many values at once. In the examples to come, you'll read about how Lou lives his values of self-care, connecting to his family, and lifelong learning every time he plays the piano. And Sarah lives her values of humor, working toward social justice and authenticity every time she directs a sketch. When you dig under that thing you want to express, what values drive you to create it? Remember them. They are what will guide you and keep you motivated when you feel stuck.

My best ideas come to me when I am running. I've been running the same road by my house for years, and it's my favorite because, even though I live in the foothills, the road is flat, carved into the mountainside with a view of the ocean a few miles away. Often I run above the fog line, and I feel my mind clearing like the sky around me. Running boosts my mood and provides me with a creative space to play with my thoughts.

What about you? When do you feel the most creative energy? Who supports your creativity? And what physical states free you the most? Is it on your morning swim, while bouncing ideas around in a team meeting, or during an evening alone tinkering in your garage? Particular contexts are creativity generators. As we explored in chapter 4, your environment, social interactions, and biology all play an essential role in your ability to choose wise effort.

It's hard to be creative if you are exhausted, hungover, or too hungry, and it's not a surprise that running outdoors opens my mind. Numerous studies have shown the link between being in nature and creative thinking.[1] Research has shown that experiencing natural environments can spark curiosity and encourage flexibility and imagination. They restore our attention and enhance the originality and variety of our creative ideas.[2]

For example, in a Stanford study on creativity, participants took a creativity test while sitting on a treadmill, walking on a treadmill, walking outside, or being wheeled outside. Walking outside produced the most novel and highest-quality analogies.[3] You can think of a hundred ways to use a button (the kind found on a shirt and the task in this study) when you are outside, but stuck at your boring desk, you may think of only one. In another study, when researchers added plants to a windowless room, participants had 12 percent quicker reactions on a computer task, experienced less stress, and felt more present.[4] Nature relaxes you, stimulates your senses, and broadens your perspective. Even looking at fractals in nature (those repeating patterns in a succulent or rose) has been shown to change your brain waves to a more relaxed, awake state.[5] If you want to boost your creativity, consider adding movement and nature. Take your grant writing to your patio, buy some roses for your desk, or walk around the block when you feel blocked.

Believe it or not, another context that supports creativity is messiness. Some people get bogged down by needing a clean space to create. I've had many clients waste hours organizing their desk before they sit down to record a podcast or cleaning out their fridge before they try out a new recipe. But actually, you may be happy (or horrified) to hear that many creative thinkers, like Albert Einstein and Mark Twain, had cluttered workspaces. Research has shown that messy rooms foster more out-of-the-box thinking, whereas orderly rooms foster conventionality.[6] But, as you may also have personally experienced, research participants in clean rooms are more likely to play by the rules and "make the healthy choice" of eating an apple rather than chocolate.

Sure, if your goal is to follow the rules, straighten up your room. But if you aim to be creative and free your genius energy, my suggestion is to let down your hair, throw your clothes on the floor, and welcome the clutter! If you were to see the floor of my room while I write this, you'd see that it's covered in books, empty tea mugs, scraps of notes, and chocolate wrappers (of course). But there's a delicate balance; excessive clutter can also cause cognitive overload, ultimately hampering creativity.[7] The take-home message is that if you are a neat freak, loosen up a bit, and if you are a hoarder, find some space to breathe. Either way, don't let cleanliness or clutter distract you from creating!

Open Up to Creativity

If you want to boost your creativity, one of the best ways to do it is to open your mind to a bit of wandering. When left unchecked, mind wandering can lead us to ruminate, worry, or plan for the future, which is why it has gotten a bad rap in psychology circles.[8] But research has shown that when mind wandering is harnessed for good, meaningful daydreams can boost innovative thinking and fantastical daydreams can enhance your creative writing.[9]

Catch yourself when you are falling into the trap of planning, ruminating, and worrying about your creative expression, and instead let yourself daydream about what could be possible. Give your mind room to breathe, to explore, and allow yourself to welcome your creative expression. Here are some daydream ideas to get your creative juices flowing. Write your answers to these questions in your Wise Effort Journal under the title "Opening Up to Creativity":

- What would you do if you had one minute to do your most creative thing?

- What would you create if you had endless amounts of time?

- What would it look like if you could design a space full of all your creations?

- If you could show one piece of (future) creative work to your childhood self, what would you want to show?

Let It Be Bad
To be creative, you must open up to the ugly, clumsy, unpolished, messy creative process. There's an initial phase where all ideas, even bad ones, need to be welcomed. If you shut down your genius by judging a rough draft that isn't stellar, avoiding doing things that feel awkward, or thinking that you failed, you close yourself to creative flow. When you are in the woods and can't find a way out, that's not the time to bail! Ask any artist, writer, or musician, and they will tell you that their best creative adventures came from wrong turns,

mistakes, and spin-offs of mediocre ideas. The key to creativity isn't being born with it but staying open to experiences supporting it.

Every weekday Sarah sits in the writers' room at *The Daily Show* with twelve directors, producers, and comedy writers. They receive the day's news stories and dive in, tossing out jokes that are hit-or-miss and collaborating on each other's creative ideas. Within a few hours, a sketch is developed, refined, and ready to be broadcast to millions of viewers.

Sarah learned a lot about focusing her energy as a camera operator. "I would be shooting a B-roll [the background footage for a scene], and my eye would catch a beautiful view. I could just drop the camera at eye level and shoot it because it's beautiful, or I could pause and ask myself, *What is it about this view?* It's the bridge and those clouds! So I would position the camera to emphasize the bridge and put the camera on time-lapse so the clouds are the focus. That type of refinement, emphasis on detail, makes a big difference."

"My job is to find interesting stories about interesting characters and creatively amp up the comedy," Sarah says. Her favorite bits are on topics she is most passionate about, like women's reproductive rights, racism, or political division. At the University of Southern California Film School, she learned that comedy is like sugarcoating a pill. You can get through to people with comedy in ways you can't with news or drama, and when someone laughs, they open up for a minute.

Sarah worked her way up to this coveted role at *The Daily Show*—and to winning a Webby and an Emmy—by being a camera operator and then directing some pretty embarrassing reality TV shows, such as *Bad Girls Club*, *Bridalplasty*, and *Celebrity Fit Club*.

For Sarah, wise effort is opening to the creative process, which involves building on her experience in what's funny and entertaining many stupid ideas until she finds better ones. She sees bad ideas as part of the journey to innovation, breakthrough moments, and a good laugh. Sarah describes this process as "sifting for gold." She takes an hour of footage with dozens of jokes and edits it to just three minutes or one punch line. She pesters the video editors to find the shot with 10 percent more disgust or 20 percent less surprise, and she sifts out extraneous stuff, which turns her sketches from good to great.

You have to let it be bad to let your genius energy flow—focusing in, seeing stories, or pulling things from thin air—into the things you want to create. Allow yourself to be a beginner. Open your mind and heart. That is where the seed of your genius energy can sprout.

> **Lou, Getting Onstage at Sixty-Five**
> Every spring, Lou starts preparing for his piano performance. He makes sure to add a few extra practices, buy a new bow tie, and structure the day of a performance for success. He goes for a swim to get his blood flowing and eats a good breakfast.
>
> Lou, sixty-five, is by far the oldest on the church stage during the recital. Surrounded by seven- and ten-year-olds wearing frilly dresses and shiny shoes, Lou sits tall and proudly plays his piece, even if his hands shake a bit with nerves. He is willing to weather the looks of surprise as he towers over the other musicians and is uplifted by seeing the pride in his wife's face in the crowd as he plays.
>
> It hasn't always been this way, though. Lou faced a lot of self-doubt when starting to play the piano again after fifty years. He carried his music books with him every time he moved, but he was hesitant to open them. He didn't want to be reminded of how long it had been since he had practiced. It seemed too hard to pick it up again. He didn't know if he had the patience for it anymore, and he was afraid of calling a piano teacher who might criticize him as his music teacher in elementary school had. Lou also thought he didn't have time to play. He was too busy working and caring for his wife, who

had recently incurred a brain injury in a car crash. Playing the piano felt secondary to more important things.

Early in our therapy sessions, I asked Lou about the activities he used to love but had put on the back burner because of stress and the business of life. The first thing he said was playing the piano, and he lit up while talking about it. Lou described how he loved playing as a teenager. It was a way to express himself when he couldn't with words, and it felt good in his body to make music during times of stress. Plus, the melodies connected Lou to his father, who had passed away two years before and whom he was still grieving. His father had loved Bach, Beethoven, and Mozart, and Lou could feel his father's presence when he pounded the keys. It soon became apparent that playing the piano wasn't secondary to other important things; it revitalized, destressed, and connected him when he needed support.

With just a short exploration of his values, Lou was motivated to start playing again—not just for the fun of it but for the psychological richness and depth it could offer him. It was then that he decided to find the right piano teacher, who was encouraging and kind, and to play recitals with children, which relieved the pressure and created the context for his creative joy.

Focus Your Creative Energy

Kurt Vonnegut wrote, "Practicing an art, no matter how well or badly, is a way to make your soul grow, for heaven's sake. Sing in the shower. Dance to the radio. Tell stories. Write a poem to a friend, even a lousy poem. Do it as well as you possibly can. You will get an enormous reward. You will have created something."[10]

There's value in working through something, toward something. You get to create your own adventure through the challenge. Be open to the natural frustration that comes with creating—come right up to it and see what happens. Sometimes creativity will flow like a firehose; other times, you may feel creatively paralyzed. This is all the creative process—energy expanding and contracting. And when the energy does flow, you'll see how creative ideas come while executing others.

So use your genius as a conduit to start (your book, your painting, your whatever) without the end goal in mind. Just start and see where the creativity takes you. The only certainty in creativity is that if you don't start, you won't create. Trust your instincts, stop running from your fears, and allow them to be some of the sources of energy that catapult you forward. You never know—those dark feelings can make for an on-point comedy sketch or a captivating piece of music. When you let go of expectations of what your creativity should look, sound, or taste like, you'll be able to make original poems, dances, and sculptures. And then, if you can link it to your deepest values, like compassion, kindness, social justice, or freedom, your creative pursuits will serve more than just you.

14

wise effort in community

I live on a little lane with seven other families in seven other houses that share a piece of land. That means when one family uses too much water, we all pay for it, but also when someone needs to be dug out of the mud, we all bring our shovels. If you read our group message thread, it says things like "Rainbow over at my house, come see!" and "Anyone have a tarp? I've got a leak." Each member has a genius energy that they bring to the lane—one neighbor is a genius at administration and keeps our fire insurance up to date, and another is a qigong master and centered us when the city came down hard on unpermitted work. Then there are the dogs, beehives, chickens, owls, bobcats, and coyotes on our lane, which remind us that we are part of a much larger web of connection.

Together, as one Community Body, we have a collective genius that makes us stronger. But that doesn't make it easy to live with each other. We've had our fair share of disagreements; *really long, boring* meetings; loss; and uncertainty as one family moves out and a new one moves in. The First Noble Truth has echoed through our lane repeatedly, much as it might have in yours: life contains inevitable ups and downs. But with wise effort, we can manage them with less friction and less suffering—including in community.

Wise effort in community helps you carry life's heavy responsibilities differently. There are your daily tasks of living, which seem to be increasingly complex and stressful, but also the big things like health crises, natural disasters, the rising cost of everything, disparity and discrimination in the workplace and the world, and increasing polarity. When you are part of wise communities—ones that are curious, open, and focusing their energy in the right places—you feel a sense of shared responsibility, taking care of others and being taken care of in return. There's a collective resilience that is stronger than any one of us has on our own.

We all share a street with someone—or an office space, a place of worship, or a pickleball court on Wednesday nights at six—and we can make these communities stronger. When we live wisely with each other, we can be happier, be freer, and experience incredible energy. It will take wise effort on your part to do this. Joining a community can be scary, and going deeper in your existing ones can make us feel vulnerable. We are asked to open ourselves, to depend on each other, to see our "interbeing," as Thich Nhat Hanh calls it.[1] As much as we like to build walls, fences, and defenses, we are never really separate. This brings us to the first step in building wiser communities: getting curious about what is making us feel so alone.

> **Trudy Goodman Founds InsightLA**
>
> Sometimes we can be surrounded by hundreds or even thousands of people yet feel like we don't belong or don't know where to start. That was the case for my good friend Trudy Goodman, whom we met earlier as my writing buddy. When Trudy moved from the East Coast to LA to care for her widowed mother and be closer to her pregnant daughter, she spent hours each day in a car. Errands that used to take her only a few minutes to complete consumed an entire Saturday afternoon because of bumper-to-bumper traffic. Trudy, a longtime meditator, would look over at the person in the car next to hers and wonder, *Do they feel as lonely as I do? They must. We aren't that different.* This was her engaging in the first step of wise effort: getting curious.
>
> She had a choice point: do nothing and stay lonely, or do something to get unstuck. So she decided to use her

genius energy and do what she knew best: teach meditation. Trudy started InsightLA in her friend's living room, where just three to five people could attend. The group grew through word of mouth, and people from all over came to hear Trudy teach. They were drawn to her, a positive energizer who had a genius for being relatable and real while transmitting deep insight. InsightLA became a community where anyone could show up as themself, share their vulnerabilities, and feel accepted.

As it grew, the community became an interdependent body—each member played an important role in keeping it running. Someone in the group had expertise in bookkeeping, another in forming a nonprofit; someone came and made tea; and others helped create community agreements. As soon as they had the resources, InsightLA opened doors in East LA, providing space for a diverse community that's traditionally underrepresented in meditation groups. Larry Yang, a senior meditation teacher and genius at creating inclusive communities, stepped in to lead. He was another positive energizer, creating affinity groups for BIPOC and LGBTQIA+ members and offering expert guidance to make InsightLA more accessible and inclusive. As a result, it grew and grew and grew.

When I joined InsightLA in 2018, it had thousands of members and had become a place of refuge, a sangha, for many of us who felt isolated or were unable to access a meditation community. I was struck by the energy exchange of giving and receiving gifts. I'd give it my all on teaching a meditation group and discussion on Tuesday nights, and I would leave feeling full for the rest of the week.

Wise communities energize us. And all of this beauty happened because Trudy Goodman was stuck in traffic and felt lonely. Sometimes it's in the most unexpected places that the most robust communities can take root.

Get Curious About What's Making You Lonely

You may be surrounded by people and numerous other living beings but still feel lonely. In 2021, 12 percent of US adults reported having no close friends, a sharp increase from 3 percent in 1990.[2] This rise in loneliness has significant health effects. Loneliness elevates your risk of heart attack and stroke and increases the chance of premature death by up to 26 percent.[3]

We are more technologically connected than ever, with some of us having "hundreds of friends," yet many of us feel like we are fending for ourselves. I believe it's more than technology creating this isolation. Many people feel *more* connected because of technology. In my view, we feel alone because we've lost touch with the truth of our interdependence, our reciprocal relationship with each other.

Think back to being a kid and all the built-in communities you had—kids you played with at recess; rode bikes with in the neighborhood; or met in the park around the corner to gossip, read the latest Baby-Sitters Club book, swap baseball cards, or maybe just lie underneath the trees. Later, you might have joined band, the volleyball team, or student government or signed up to work at the local Humane Society. These were communities where you could go in order to feel less alone. But as we grow older, we play less, work more, and leave little room for conversation or tree gazing. We get on the subway and pull out our phones or look down when we are walking because it's uncomfortable to look someone in the eye. Often we don't notice the people who are headed to the same place or sharing the same space.[4] Research has shown that weak ties are surprisingly beneficial for our well-being.[5] In fact, you're more likely to secure a job through acquaintances than friends because they connect you to different social circles.[6] Even something as simple as striking up a conversation during a daily commute can boost your happiness level.[7]

Many of us crave communities but don't see that we are already part of them.

So to start, I encourage you to get curious about the communities right in front of you. Look around your workplace, regular sandwich stop, walking trail, gym, or place of worship. Your group texts might say a lot about the communities you are already part of. Endless texts about arranging carpool or golf tee times? A family group text that weaves together cousins in six different time zones? Those are communities.

If you come up short or yearn for a deeper sense of community, make a brainstorm of possibilities. Start with your interests. Do you love music, vintage cars, video games, cooking, or self-help books? Communities can form around any of these passions. But communities don't arise just from shared joys; they can also emerge from shared worries and a desire for change.

What are the issues that weigh on your heart? Do you worry about climate change or the direction of your country's leadership? Do you feel powerless when reading about acts of violence against people of color? Does your stomach drop when you hear news of suffering in places like the Middle East, Sudan, or Congo or when you hear reports of children who are hungry? There are communities working tirelessly to address these challenges, and they need your genius energy.

Get Curious About What's Holding You Back

Community satisfies our core human yearning to belong and feel like we matter. And it's this very yearning—the fact that we want to be connected—that makes putting ourselves out there so hard sometimes. Remember the koan about the woman running from tigers? You might want to sign up for that cooking class or work in the community garden, but as the date gets closer, you feel more and more anxious until finally you cancel. Or maybe you are in a community where a conflict is brewing, and you bail or get too overbearing because it's too hard to listen to other people's perspective. When the tigers show up, we tend to run away or try to control the situation, and in doing so, we miss out on the strawberries of connection.

Many of us underuse our genius energy in communities because it's uncomfortable to connect. Take my client Daniel, whom we first met in chapter 5. When Daniel was diagnosed with cancer, he was hesitant to ask for support. He put off joining a cancer support group and didn't want to lean too much on his friends. Daniel had grown increasingly isolated over the years, as many of us have. A survey conducted by the Survey Center on American Life in 2021 found that the percentage of men reporting having no close friends had quintupled over the previous three decades.[8] Daniel found school functions and dinner parties uncomfortable, hated small talk, and often felt that he didn't relate to others. So we began to get curious: What was he afraid of?

Daniel said he feared that his friends wouldn't be able to handle it if he told them about his struggles. That it would make them uncomfortable and they would not be able to offer helpful support. When I suggested a cancer support group, he said he worried that he would be stuck there hating it, not sure that these would be his "people," judging himself and the people who were there. It seemed easier to keep to himself. At the same time, he longed to not be alone in his diagnosis. Plus, as a medic with cancer, he had a unique perspective to offer others, and he could imagine giving and getting support if he could just stop running away from the situation and getting lost in stories.

To figure out your own blocks to being part of communities around you, get curious about the three ways your genius energy can get misdirected: Are you running away, holding on too tightly, or stuck in a story? Get out your Wise Effort Journal and title a page "What's Holding Me Back from Community?" Then answer these questions:

> **Are you running away from discomfort?** Do you fear you won't fit in or that you won't be welcomed into the group? Or maybe you don't trust your social skills and fear that you will be awkward? Do you worry about becoming too dependent on others or fear that people will depend too much on you? Does conflict or disagreement in a group make

you uncomfortable? What do you do when these fears show up? Do you leave events early, stay in your office, avoid eye contact, remain quiet, say no to social engagements, or blame yourself for having something "wrong with you"? Get curious about the ways you avoid fully participating in groups.

Then there are the things **we hold on too tightly to** that keep us separate. Do you cling to familiar routines and want to stay in your comfort zone? Maybe you won't go to the meetup because it's "past your bedtime" or starts too early in the morning. Or you want to be in control and you feel uneasy about the unpredictability that comes with groups. Possibly you're attached to your identity of "I'm not the type of person who . . ." Or maybe you are presenting yourself with a fake facade, holding too tightly to impressing people, which in turn keeps them at a distance. How is holding on too tightly preventing you from being part of a community?

Finally, groups can be intimidating, breeding grounds for us to **get stuck in stories**. We believe the things our mind is saying, like *They already have their friend group; I have nothing to offer. I don't have time. I'm an impostor. No one will care. No one is like me.* And in our world of increasing divisiveness, we make up stories about others that keep us separate: *Oh, you live there? You voted for whom? You drive what type of car? You look like that? We can't be in the same circle.* What stories are keeping you separate?

Running away, holding on too tightly, and being stuck in a story blocks us from getting the community we need. Get to know these traps, and when you spot one, see it as a choice point—a chance to do something different. Answer some of the questions we explored earlier in the book in relation to joining or deepening your community. Title this "Letting Go of My Story About Community."

- If fear weren't such a problem for me, I would _____.

- If I accepted _____, I could _____.

- If I were to loosen the story that they are _____, I could _____.

Here are Daniel's responses:

- **If fear weren't such a problem for me, I would** ask for help when I feel isolated.

- **If I accepted** that I cannot do this all on my own, **I could** see that people want to help.

- **If I were to loosen up the story** that somehow asking for help is giving up, **I could** get some relief during the hardest times and invite people to come to me when I really need it.

Open Up to Feelings That Happen in Community

A community functions as a Second Body. If you are part of a Community Body, that means that when one arm is hurting, the whole body feels it. And it means that if you are feeling awkward, vulnerable, or scared of being part of a group, someone else is surely feeling that as well—or did when they first joined.

On my son's first day of preschool, his sixty-five-year-old teacher told me that even after thirty years of teaching, she still can't sleep the night before school starts. It's normal to be anxious about being judged or about starting something new. If you are worried about walking into a new class, joining a support group, moving into a new neighborhood, or your first day back at work after being away, you can bet there's someone else worried right along with you. Your worry actually points to the power of community. Community offers us a chance to see that we all worry about fitting in and gives us a chance to enter the flow of compassion. Start with compassion for yourself, then offer it to others, and finally open up to receive the gifts of being supported by a larger whole. Here are a few practices from the Wise Effort method that can help.

Get Centered

Use your grounding practices from chapter 7 to take care of your nervous system. The more centered you are, the more likely you are to send those signals to others through what's called "neuroception"—the unconscious ways our bodies communicate with each other through the muscles around our eyes, the tone of our voice, or how we lean in and offer a gentle pat on the back.[9] Taking a few slow breaths or repeating an encouraging mantra—*Just this moment, I can handle this*—as you walk into a group can do wonders. And if you are already part of a group, start integrating some centering practices to kick off your gathering. Start your meeting with a moment of silence, a group check-in, or a grounding poem or prayer. The most successful long-term communities like twelve-step meetings, Quaker meetings, and even competitive sports teams center themselves before they get started. That's because when the group is centered, members can better hear each other, support each other's geniuses, and work synergistically as a Wise Self.

Drop into Your Body

Remember that making space for feelings starts with opening to them in your body. This is very helpful if you tend to get in your head in social situations. Stay at the level of pure sensation—what are you feeling in your belly, your chest, your throat? Then, give your feeling a name and ask it what it needs. To remind yourself of all the other times you have done something hard and gotten through? To look for someone who seems on the outskirts and invite them in? This is the flow of compassion: take in compassion from others, give it to yourself, and offer it outward. When you allow compassion to flow in community, it only gets stronger.

They Are Just Like Me
One of the most powerful ways to dissolve the illusion of separateness is to remember that despite our many differences, all humans share the same fundamental experiences. We all know vulnerability and joy, we all long to be loved, and we all carry worries that sometimes keep us awake at night. The Just Like Me practice is a simple way to remember that you are not alone in your experience.[10] The next time you feel anxious, disconnected, or out of place, try this practice. Look at the face of someone you love, an acquaintance, a stranger, or even someone you are having a conflict with and remind yourself of the following:[11]

> Just like me, this person has things about their life that are hard.
>
> Just like me, this person has hopes and fears.
>
> Just like me, this person was a child once.
>
> Just like me, this person sometimes struggles to connect.
>
> Just like me, this person gets stuck in their head sometimes.
>
> Just like me, this person wants to be seen, heard, and valued.
>
> Just like me, this person longs to be happy.
>
> Just like you, everyone you encounter has a human mind, body, and heart. When you see this in strangers, people you are angry at, or people you are anxious around, it expands you to a Wise Self. *Just like me,*

they struggle, even though their circumstances and history are different than mine.

Tara Brach puts it this way: "Believing we are separate selves is one of our deepest illusions and the source of our suffering. If we try to hide our feelings of unworthiness or unlovableness, we deepen the sense of separation from others. Taking the risk to be vulnerable and real reveals the truth of our belonging—to each other, to ourselves, and to this world we share."[12]

Open to the Many Minds in Your Community

We began this book with the metaphor of a bird stuck in a kitchen, flying at a closed window. Its genius energy is headed in the wrong direction. The benefit of being in community is that you don't have to find your way out alone. There are people there who can see things you can't and who have had experiences you lack. And when you open yourself to others' perspectives, you just might find that open door waiting for you to fly out. You've experienced this when your online group is global and you learn how different cultures solve problems. Or when your AA meeting connects you with people from diverse backgrounds and cultures, offering you the chance to learn about different traditions, perspectives, and ways of celebrating. Diverse groups shake up our thinking, broaden our worldview, and widen the door out of that little kitchen we've been stuck in. But taking another person's point of view into consideration doesn't always come naturally to us, especially when we are in positions of power.

Take psychologist Adam Galinsky's "E" test, for example.[13] When research participants were asked to "draw the letter E on their forehead," they were more likely to draw an E that faced them if they were primed to be in a position of power. You are less likely to consider another person's perspective when you are at the helm. Remember this in the spaces where you have privilege, and make an effort to turn your "E" around to understand another person's world-view. Although you will never truly understand what it is like to be another person, we can all use wise effort to open our minds to more perspectives than just our own.

As David Brooks writes, "Remember that the person who is lower in any power structure than you are has a greater awareness of the situation than you do.... Someone who is being sat on knows a lot about the sitter—the way he shifts his weight and moves—whereas the sitter may not be aware that the sat-on person is even there."[14]

Here are some practices from the Wise Effort method that will help you open up to new perspectives in your communities:

- **Question your thoughts:** To overcome your biases and your tendency to quickly judge others (which we all have), ask yourself, *Are you sure?* This is especially important if you are leading a community or are in a position of privilege.

- **Enter the paradox:** Remember that multiple viewpoints can be true at once. A wise person can hold many perspectives and integrate them.

- **Remember your Many Bodies:** Every person in your group brings a unique genius that will make your organization, team, or family stronger. Make it your job to highlight their energy and encourage them to find ways to put it to use.

- **Share your genius:** One of the joys of being in community is mutual exchange—feeling like you are giving and receiving. What genius do you have to offer community? When have you felt most connected and valued in a community, and what were you contributing in those moments?

Be an Energizing Leader

When Adelle's West African dance teacher moved away, she realized the class wouldn't continue unless someone stepped up. Though hesitant, she leaned into her genius for breaking things down (she is an occupational therapist) and her deep respect for the culture of West African dance. Each Sunday, ten to twenty people gathered on the beach for Adelle's class, where she taught dances like the Yankadi, a sensual Susu dance that starts slow before bursting with vibrant energy. She began each gathering by sharing the cultural roots of the dance, and her gift for simplifying steps made everyone feel like they could follow. At the end of each class, Adelle invited participants to step into the circle for solos, to *do their thing*. It wasn't just a dance class; it was a place where people of diverse ages and backgrounds could express themselves, leaving sweaty, exhilarated, and feeling that they were part of something bigger.

Adelle is a positive energizer. Emma Seppälä, a leadership researcher at the Yale School of Management, describes leaders like this as akin to the sun, walking into a room and making it glow.[15] When Seppälä empirically examined what makes an effective organization, she found that the most significant predictor of success was not the leader's influence, personality, charisma, or power but rather their relational energy. This capacity to uplift, energize, and renew others makes a team thrive. Research has shown that if you are a positive energizer, your team will have higher performance and innovation; greater cohesion, loyalty, and engagement; enhanced well-being; and even more positive relationships with their families.[16] We all can step up and lead as positive energizers in our communities. Consider where leadership is needed in your community. Are there places where someone needs to step up, and could that person be you? If so, what genius energy can you bring? Are there places where you could be more bold?

Open Up to Wise Habits

Ultimately, wise effort in community is taking action toward your values, even when it's hard. When the going gets tough, how do you want to show up for others? As respectful? Inclusive? Generous? You can put these values at the front of your mind, let them guide you, and make them a habit.

Our wise habits don't just impact us—they ripple outward, shaping the communities we live in. Remember that wise habits have three simple steps: notice the choice point, act on your values, and savor the reward. You're at the airport and you notice a fellow traveler looking frazzled, checking their watch nervously. Instead of staying in your own bubble, you offer to let them move ahead of you in the security line. They breathe a sigh of relief, thank you, and then offer a smile to the person in front of them in line. It's a small gesture, but wise habits like this shift the energy of the room. Or maybe there's tension rising in your neighborhood over limited parking spaces. Instead of letting frustration simmer, you see it as a choice point and use your genius for gathering people to host a casual taco night at your house where neighbors can talk, share concerns, and come to a solution together. You're grateful to have played a part in bringing them together.

Every day, we have these choice points—moments when we can focus our genius energy on our values and connect.

Consider the communities you are in. Where are choice points for you to make them better? What genius energy do you have to offer? What are your community values? And what are you willing to feel to embrace mutual understanding? It takes a shift in mindset—believe that solutions are possible; see opportunities, not limits; and care for both personal and community well-being. This is the foundation of community change.

Middle Schoolers Take the Lead

The motto at Santa Barbara Middle School is "Carpe diem": seize the day! On Friday mornings at 6:45 a.m., with brave hearts, students, teachers, families, and dogs gather at

Leadbetter Beach for a sunrise swim. Unlike most middle schoolers, who need to be dragged out of bed, these students eagerly show up to lead the swim. These students are positive energizers, and the parents and teachers feel it.

Even though it's early, we're cold, and it takes a lot of effort to get showered and ready for school or work by 8 a.m., we don't rush it. There's a relaxed and unhurried vibe at the start of our morning circle, emphasizing that this gathering and our presence with each other are what truly matter. We all take the time to talk to each other—parents check in about how each other's kids are adjusting to school, students chat with teachers about their lives outside school, and we all feel like we've seized the day by beginning it together with the rising sun.

The ritual begins with getting centered. Everyone forms a circle, with the ninth graders in the center leading the group in singing songs, celebrating birthdays, reading poems, and observing a minute of shivering silence before everyone, dogs included, plunges into the ocean. Sure, it's uncomfortable, but we are open to feeling it. There's a unique energy that comes with doing hard things with people you care about. And gathering in this way is a living expression of the community's stated values of lifelong learning, self-trust, strength, courage, compassion, and respect for others.

The sunrise swim is a cherished tradition at SBMS that has been happening for over thirty-four years and is a perfect example of wise effort in community. Having a middle schooler is a rocky road, and this ritual is a model that students can apply to other challenges they will face. They are learning to open to discomfort, remember their values, expand their sense of self, and, most importantly, use their genius to seize the day!

Ultimately, learning how to practice wise effort in your life makes you feel energetic, alive, and like your best talents are being put to work. When you do this in community, whether it's sharing a donut after a swim or creating global connections, you feel a buzz. You are working and growing with others in meaningful ways. We all have a genius, and when we learn how to direct it, we make the world a better place to live in together. It's life at its most life-y.

Practice Focusing Your Energy

Wise effort is a practice. Slowly, over the course of time, it will become a way of being. When you choose to use your energy wisely, you know and feel in your bones the power of it. This is your life force being pointed in the right direction.

Everyone has a genius energy, but few take the opportunity to get to know it as you have. Go back to the end of chapter 1 and complete the Wise Effort Self-Assessment to see just how far you've come! Compare your sum scores in each category. Where have you improved the most? Are there areas of the book you want to revisit and keep strengthening? Wise effort never ends.

You have done the exciting work of opening yourself to your genius energy—learning about how it drives you, propels you forward, and makes you uniquely you. And you have done the hard work of looking inside and seeing the ways that this very energy gets misdirected. You've met your frenemy eye to eye. Remember, the first task is to **get curious**: when you find yourself stuck, sit on the kitchen floor of your life, dear bird, and let yourself wonder, *Huh? What is happening here? How is my genius misdirected? Where do I really want to head?*

You've bravely faced the second life task, too: **open up**. By opening to feelings, you've made your life deeper and revealed what you care most about. You've practiced naming your feelings, bringing them into the room, and being there for them. And you have opened your mind, which makes you freer to choose where you want to place your energy. Remember to resist the temptation to believe everything your mind tells you is true. Keep asking, *Are you sure?* And you've also opened up to your Wise Self, creating a bigger container for your genius energy to thrive. Your Wise Self is expansive, compassionate, and ready to do BIG things. You can open up to change.

The third life task is to **focus your genius energy** where it matters most. You've practiced recognizing the moments when you have a choice to use your genius energy in the most compassionate, effective, creative, and powerful ways—to create better relationships, physical health, creative projects, and community.

The power of your genius energy is abundantly clear when you start harnessing it for good, like letting go of resentments that weigh you down, pulling out your computer to write, or being a leader in a community that's going somewhere great.

Wise effort is a matter of discipline, a word whose root means "to be a student." And as you know, the best students practice. When you practice wise effort, you will become more psychologically flexible. Hard things will not bother you so much. Difficult people will not irritate you so much. You will feel a sense of flow in your life. When you practice wise effort, energy will flow back to you. You will know what is worth doing and where to let go, and you can depend on a greater sense of interbeing to get you through. When you practice wise effort, you set your genius energy free. Where once it was your problem, now it becomes your solution.

Keep practicing. You know the way now.

conclusion

wise effort is now

I woke up in the middle of the night last night, worried about so many things—this book, my kids starting school, the state of our world. In the past, I would have gone to the kitchen to search for answers. But last night, I knew what to do instead. I stepped outside, felt the cold concrete under my bare feet, and looked up at the moon. That was enough. After a while, I got tired again and went back to sleep.

There's one last Zen koan I want to leave you with. After all we have done together here, I am confident that if you wake in the night or come to important choice points in your life, you will have *plenty* of ideas from this book to support you in choosing wise effort. You have a path—get curious, open up, and focus your energy—that you can apply almost anywhere to reclaim your genius. But this koan is about more than that; it's about your genius itself. Here it is: *The finger pointing at the moon is not the moon.*

Linger on it for a bit and what this means for you.

What you have learned here are practices to point yourself toward your genius, as the finger points to the moon. But the finger isn't the moon itself; it's just a pointer. It's up to you to experience the force of the moon—your genius energy—for yourself. All these ideas are nothing in comparison to the power of using your genius wisely. And when you do, you will have tremendous power, as I had when I knew to step outside and look up. If we ever meet, I'm fairly certain it will feel a bit like pointing at the moon. We'll see a beautiful genius in each other—two humans doing their best to be curious, open, and wise.

acknowledgments

I wouldn't describe myself as having a genius for writing; it doesn't come easily to me. As Kurt Vonnegut said, "When I write, I feel like an armless, legless man with a crayon in his mouth." That's why I'm lucky to have had so many bodies to support, guide, and inspire this book.

Thank you to Rick Hanson for your wise guidance in all things—spirituality, book writing, business, and life. You saw this book coming years ago, inspired me to play big, and always amplify the good in me. Thank you to my editing bodies: the brilliant Jennie Nash, my book coach extraordinaire, who made it her mission to not let *Wise Effort* turn into my Nightmare Review. You are a genius at untangling frameworks and pushing authors to places they don't think they can go. Not only did you help me find my writing voice, but you helped me learn to like it. To my editors at Sounds True—Sarah Stanton, thank you for trusting my brainstorm of possibility, and Lyric Dodson, I've so appreciated your gentle way of giving spot-on feedback. Your patience and flexibility in this process made all those revisions worth it. Thank you to Jess Beebe for helping me set the foundation and Anna Gilmour for checking the science.

Thank you to my clients who've bravely offered their personal stories and experience as they worked through the method with me. Daniel, Giselle, Amy, and Lou, you know who you are, and all the clients who've sat in my casita under the oak trees, you are my coauthors.

To my Second Bodies—the many friends and colleagues who took my early-morning phone calls: Giulia Preziuso, Aaron Bright, Elissa Epel, Trudy Goodman, Sonya Looney, Katharine

Foley-Saldeña, Isa Hendry, Christy Peterson, Beth Bemis, Alisha Brosse, Liz Boyer, Meg McKelvie, Alexis Karris, Lara Fielding, Katy Bowman, Christina Schneider, Adelle Kurstin, Elyse Grossman, Luca Cupery, Susan Moe, Jenny Schatzle, Jane Chapman, Bri Pettit, Jay and Kristen Ruskey, and Cassie Hendry. And my Community Bodies—El Rancho Hacienda, Yoga Soup, Santa Barbara Middle School, and, of course the Mandala Mamas. You are the lungs that gave me enough breath to keep going.

To my mentor bodies. To Kelly Wilson for introducing me to ACT and what could be possible when values and vulnerability are poured from the same person. Steven Hayes and Joseph Ciarrochi, your work is the future of psychology, and it makes me hopeful for everyone who suffers; your research and mentorship are on every page of this book. To my doctoral advisers, Linda Craighead and Debra Safer, you charted my early path toward acceptance-based interventions, and I am ever grateful to you for giving me a second chance. And to Robyn Walser and Miranda Morris, thank you for deepening my understanding of what it means to practice ACT with heart and spunk.

Then there are the many bodies behind the microphone. Thank you to the *Wise Effort* podcast guests who informed and inspired this framework, including Matthew McKay, Michael Herold, Anna Lembke, Robert Waldinger, Sarah Hamblin, Nedra Tawwab, Dalya Sarkeys, Terry Real, Christiana Figueres, Jud Brewer, Nedra Tawaab, Lama Tsultrim Allione, Darcia Narvaez, Christina Maslach, Ann Kelley, Stephen Batchelor, Stephen Porges, Jack Kornfield, and Kate Johnson. And thank you to Christina Butt, Ashley Hiatt, Tina Goyzueta, Whitney Cubbison, and Michelle Keane for content strategy.

In deep gratitude to my spiritual body, Thich Nhat Hanh: your peace is in every one of my steps of this project.

Finally, thank you to my family bodies. To Craig, I am so lucky your genius is patience. From the first time we met, you saw something in me that I couldn't see in myself. You are the love of my life and show me what it means to love wisely. And to my boys, Henry and Walker, all those early mornings writing this book while you were sleeping, I felt connected to you. You are my daily reminders of what matters most. To Ashley, Dave, Ellie, Lulu, and Xan, I am so grateful to have you as family. To my dad, listening to all those long stories finally paid off; thank you for your deep wisdom. And to my mom, for your genius in offering me endless unconditional love. Is that a genius? I think it is.

additional resources: overview of wise effort skills

GET CURIOUS	OPEN UP YOUR MIND	OPEN UP YOUR FEELINGS	OPEN UP YOUR WISE SELF	OPEN UP TO CHANGE
1. What is my genius? 2. How am I overusing, underusing, or misusing my genius? 3. How is my environment impacting my genius? 4. What are my values?	1. Make space for your thoughts 2. Question your thoughts 3. Enter the paradox 4. Savor what's good 5. Trust your heart-mind	1. Center yourself 2. Make room for what's hard 3. Take care of your feeling 4. Give it a name 5. Ask, *What do I need?* 6. Act from your values	1. Remember that you are already wise 2. Ask, *Who am I?* 3. Let go of your story 4. Find your many bodies 5. Expand your sense of self 6. Act with compassion	1. Radically accept 2. See the choice point 3. Try something different 4. Use wise effort skills 5. Develop wise habits 6. Do it again

notes

Introduction: What Is Wise Effort?
1. Sylvia Boorstein, *It's Easier Than You Think: The Buddhist Way to Happiness* (New York: HarperCollins, 2011).
2. E. O. Wilson, *Consilience: The Unity of Knowledge* (New York: Vintage Books, 1998).

Chapter 1: What Is Your Genius?
1. Stephen Porges, "The Polyvagal Theory: Phylogenetic Substrates of a Social Nervous System," *International Journal of Psychophysiology* 42, no. 2 (2001): 123–146, doi.org/10.1016/S0167-8760(01)00162-3.
2. "How to Use Polyvagal Theory to Re-tune Your Nervous System with Dr. Stephen Porges," episode 51 of *Your Life in Process*, podcast, January 22, 2023, available at drdianahill.com/podcasts/.
3. Karen Bush Gibson, *The Chumash: Seafarers of the Pacific Coast* (Mankato, MN: Capstone Press, 2003); Aldona Jonaitis and Aaron Glass, *The Totem Pole: An Intercultural History* (Seattle: University of Washington Press, 2010).
4. "Genius," Merriam-Webster, accessed October 23, 2024, merriam-webster.com/dictionary/genius.
5. Betsy Wills and Alex Ellison, *Your Hidden Genius: The Science-Backed Strategy to Uncovering and Harnessing Your Innate Talents* (New York: HarperCollins, 2025).
6. PDP group and Daniel Siegel, *Personality and Wholeness in Therapy: Integrating 9 Patterns of Developmental Pathways in Clinical Practice* (New York: W. W. Norton, 2024).

7. You can assess your aptitude at youscience.com.
8. Mihaley Csikszentmihalyi, *Flow: The Psychology of Optimal Experience* (New York: Harper & Row, 1990).
9. Christopher Peterson and Martin E. P. Seligman, *Character Strengths and Virtues: A Handbook and Classification* (New York: Oxford University Press, 2004).
10. For a scientifically validated measure of your character strengths, visit VIAcharacter.org.
11. Peter Wohlleben, *The Hidden Life of Trees: What They Feel, How They Communicate—Discoveries from a Secret World* (Vancouver, BC: Greystone Books, 2015), 222–223.
12. David Andréen and Rupert Soar, "Termite-Inspired Metamaterials for Flow-Active Building Envelopes," *Frontiers in Materials* 10 (2023), doi.org/10.3389/fmats.2023.1126974; Sam Stier, "The Beak That Inspired a Bullet Train: Kingfishers," AskNature.org, last updated November 9, 2020, asknature.org/strategy/beak-provides-streamlining/.

Chapter 2: What Is Your Struggle?

1. "Getting Curious and Choosing Meaningful Passions with Dr. Judson Brewer," episode 77 of *Wise Effort*, podcast, July 31, 2023, available at drdianahill.com/podcasts/; Judson Brewer, *The Craving Mind: From Cigarettes to Smartphones to Love; Why We Get Hooked and How We Can Break Bad Habits* (New Haven, CT: Yale University Press, 2017).
2. Todd B. Kashdan et al., "The Five-Dimensional Curiosity Scale Revised (5DCR): Briefer Subscales While Separating Overt and Covert Social Curiosity," *Personality and Individual Differences* 157 (2020), doi.org/10.1016/j.paid.2020.109836; Sophie Von Stumm et al., "The Hungry Mind: Intellectual Curiosity Is the Third Pillar of Academic Performance," *Perspectives on Psychological Science* 6, no. 6 (2011): 574–588, doi.org/10.1177/1745691611421204.

3. Jordan A. Litman and Paul J. Silvia, "The Latent Structure of Trait Curiosity: Evidence for Interest and Deprivation Curiosity Dimensions," *Journal of Personality Assessment* 86, no. 3 (2006): 318–328, doi.org/10.1207/s15327752jpa8603_07; Matthias J. Gruber et al., "States of Curiosity Modulate Hippocampus-Dependent Learning via the Dopaminergic Circuit," *Neuron* 84, no. 2 (2014): 486–496, doi.org/10.1016/j.neuron.2014.08.060.
4. "Living Life on Your Own Terms (Real Play) with Michael Herold," episode 116 of *Your Life in Process*, podcast, May 13, 2024, available at drdianahill.com/podcasts/.
5. Anita Karekla, "Acceptance and Commitment Therapy Exceeds 1,000 Randomized Controlled Trials!," Association for Contextual Behavioral Science, December 22, 2022, contextualscience.org/news/acceptance_and_commitment_therapy_exceeds_1000_randomized_controlled_trialso.
6. Steven Hayes et al., "Evolving an Idionomic Approach to Processes of Change: Towards a Unified Personalized Science of Human Improvement," *Behaviour Research and Therapy* 156 (2022): doi.org/10.1016/j.brat.2022.104155.
7. Joseph Ciarrochi et al., "Process-Based Therapy: A Common Ground for Understanding and Utilizing Therapeutic Practices," *Journal of Psychotherapy Integration* 34, no. 3 (2024): 265–290, doi.org/10.1037/int0000348.
8. Steven C. Hayes, *A Liberated Mind: How to Pivot Toward What Matters* (New York: Avery, 2019).

Chapter 3: How Is Your Genius Also Your Problem?

1. Bessel Van der Kolk, *The Body Keeps the Score: Brain, Mind, and Body in the Healing of Trauma* (New York: Penguin Publishing Group, 2014).
2. Russ Harris, *The Happiness Trap: Stop Struggling, Start Living* (Wollombi, Australia: Exisle Publishing, 2007).

3. Rick Hanson and Richard Mendius, *Buddha's Brain: The Practical Neuroscience of Happiness, Love and Wisdom* (Oakland, CA: New Harbinger Publications, 2009).
4. "Suffer," Online Etymology Dictionary, accessed August 29, 2024, etymonline.com/word/suffer.
5. Sylvia Boorstein, *Pay Attention, for Goodness' Sake* (New York: Penguin Random House, 2003).
6. Rick Hanson with Forrest Hanson, *Resilient: How to Grow an Unshakable Core of Calm, Strength, and Happiness* (New York: Harmony Books, 2018).
7. Richard G. Tedeschi and Lawrence G. Calhoun, "The Posttraumatic Growth Inventory: Measuring the Positive Legacy of Trauma," *Journal of Traumatic Stress* 9 (1996): 455–471.
8. Adam M. Grant and Barry Schwartz, "Too Much of a Good Thing: The Challenge and Opportunity of the Inverted U," *Perspectives on Psychological Science* 6, no. 1 (2011): 61–76, doi.org/10.1177/1745691610393523.
9. Ryan M. Niemiec, "Finding the Golden Mean: The Overuse, Underuse, and Optimal Use of Character Strengths," in *A Second-Wave Positive Psychology in Counselling Psychology* (London, UK: Routledge, 2023), 183–201.
10. Robert B. Kaiser and Darren V. Overfield, "Strengths, Strengths Overused, and Lopsided Leadership," *Consulting Psychology Journal: Practice and Research* 63, no. 2 (2011): 89–109, doi.org/10.1037/a0024470.
11. Sharon Salzberg, *Lovingkindness: The Revolutionary Art of Happiness* (Boston, MA: Shambhala Publications, 1995).
12. Pema Chödrön, *Comfortable with Uncertainty: 108 Teachings on Cultivating Fearlessness and Compassion* (Boulder, CO: Shambhala Publications, 2002), 111.
13. Steven C. Hayes et al., "Experiential Avoidance and Behavioral Disorders: A Functional Dimensional Approach to Diagnosis and Treatment," *Journal of Consulting and Clinical Psychology* 64, no. 6 (1996): 1152, doi.org/10.1037/0022-006X.64.6.1152;

Mehdi Akbari et al., "Experiential Avoidance in Depression, Anxiety, Obsessive-Compulsive Related, and Posttraumatic Stress Disorders: A Comprehensive Systematic Review and Meta-Analysis," *Journal of Contextual Behavioral Science* 24 (2022): 65–78, doi.org/10.1016/j.jcbs.2022.03.007.

14. Anna Lembke, *Dopamine Nation: Finding Balance in the Age of Indulgence* (New York: Penguin, 2021), 40.
15. David Nguyen et al., "Positive Affect: Nature and Brain Bases of Liking and Wanting," *Current Opinion in Behavioral Sciences* 39, no. 4 (2021): 72–78, doi.org/10.1080/00201740903087359.
16. Patrick Anselme and Mike J. F. Robinson, "'Wanting,' 'Liking,' and Their Relation to Consciousness," *Journal of Experimental Psychology: Animal Learning and Cognition* 42, no. 2 (2016): 123–140, dx.doi.org/10.1037/xan0000090.
17. Kent C. Berridge, "A Liking Versus Wanting Perspective on Emotion and the Brain," in *The Oxford Handbook of Positive Emotion and Psychopathology* (Oxford, UK: Oxford University Press, 2019), 184–196.
18. Jennifer Crocker and Lora E. Park, "The Costly Pursuit of Self-Esteem," *Psychological Bulletin* 130, no. 3 (2004): 392–414, doi.org/10.1037/0033-2909.130.3.392.
19. Daniel Kahneman, *Thinking, Fast and Slow* (New York: Farrar, Straus and Giroux, 2011), 24.

Chapter 4: How Does Your Environment Impact Your Genius?

1. Jue Lin and Elissa Epel, "Stress and Telomere Shortening: Insights from Cellular Mechanisms," *Ageing Research Reviews* 73 (2022), doi.org/10.1016/j.arr.2021.101507.
2. Seolbin Han et al., "Association of Sleep Quality and Mitochondrial DNA Copy Number in Healthy Middle-Aged Adults," *Sleep Medicine* 113 (2024): 19–24, doi.org/10.1016/j.sleep.2023.11.011.

3. Daniel J. Siegel and the PDP Group, *Personality and Wholeness in Therapy: Integrating 9 Patterns of Developmental Pathways in Clinical Practice* (New York: W. W. Norton, 2024).
4. Gallup, "State of the Global Workplace," accessed December 18, 2024, gallup.com/workplace/349484/state-of-the-global-workplace.aspx.
5. World Health Organization, "Burn-out an 'Occupational Phenomenon': International Classification of Diseases," May 2019, who.int/news/item/28-05-2019-burn-out-an-occupational-phenomenon-international-classification-of-diseases.
6. Christina Maslach, *The Burnout Challenge: Managing People's Relationships with Their Jobs* (Cambridge, MA: Harvard University Press, 2022).
7. Maslach, *The Burnout Challenge*.
8. "What Is PTSD, and Who Does It Affect?," Disabled Veterans National Foundation, accessed January 27, 2025, ptsd.va.gov/understand/common/common_adults.asp.

Chapter 5: What Are Your Values?
1. Stephen R. Covey, *The 7 Habits of Highly Effective People*, 30th anniversary ed. (New York: Simon and Schuster, 2020), 112.
2. Jared A. Chase et al., "Values Are Not Just Goals: Online ACT-Based Values Training Adds to Goal Setting in Improving Undergraduate College Student Performance," *Journal of Contextual Behavioral Science* 2, no. 3–4 (2013): 79–84, doi.org/10.1016/j.jcbs.2013.08.002.
3. adrienne maree brown, *Emergent Strategy: Shaping Change, Changing Worlds* (Chico, CA: AK Press, 2017), 41.
4. Diana Hill and Debbie Sorenson, *ACT Daily Journal: Get Unstuck and Live Fully with Acceptance and Commitment Therapy* (Oakland, CA: New Harbinger Publications, 2021), 108.
5. Daniel Pink, *The Power of Regret: How Looking Backward Moves Us Forward* (New York: Penguin Publishing Group, 2022), 14.

6. "The Power of Regret with Daniel Pink," episode 28 of *Your Life in Process*, podcast, July 10, 2022, available at drdianahill.com/podcasts/.

Chapter 6: Open Up Your Mind

1. Daniel M. Wegner et al., "Paradoxical Effects of Thought Suppression," *Journal of Personality and Social Psychology* 53, no. 1 (1987): 5–13, doi.org/10.1037/0022-3514.53.1.5.
2. Deming Wang et al., "Ironic Effects of Thought Suppression: A Meta-Analysis," *Perspectives on Psychological Science* 15, no. 3 (2020): 778–793, doi.org/10.1177/1745691619898795.
3. Not the most professional thought, but therapists are human, too.
4. Lucas S. LaFreniere and Michelle G. Newman, "Exposing Worry's Deceit: Percentage of Untrue Worries in Generalized Anxiety Disorder Treatment," *Behavior Therapy* 51, no. 3 (2020): 413–423, doi.org/10.1016/j.beth.2019.07.003.
5. Jeffrey A. Hayes et al., "Managing Countertransference," *Psychotherapy* 48, no. 1 (2011): 88–97, doi.org/10.1037/a0022182.
6. Yael Schonbrun, *Work, Parent, Thrive: 12 Science-Backed Strategies to Ditch Guilt, Manage Overwhelm, and Grow Connection (When Everything Feels Like Too Much)* (Boulder, CO: Shambhala Publications, 2022).
7. Rick Hanson, *Hardwiring Happiness: The New Brain Science of Contentment, Calm, and Confidence* (New York: Harmony/Rodale, 2016), 31.
8. Martin Picard and Bruce S. McEwen, "Psychological Stress and Mitochondria: A Systematic Review," *Psychosomatic Medicine* 80, no. 2 (2018): 141–153, doi.org/10.1097/psy.0000000000000545; Technology Networks: Neuroscience News and Research, "Positive Life Linked to Mitochondria: Do Mitochondria Change Mood, or Does Mood Change Mitochondria?," June 21, 2024, technologynetworks.com/neuroscience/news/positive-life-linked-to-mitochondria-388052.

9. Jack Kornfield, *The Wise Heart: A Guide to the Universal Teachings of Buddhist Psychology* (New York: Bantam Books, 2009); Darcia Narvaez, *Neurobiology and the Development of Human Morality: Evolution, Culture, and Wisdom* (New York: W. W. Norton, 2014).
10. John A. Armour, "Anatomy and Function of the Intrathoracic Neurons Regulating the Mammalian Heart," in *Reflex Control of the Circulation* (Boca Raton, FL: CRC Press, 1991).

Chapter 7: Open Up Your Feelings

1. Francis Weller, *The Wild Edge of Sorrow: Rituals of Renewal and the Sacred Work of Grief* (Berkeley, CA: North Atlantic Books, 2015), 110.
2. Jack Saul, *Collective Trauma, Collective Healing: Promoting Community Resilience in the Aftermath of Disaster* (New York: Taylor & Francis, 2022).
3. Paul Gilbert and Choden, *Mindful Compassion: How the Science of Compassion Can Help You Understand Your Emotions, Live in the Present, and Connect Deeply with Others* (Oakland, CA: New Harbinger Publications, 2014); Paul Gilbert, *The Compassionate Mind: A New Approach to Life's Challenges* (Oakland, CA: New Harbinger Publications, 2009).
4. Alexandra D. Crosswell et al., "Deep Rest: An Integrative Model of How Contemplative Practices Combat Stress and Enhance the Body's Restorative Capacity," *Psychological Review* 131, no. 1 (2024): 247–270, doi.org/10.1037/rev0000453.
5. Robin Blades et al., "A Randomized Controlled Clinical Trial of a Wim Hof Method Intervention in Women with High Depressive Symptoms," *Comprehensive Psychoneuroendocrinology* 20 (2024), doi.org/10.1016/j.cpnec.2024.100272.
6. Nikolai A. Shevchuk, "Adapted Cold Shower as a Potential Treatment for Depression," *Medical Hypotheses* 70, no. 5 (2008): 995–1001, doi.org/10.1016/j.mehy.2007.04.052.

7. Tomoko Kinoshita et al., "Cold-Water Face Immersion Per Se Elicits Cardiac Parasympathetic Activity," *Circulation Journal* 70, no. 6 (2006): 773–776, doi.org/10.1253/circj.70.773.
8. Matthew A. Killingsworth and Daniel T. Gilbert, "A Wandering Mind Is an Unhappy Mind," *Science* 330, no. 6006 (2010): 932, doi.org/10.1126/science.1192439.
9. Petra Levinger et al., "What Doesn't Kill You Makes You Fitter: A Systematic Review of High-Intensity Exercise on Mood," *Journal of Clinical Medicine* 9, no. 3 (2020): 652.
10. James D. Lane et al., "Binaural Auditory Beats Affect Vigilance Performance and Mood," *Physiology and Behavior* 63, no. 2 (1998): 249–252, doi.org/10.1016/S0031-9384(97)00436-8.
11. Stephen W. Porges, "The Polyvagal Theory: Phylogenetic Substrates of a Social Nervous System," *International Journal of Psychophysiology* 42, no. 2 (2001): 123–146, doi.org/10.1016/S0167-8760(01)00162-3.
12. Peter Levine and Ann Frederick, *Waking the Tiger: Healing Trauma* (Berkeley, CA: North Atlantic Books, 1997).
13. Kristen Neff, *Self-Compassion: The Proven Power of Being Kind to Yourself* (New York: HarperCollins, 2011).
14. Matthew D. Lieberman et al., "Putting Feelings into Words: Affect Labeling Disrupts Amygdala Activity in Response to Affective Stimuli," *Psychological Science* 18, no. 5 (2007): 421–428, doi.org/10.1111/j.1467-9280.2007.01916.x.
15. Lama Tsultrim Allione, *Wisdom Rising: Journey into the Mandala of the Empowered Feminine* (Ojai, CA: Atria/Enliven Books, 2018); "Feeding Your Inner Demons with Lama Tsultrim Allione," episode 54 of *Wise Effort*, podcast, February 13, 2022, available at drdianahill.com/podcasts/.
16. Eve Ekman et al., "Transforming Adversity into an Ally: A Qualitative Study of 'Feeding Your Demons' Meditation," *Frontiers in Psychology* 13 (2022), doi.org/10.3389/fpsyg.2022.806500.
17. Caroline Hickman et al., "Climate Anxiety in Children and Young People and Their Beliefs about Government Responses to

Climate Change: A Global Survey," *The Lancet Planetary Health* 5, no. 12 (2021): e863–e873.
18. Elissa Epel et al., "Outcomes of a Novel Experiential Psychosocial Climate Resilience Course for Young Adults," manuscript in preparation, 2024.

Chapter 8: Open Up Your Wise Self

1. Diana Hill, *The Self-Compassion Daily Journal: Let Go of Your Inner Critic and Embrace Who You Are with Acceptance and Commitment Therapy* (Oakland, CA: New Harbinger Publications, 2024).
2. The Berlin Wisdom Paradigm: An Expert Knowledge System, Evidence-Based Wisdom, evidencebasedwisdom.com/2015/09/20/the-berlin-wisdom-paradigm-an-expert-knowledge-system/.
3. Monika Ardelt, "Wisdom and Life Satisfaction in Old Age," *Journals of Gerontology Series B: Psychological Sciences and Social Sciences* 58, no. 5 (2003): P232–P239, doi.org/10.1093/geronb/52B.1.P15; J. Glück and S. Bluck, "The MORE Life Experience Model: A Theory of the Development of Personal Wisdom," in M. Ferrari and N. M. Weststrate, editors, *The Scientific Study of Personal Wisdom: From Contemplative Traditions to Neuroscience* (Dordrecht, Netherlands: Springer, 2013), 75–97.
4. Kaili Zhang et al., "Wisdom: Meaning, Structure, Types, Arguments, and Future Concerns," *Current Psychology* 42, no. 18 (2023): 15030–15051, doi.org/10.1007/s12144-022-02816-6; Paul B. Baltes and Ursula M. Staudinger, "Wisdom: A Metaheuristic (Pragmatic) to Orchestrate Mind and Virtue Toward Excellence," *American Psychologist* 55, no. 1 (2000): 122–136, doi.org/10.1037//0003-066X.55.1.122.
5. Annie Murphy Paul, *The Extended Mind: The Power of Thinking Outside the Brain* (Boston, MA: Houghton Mifflin Harcourt, 2021).
6. Darcia Narvaez et al., eds., *Indigenous Sustainable Wisdom: First-Nation Know-How for Global Flourishing* (Vienna, Austria: Peter Lang, 2019), 27–28.

7. Paul Gilbert and Choden, *Mindful Compassion: How the Science of Compassion Can Help You Understand Your Emotions, Live in the Present, and Connect Deeply with Others* (Oakland, CA: New Harbinger Publications, 2014); Paul Gilbert, *The Compassionate Mind: A New Approach to Life's Challenges* (Oakland, CA: New Harbinger Publications, 2009).
8. Richard C. Schwartz, *No Bad Parts: Healing Trauma and Restoring Wholeness with the Internal Family Systems Model* (Boulder, CO: Sounds True, 2021).
9. I first learned a version of this exercise from Steven Hayes in an ACT training. He describes a similar practice in *A Liberated Mind: How to Pivot Toward What Matters* (New York: Avery, 2019).
10. Simone Schnall et al., "Social Support and the Perception of Geographical Slant," *Journal of Experimental Social Psychology* 44, no. 5 (2008): 1246–1255, doi.org/10.1016/j.jesp.2008.04.011.
11. Daniel J. Siegel, *IntraConnected: MWe (Me + We) as the Integration of Self, Identity, and Belonging* (New York: W. W. Norton, 2022), 88.
12. Dacher Keltner, *Awe: The Transformative Power of Everyday Wonder* (New York: Penguin, 2023).
13. Judson A. Brewer et al., "Meditation Experience Is Associated with Differences in Default Mode Network Activity and Connectivity," *Proceedings of the National Academy of Sciences* 108, no. 50 (2011): 20254–20259, doi.org/10.1073/pnas.1112029108.
14. Robin L. Carhart-Harris et al., "Neural Correlates of the Psychedelic State as Determined by fMRI Studies with Psilocybin," *Proceedings of the National Academy of Sciences* 109, no. 6 (2012): 2138–2143, doi.org/10.1073/pnas.1119598109.
15. "(Most) Everything You Want to Know About Psychedelic-Assisted Therapy with Brian Pilecki," episode 29 of *Wise Effort*, podcast, July 18, 2022, available at drdianahill.com/podcasts/.
16. If you are a mental health professional interested in learning more, I recommend checking out truenorthact.com.

17. Michael Pollan, *How to Change Your Mind: What the New Science of Psychedelics Teaches Us About Consciousness, Dying, Addiction, Depression, and Transcendence* (New York: Penguin Publishing Group, 2018).
18. Jennifer L. Goetz et al., "Compassion: An Evolutionary Analysis and Empirical Review," *Psychological Bulletin* 136, no. 3 (2010): 351–374, doi.org/10.1037/a0018807.
19. Gilbert, *The Compassionate Mind*.
20. Paul Gilbert et al., "Fears of Compassion: Development of Three Self-Report Measures," *Psychology and Psychotherapy: Theory, Research and Practice* 84, no. 3 (2011): 239–255, doi.org/10.1348/147608310X526511.
21. Marcela Matos et al., "Compassion Protects Mental Health and Social Safeness During the COVID-19 Pandemic Across 21 Countries," *Mindfulness* 13, no. 4 (2022): 863–880, doi.org/10.1007/s12671-021-01822-2.

Chapter 9: Open Up to Change

1. Jon Arcelus et al., "Mortality Rates in Patients with Anorexia Nervosa and Other Eating Disorders: A Meta-Analysis of 36 Studies," *Archives of General Psychiatry* 68, no. 7 (2011): 724–731, doi.org/10.1001/archgenpsychiatry.2011.74.
2. "Values, Vulnerability, and Forgiveness with ACT Co-founder Kelly Wilson," episode 33 of *Wise Effort*, podcast, September 5, 2022, available at drdianahill.com/podcasts/.
3. Tara Brach, *Radical Acceptance: Embracing Your Life with the Heart of a Buddha* (New York: Random House Publishing, 2004), 5.
4. Joseph Ciarrochi et al., *The Weight Escape: How to Stop Dieting and Start Living* (Boulder, CO: Shambhala Publications, 2014).
5. Sogyal Rinpoche, *The Tibetan Book of Living and Dying: A Spiritual Classic from One of the Foremost Interpreters of Tibetan Buddhism to the West* (London, UK: Ebury Publishing, 2012).

6. Pema Chödrön, *How We Live Is How We Die* (Boulder, CO: Shambhala Publications, 2022), 14.
7. Charles Duhigg, *The Power of Habit: Why We Do What We Do in Life and Business* (New York: Random House Publishing, 2012).
8. James O. Prochaska and Carlo C. DiClemente, *The Transtheoretical Approach Crossing Traditional Boundaries of Therapy* (Malabar, FL: Krieger Publishing Company, 1994).

Chapter 10: Wise Effort in Relationships

1. Robert Waldinger, "What Makes a Good Life? Lessons from the Longest Study on Happiness," TEDxBeaconStreet, November 2015, ted.com/talks/robert_waldinger_what_makes_a_good_life_lessons_from_the_longest_study_on_happiness?subtitle=en.
2. "Lessons from the Harvard Health Study on Happiness with Robert Waldinger," episode 53 of *Your Life in Process*, podcast, February 6, 2023, available at drdianahill.com/podcasts/.
3. "Lessons from the Harvard Health Study on Happiness with Robert Waldinger."
4. Robert Waldinger and Marc Schulz, *The Good Life: Lessons from the World's Longest Scientific Study of Happiness* (New York: Simon & Schuster, 2023).
5. "The Power of Acceptance & Commitment (ACT Therapy) with Dr. Diana Hill," episode 252 of *Therapist Uncensored*, podcast, December 3, 2024, available at therapistuncensored.com/episodes-2/.
6. Morris Rosenberg and Claire B. McCullough, "Mattering: Inferred Significance and Mental Health Among Adolescents," *Research in Community & Mental Health* 2 (1981): 163–182.
7. "Power of Empathy and Motivational Interviewing with Stephen Rollnick," episode 135 of *Psychologists Off the Clock*, podcast, April 8, 2020, available at offtheclockpsych.com/power-of-empathy-motivational-interviewing/.
8. Terrence Real, *Us: Getting Past You and Me to Build a More Loving Relationship* (New York: Harmony Books, 2022).

9. Karl Pillemer, *Fault Lines: Fractured Families and How to Mend Them* (New York: Penguin Publishing Group, 2022).
10. Anne Lamott, *Traveling Mercies: Some Thoughts on Faith* (New York: Knopf Doubleday Publishing Group, 2000), 134.

Chapter 11: Wise Effort with Your Body

1. Beate M. Herbert et al., "Intuitive Eating Is Associated with Interoceptive Sensitivity: Effects on Body Mass Index," *Appetite* 70 (2013): 22–30, doi.org/10.1016/j.appet.2013.06.082.
2. Annie Murphy Paul, *The Extended Mind: The Power of Thinking Outside the Brain* (Boston, MA: Houghton Mifflin Harcourt, 2021); Narayanan Kandasamy et al., "Interoceptive Ability Predicts Survival on a London Trading Floor," *Scientific Reports* 6, no. 1 (2016): doi.org/10.1038/srep32986.
3. Shari M. Geller, "Therapeutic Presence and Polyvagal Theory: Principles and Practices for Cultivating Effective Therapeutic Relationships," in *Clinical Applications of the Polyvagal Theory: The Emergence of Polyvagal-Informed Therapies*, ed. Deb Dana and Stephen Porges (New York: W. W. Norton, 2018), 106–126; Wolf E. Mehling et al., "The Multidimensional Assessment of Interoceptive Awareness (MAIA)," *PloS One* 7, no. 11 (2012): e48230, doi.org/10.1371/journal.pone.0048230; Manos Tsakiris and Hugo Critchley, "Interoception Beyond Homeostasis: Affect, Cognition and Mental Health," *Philosophical Transactions of the Royal Society B: Biological Sciences* 371, no. 1708 (2016): doi.org/10.1098/rstb.2016.0002.
4. Diana M. Hill et al., "Appetite-Focused Dialectical Behavior Therapy for the Treatment of Binge Eating with Purging: A Preliminary Trial," *International Journal of Eating Disorders* 44, no. 3 (April 2011): 249–261, doi.org/10.1002/eat.20812.
5. Linda Stone, "Are You Breathing? Do You Have Email Apnea?," Lindastone.net, February 2008, lindastone.net/2014/11/24/are-you-breathing-do-you-have-email-apnea/.

6. Daniel Kahneman, *Thinking, Fast and Slow* (New York: Farrar, Straus and Giroux, 2011).
7. Geneen Roth, *When You Eat at the Refrigerator, Pull Up a Chair: 50 Ways to Feel Thin, Gorgeous, and Happy (When You Feel Anything But)* (New York: Hachette Books, 2010).
8. "New Contemplations for Eating," Plum Village. January 15, 2014, plumvillage.org/articles/news/new-contemplations-before-eating.
9. Nazik Elgaddal et al., "Physical Activity Among Adults Aged 18 and Over: United States, 2020," NCHS Data Brief 443 (2022): cdc.gov/nchs/products/databriefs/db443.htm.
10. Diana Hill and Katy Bowman, *I Know I Should Exercise But . . . : 44 Reasons We Don't Move and How to Get Over Them* (Sequim, WA: Uphill Books, 2025).
11. Tricia Hersey, *Rest Is Resistance: A Manifesto* (Boston, MA: Little, Brown, 2022), 3.
12. Pilar Gerasimo, *The Healthy Deviant* (Berkeley, CA: North Atlantic Books, 2020).; "How to Be a Healthy Deviant with Pilar Gerasimo," episode 38 of *Wise Effort*, podcast, October 10, 2022, available at drdianahill.com/podcasts/.
13. Alexandra D. Crosswell et al., "Deep Rest: An Integrative Model of How Contemplative Practices Combat Stress and Enhance the Body's Restorative Capacity," *Psychological Review* 131, no. 1 (January 2024): 247–270, doi: 10.1037/rev0000453.
14. Esther Perel, *Where Should We Begin: A Game of Stories*, 2nd ed., game.estherperel.com/products/where-should-we-begin-a-game-of-stories-2nd-edition.
15. Emily Nagoski, *Come as You Are: The Surprising New Science That Will Transform Your Sex Life* (Melbourne, Australia: Scribe, 2015).
16. adrienne maree brown, *Pleasure Activism: The Politics of Feeling Good* (Chico, CA: AK Press, 2019), 26.

Chapter 12: Wise Effort at Work

1. Timothy Butler and James Waldroop, "Job Sculpting: The Art of Retaining Your Best People," *Harvard Business Review* 77, no. 5 (1999), 144–152.
2. Amy Wrzesniewski et al., "Turn the Job You Have into the Job You Want." *Harvard Business Review* 88, no. 6 (2010): 114–117.
3. Susan Sorenson, "How Employees' Strengths Make Your Company Stronger," Gallup, accessed December 17, 2024, gallup.com/workplace/231605/employees-strengths-company-stronger.aspx.
4. Kelly McGonigal, *The Upside of Stress: Why Stress Is Good for You and How to Get Good at It* (New York: Avery, 2015).
5. Michael F. Steger et al., "Measuring Meaningful Work: The Work and Meaning Inventory (WAMI)," *Journal of Career Assessment* 20, no. 3 (2012): 322–337, doi.org/10.1177/1069072711436160; Richard M. Ryan and Edward L. Deci, "Intrinsic and Extrinsic Motivations: Classic Definitions and New Directions," *Contemporary Educational Psychology* 25, no. 1 (2000): 54–67, doi.org/10.1006/ceps.1999.1020; Blake A. Allan et al., "Helping Others Increases Meaningful Work: Evidence from Three Experiments," *Journal of Counseling Psychology* 65, no. 2 (2018): 155–165, psycnet.apa.org/doi/10.1037/cou0000228.

Chapter 13: Wise Effort in Creativity

1. Chin-Wen Yeh et al., "The Influence of Natural Environments on Creativity," *Frontiers in Psychiatry* 13 (2022), doi.org/10.3389/fpsyt.2022.895213.
2. Ruth Ann Atchley et al., "Creativity in the Wild: Improving Creative Reasoning Through Immersion in Natural Settings," *PloS One* 7, no. 12 (2012): e51474, doi.org/10.1371/journal.pone.0051474.

3. Marily Oppezzo and Daniel L. Schwartz, "Give Your Ideas Some Legs: The Positive Effect of Walking on Creative Thinking," *Journal of Experimental Psychology: Learning, Memory, and Cognition* 40, no. 4 (2014): 1142–1152, doi.org/10.1037/a0036577.
4. Virginia I. Lohr et al., "Interior Plants May Improve Worker Productivity and Reduce Stress in a Windowless Environment," *Journal of Environmental Horticulture* 14, no. 2 (1996): 97–100, doi.org/10.24266/0738-2898-14.2.97.
5. Caroline M. Hagerhall et al., "Investigations of Human EEG Response to Viewing Fractal Patterns," *Perception* 37, no. 10 (2008): 1488–1494, doi.org/10.1068/p5918.
6. Kathleen D. Vohs et al., "Physical Order Produces Healthy Choices, Generosity, and Conventionality, Whereas Disorder Produces Creativity," *Psychological Science* 24, no. 9 (2013): 1860–1867, doi.org/10.1177/0956797613480186.
7. Stephanie McMains and Sabine Kastner, "Interactions of Top-down and Bottom-up Mechanisms in Human Visual Cortex," *Journal of Neuroscience* 31, no. 2 (2011): 587–597, doi.org/10.1523/JNEUROSCI.3766-10.2011.
8. Cristina Ottaviani et al., "Flexibility as the Key for Somatic Health: From Mind Wandering to Perseverative Cognition," *Biological Psychology* 94, no. 1 (2013): 38–43, doi.org/10.1016/j.biopsycho.2013.05.003.
9. Benjamin Baird et al., "Inspired by Distraction: Mind Wandering Facilitates Creative Incubation," *Psychological Science* 23, no. 10 (2012): 1117–1122, doi.org/10.1177/0956797612446024.
10. Kurt Vonnegut, *A Man Without a Country* (New York: Penguin Random House, 2005), 24.

Chapter 14: Wise Effort in Community
1. Thich Nhat Hanh, *Interbeing: Fourteen Guidelines for Engaged Buddhism* (Oklahoma City, OK: Full Circle, 2003).

2. Daniel A. Cox, "The State of American Friendship: Change, Challenges, and Loss," Survey Center on American Life, June 8, 2021, americansurveycenter.org/research/the-state-of-american-friendship-change-challenges-and-loss/.
3. Julianne Holt-Lunstad et al., "Loneliness and Social Isolation as Risk Factors for Mortality: A Meta-Analytic Review," *Perspectives on Psychological Science* 10, no. 2 (2015): 227–237, doi.org/10.1177/1745691614568352.
4. Mark S. Granovetter, "The Strength of Weak Ties," *American Journal of Sociology* 78, no. 6 (1973): 1360–1380, doi.org/10.1086/225469.
5. Granovetter, "The Strength of Weak Ties."
6. Gillian M. Sandstrom and Elizabeth W. Dunn, "Social Interactions and Well-Being: The Surprising Power of Weak Ties," *Personality and Social Psychology Bulletin* 40, no. 7 (2014): 910–922, doi.org/10.1177/0146167214529799.
7. Nicholas Epley and Juliana Schroeder, "Mistakenly Seeking Solitude," *Journal of Experimental Psychology: General* 143, no. 5 (2014): 1980–1999, doi.org/10.1037/a0037323.
8. Cox, "The State of American Friendship."
9. Stephen W. Porges, "Neuroception: A Subconscious System for Detecting Threats and Safety," *Zero to Three (J)* 24, no. 5 (2004): 19–24.
10. "'Just Like Me' Guided Meditation," episode 125 of *Heart Wisdom*, podcast, March 24, 2021, available at jackkornfield.com/ep-125-just-like-me-guided-meditation/.
11. "'Just Like Me' Guided Meditation."
12. Tara Brach, *Trusting the Gold: Uncovering Your Natural Goodness* (Boulder, CO: Sounds True, 2021), 41.
13. Adam D. Galinsky, et al., "Power and Perspectives Not Taken," *Psychological Science* 17, no. 12 (2006): 1068–1074, doi.org/10.1111/j.1467-9280.2006.01824.x.
14. David Brooks, *How to Know a Person: The Art of Seeing Others Deeply and Being Deeply Seen* (New York: Random House Publishing Group, 2023), 115.

15. "The Future of Wise Leadership with Emma Seppälä," episode 122 of *Wise Effort*, podcast, June 24, 2024, available at drdianahill.com/podcasts/.
16. Emma Seppälä and Kim Cameron, "The Best Leaders Have a Contagious Positive Energy," *Harvard Business Review*, April 18, 2022, hbr.org/2022/04/the-best-leaders-have-a-contagious-positive-energy.

about the author

Diana Hill, PhD, is a clinical psychologist, speaker, and ACT expert helping people direct their energy toward what matters most. Through her Wise Effort programs and podcast, she helps people play big in their careers, health, and relationships. Her books include *I Know I Should Exercise But . . .* , *The Self-Compassion Daily Journal*, and *ACT Daily Journal*. NPR, the *Wall Street Journal*, and *Mindful* magazine have featured her work. She resides in Santa Barbara, California. For more, visit drdianahill.com.

about sounds true

Sounds True was founded in 1985 by Tami Simon with a clear mission: to disseminate spiritual wisdom. Since starting out as a project with one woman and her tape recorder, we have grown into a multimedia publishing company with a catalog of more than 3,000 titles by some of the leading teachers and visionaries of our time, and an ever-expanding family of beloved customers from across the world.

In more than three decades of evolution, Sounds True has maintained our focus on our overriding purpose and mission: to wake up the world. We offer books, audio programs, online learning experiences, and in-person events to support your personal growth and awakening, and to unlock our greatest human capacities to love and serve.

At SoundsTrue.com you'll find a wealth of resources to enrich your journey, including our weekly *Insights at the Edge* podcast, free downloads, and information about our nonprofit Sounds True Foundation, where we strive to remove financial barriers to the materials we publish through scholarships and donations worldwide.

To learn more, please visit SoundsTrue.com/freegifts or call us toll-free at 800.333.9185.

Together, we can wake up the world.